SURVIVE AND THRIVE 2-IN-1 COLLECTION

PREPARE YOUR HOME FOR A SUDDEN GRID-DOWN SITUATION + THE BUG OUT BOOK - PROVEN STRATEGIES TO THRIVE IN A GRID-DOWN CRISIS AND MASTER THE ART OF BUG OUT PLANNING

TED RILEY

Copyright © 2023 Ted Riley. All rights reserved.

The content contained within this book may not be reproduced, duplicated, or transmitted without direct written permission from the author or the publisher.

Under no circumstances will any blame or legal responsibility be held against the publisher, or author, for any damages, reparation, or monetary loss due to the information contained within this book, either directly or indirectly.

Legal Notice:

This book is copyright protected. It is only for personal use. You cannot amend, distribute, sell, use, quote, or paraphrase any part, or the content within this book, without the consent of the author or publisher.

Disclaimer Notice:

Please note the information contained within this document is for educational and entertainment purposes only. All effort has been executed to present accurate, up-to-date, reliable, complete information. No warranties of any kind are declared or implied. Readers acknowledge that the author is not engaged in the rendering of legal, financial, medical, or professional advice. The content within this book has been derived from various sources. Please consult a licensed professional before attempting any techniques outlined in this book.

By reading this document, the reader agrees that under no circumstances is the author responsible for any losses, direct or indirect, that are incurred as a result of the use of the information contained within this document, including, but not limited to, errors, omissions, or inaccuracies.

CONTENTS

PREPARE YOUR HOME FOR A SUDDEN GRID-DOWN SITUATION

Introduction — 13

1. **WHEN THE GRID GOES DOWN** — 17
   What It Means for You
   - Potential Causes of Prolonged Grid Failure — 17
   - What Would Happen If the Grid Went Down? — 19
   - Remembering Your Survival Priorities — 20

2. **THE POWER'S OUT!** — 22
   Immediate Short-Term Solutions
   - Essential Power Outage Supplies — 22
   - Warm Weather Power Outage Tips — 28
   - Cold Weather Power Outage Tips — 30
   - Grid-Down Action Plan — 32
   - Take Action: Checklists and Plans — 34

3. **A CLOSER LOOK AT OFF-GRID POWER** — 35
   - A Quick Note on Going Fully Off-Grid — 36
   - Off-Grid Power Options — 37
   - Storing Electricity — 44
   - Preparing an On-Grid Property for an Off-Grid Situation — 45
   - Take Action: DIY Emergency Solar Panel Battery Charger — 46

4. **LONGER-TERM SOLUTIONS** — 50
   Heating and Cooling
   - Whole-House Systems — 50
   - Backup Systems for Grid-Reliant Homes — 54
   - Take Action: DIY Compost Water Heater — 62

5. **LONGER-TERM SOLUTIONS**   64
   Lighting
   Backup Lighting Solutions   65
   Take Action: DIY Emergency Light   70

6. **LONGER-TERM SOLUTIONS**   72
   Water Filtration and Storage
   Why Water Is a Priority If the Grid Goes Down   72
   What You Can Do in Advance of a Crisis   73
   Water Storage Options   74
   If the Grid Goes Down: What to Do Immediately   77
   The Water You Should Never Drink   78
   Sourcing Water from the Wild   78
   Conserving Water   81
   Take Action: Calculate Your Family's Water Needs   82

7. **LONGER-TERM SOLUTIONS**   84
   Food and Cooking
   Off-Grid Cooking Options   85
   Off-Grid Cooking Essentials   96
   Fueling the Fire   98
   Fuel Conservation Techniques   100
   Grid-Down Cooking Safety   101
   Sourcing Food   102
   Take Action: Make a Crossbow   106

8. **LONGER-TERM SOLUTIONS**   122
   Medical Care
   Minimizing Risk   123
   Medicine to Stock Up On   125
   Natural Medicine   130
   Take Action: Emergency First Aid Kit Checklist   134

9. **LONGER-TERM SOLUTIONS**   136
   Sanitation and Hygiene
   Essential Sanitation Supplies   136
   Toileting   137
   Personal Hygiene   143
   Waste Management   145

Pest Control	147
Take Action: DIY Hand Sanitizer	148
10. LONGER-TERM SOLUTIONS	149
Laundry and Dishwashing	
Dishwashing	149
Laundry	151
Take Action: DIY Laundry Detergent	157
11. LONGER-TERM SOLUTIONS	159
Communication	
goTenna	160
CB Radios	160
FRS/GMRS	161
Satellite Phones	161
Ham Radio	162
Walkie Talkie	163
Powering Communication	163
Take Action: Know the Emergency Frequencies	164
12. LONGER-TERM SOLUTIONS	169
Security	
Seeing through the Eyes of an Intruder	169
Off-Grid Security	170
Take Action: Plan Your Escape Routes	178
Escape Route Checklist	178
13. IN THE EVENT OF ECONOMIC COLLAPSE	180
What's Valuable Now: Cash	180
If Cash Loses Its Value	182
Bartering Tips	183
Take Action: DIY Dry Bag	184
Conclusion	189
References	191

THE BUG OUT BOOK

Introduction — 205

1. TO BUG OUT OR TO BUG IN? HOW YOU KNOW WHEN IT'S TIME TO GO — 209
   When It's Better to Stay Put — 210
   When Bugging Out Is Best — 216
   Bug In or Bug Out—How to Decide — 218
   ★ Take Action! — 221

2. WHERE ARE YOU GOING WITH THAT BUG-OUT BAG? — 223
   What Makes a Good Bug-Out Location? — 224
   Choosing Your Structure — 229
   ★ Take Action! — 241

3. MEET BOB: PREPARING YOUR BUG-OUT BAG — 243
   What Is a Bug-Out Bag? — 243
   Getting Your Gear — 245
   Packing on a Limited Budget — 253
   How to Pack Your Bag — 254
   Evaluating Your Bag — 256
   ★ Take Action! — 257

4. BUG-OUT BOOT CAMP: TRAINING UP FOR AN EMERGENCY — 265
   The Importance of Physical Fitness — 266
   Making a Trial Run — 279
   ★ Take Action! — 280

   A Quick Breather to Focus on What You've Achieved — 283

5. WHICH WAY... AND HOW? PLANNING YOUR TRANSIT — 285
   Why It's Important to Have Different Options — 286
   What Are Your Options? — 287
   Planning Your Route — 292
   Creating a Family Evacuation Plan — 296
   ★ Take Action! — 296

6. HOME AWAY FROM HOME: PREPARING
   YOUR BUG-OUT SPOT 300
   The Fundamentals of Preparation 300
   ★ Take Action! 306

7. NO PERSON (OR DOG!) LEFT BEHIND:
   BUGGING OUT WITH VULNERABLE
   PEOPLE AND ANIMALS 309
   Bugging Out With Children 309
   Bugging Out With Elderly People 317
   Bugging Out With Someone With a Health
   Condition 318
   Bugging Out With Animals 319
   ★ Take Action! 321

8. TREASURES ON THE ROAD: PREPARE YOUR
   SURVIVAL CACHE 323
   What Is a Survival Cache? 324
   What Should Your Survival Cache Contain? 324
   The Container 326
   The Advantage of Having Multiple Caches 331
   The Best Locations for a Survival Cache 332
   Choosing a Hiding Place 333
   Protecting and Finding Your Cache 335
   ★ Take Action! 336

9. SECURING YOUR BASES ... BOTH AT HOME
   AND ON THE ROAD 338
   Additional Security Precautions 339
   Beyond Physical Precautions 342
   Securing Yourself and Your Family 343
   ★ Take Action! 345

10. MAKE A SWIFT EXIT WITHOUT CUTTING
    YOURSELF OFF: PLANNING AND
    COMMUNICATION 348
    Pre-Planning 348
    Finalizing an Exit Plan 350
    Key Questions to Ask Yourself 351
    Communication Planning 352
    ★ Take Action! 355

Conclusion	359
References	367
About the Author	373

A Special Gift to My Readers

Included with your purchase of this book is your free copy of the *Emergency Information Planner*

Follow the link below to receive your copy:
www.tedrileyauthor.com
Or by accessing the QR code:

You can also join our Facebook community **Suburban Prepping with Ted**, or contact me directly via ted@tedrileyauthor.com.

PREPARE YOUR HOME FOR A SUDDEN GRID-DOWN SITUATION

TAKE SELF-RELIANCE TO THE NEXT LEVEL WITH PROVEN METHODS AND STRATEGIES TO SURVIVE A GRID-DOWN CRISIS

INTRODUCTION

> *"Remember: When disaster strikes, the time to prepare has passed."*
>
> — STEVEN CRYOS

Picture the scene: The whole family's snuggled up on the sofa watching a movie, and the kids are wolfing down popcorn like there's no tomorrow. The heating's on, the lights are glowing, and you're considering hot chocolate all around. Then suddenly, the TV screen is black, the lights are off, the heating's cut out, and boiling water for hot chocolate has become a serious mission. Plus the kids have lost the plot, and your wife's panicking about how you're all going to navigate the morning routine.

That was my house a couple of weeks ago.

It was all totally fine—over within a few hours, in fact. It was just a short-term power outage; no doubt you've had them yourself. And if you're anything like me, you've got everything you need to handle them. We actually had a good evening. Once the kids had calmed down, we filled the front room with candles, wrapped ourselves in blankets, and cracked open the board games. And we made that hot chocolate over a camping stove, found in the back of a cupboard with the help of a flashlight. The kids loved it. Arguably we had a better night than we would have had watching the movie.

It got me thinking though. We were fine for a few hours. We had everything we needed to see us through an immediate problem with the grid… But would we have coped if it had gone on for weeks? The answer, unfortunately, was no. We'd have been fine for a little while, but if we had to live without power for more than a couple of weeks, we'd have struggled.

There have been disasters and power outages all across America over the last few years, and the same is true in Europe, Asia, and Oceania. The problem isn't getting better. In fact, it's only getting worse. We're facing more and more extreme weather, and the grid is subject to increasing pressure. The chances of a longer-term grid-down situation are becoming ever more likely.

That small-scale power outage made me realize: We need to be more prepared. And if my family, a family for whom being prepared is second nature, needed to work on this, how many other families would struggle if the grid was to go down?

And this, I know, is why you're here.

We're all afraid that we won't be able to keep our families safe and healthy if the comforts we currently rely on suddenly become unavailable. Most of us are fully dependent on the grid, and if you're wondering how you'd cope without it, you're certainly not alone. We haven't had to think about how to meet the demands of a busy household without it, so most of us haven't. You might not be aware of what equipment you need to have in backup, how you'll keep up with your family's personal hygiene and medical needs, what you'll do about cooking, or how you'll communicate with the outside world. You might have worried about what you'll do if you get caught without power, but are you equipped for it? Do you even fully understand what it means?

Perhaps, like me, a power outage woke you up to the fact that you need to be more prepared, or perhaps you were taking stock of the supplies you've already prepared for a disaster, only to realize that all that rice isn't going to be much use without a way to cook it. You're looking for solutions, and let me tell you, you've come to the right place. Once I get a whiff of a hole in my own preparedness plan, I'm obsessive, so I can tell you I've thought all this through thoroughly.

You're going to come away with practical advice you can implement straight away to make sure your family's prepared no matter what happens. You'll have a clear idea of the essential supplies you'll want to get hold of in case we find ourselves faced with a grid-down emergency, and you'll have a better understanding of the bases you need to cover. You'll learn strategies that will help you in a range of different disasters, and you'll recognize exactly what you currently rely on the grid for so that you're better equipped to think around it.

I've spent years studying wilderness and urban survival, and my family and I have been preparing our homestead for the worst for years. I might have left a few gaps in my original plan, but we're on it now, and I promise you can trust the information I'm going to share with you. If wilderness survival is possible, then urban survival is possible—even without the grid. In fact, there are plenty of people who live off the grid by choice. I read about one man in Florida who's been living in a camper van, completely independent from the grid, for 20 years. He's going to be fine if the grid goes down… But don't worry: It won't be long before you will be too.

Those short-term power outages will be a piece of cake, but better yet, you'll be ready to face something much more serious. I've taken all the hard work out for you: You don't have to think about a thing. Just assess your family's needs, gather your supplies, and stock up. And you might want to practice a few things too, but don't worry: We'll get to that.

So let's not waste any more time. Let's make sure we're ready for whatever the world wants to throw at us next. Preparedness is a journey, and this is the next step on the path to surviving comfortably, no matter what.

1

WHEN THE GRID GOES DOWN

WHAT IT MEANS FOR YOU

What comes to mind when you think of the grid going down? The chances are it's something like my recent power outage. You may think of a time without lights, heating, and cooking facilities; you probably realize that hot water and laundry are going to be an issue. But a true grid-down scenario has a far greater impact than most people realize. Let's take a step back for a second and think about the kinds of events that could cause a grid-down scenario. I think if you're to be truly prepared, it's important to think about cause as well as effect.

POTENTIAL CAUSES OF PROLONGED GRID FAILURE

My aim isn't to go into a lot of depth about each of these potential disasters. It's simply to help you build an awareness of the sorts of things that could affect the grid. In my experience, most people are aware of the physical consequences of many of these things, but imagining a life without power is so alien to us that many people overlook it.

The most obvious causes of grid failure are natural disasters and environmental events. At the minor end of the scale, that's regional weather; at the extreme end, it's tsunamis, floods, and earthquakes. Generally speaking, regional weather events are less likely to affect the grid for a prolonged period of time. However, an intense storm or a tornado could cause significant damage to a distribution system, and it could mean an area is without power for a while. With an event like an earthquake, there's even greater potential for disruption. Transmission poles, distribution poles, and substations are all vulnerable to damage, and there's a significant risk of fuel loss. Flooding, ice storms, volcanic activity, wildfires, and drought can also cause great damage, and the problem with all of these weather events is that as the climate warms, they become much more likely to occur in areas where the infrastructure isn't prepared for them.

Extreme weather on Earth isn't the only risk to the grid, though. What happens in space also affects our environment. Storms on the sun, for example, cause eruptions of charged particles known as coronal mass ejections, and these can result in fluctuations in the Earth's magnetic field. There's a lot of science we could go into here, but the simple story is that these fluctuations can damage the whole power system. And unfortunately, coronal mass ejection isn't the only space event that can impact the magnetic field here on Earth.

Much as we may like to think that all threats to the grid are natural occurrences, sadly, this is not the case, and we are at the mercy of deliberate interference too. Terrorist attacks and cyberattacks are a risk, and even if the grid is not an intentional target, war and conflict can also have devastating effects. Many of us are lucky enough not to be affected by these things in our daily lives, but the harsh reality is that life can change in an instant, and we should be prepared for every possibility.

WHAT WOULD HAPPEN IF THE GRID WENT DOWN?

If any of these events did shut down the grid, the impact would be immense. There are 3 things we rely on to function day-to-day: food, water, and money. All of these things would be affected. Water supplies would shut down without the grid to power them. Backup generators would keep them going for a while, but there's a limit, and it wouldn't be long before the faucets would run dry and the sewage system would back up. Access to food, meanwhile, would become much more difficult. Many producers rely on automated services, which would cease to function without power. Refrigeration and delivery would be impossible, and even if delivery trucks could run, stores would soon be unable to keep up with demand, and the shelves would empty quickly. And for us at home, refrigeration, preparation, and cooking would all require an emergency backup plan to be in place.

Money may seem like less of a necessity in this context, but the world revolves around it, and in our current system, we need it in order to access goods and services. We live in an increasingly cashless society, and that means our ability to use money is almost entirely dependent on electricity.

These are perhaps the most significant problems, but they're not the only ones. In a large-scale grid-down situation, the gas supply would run out, cell phone service would cease, mail wouldn't be delivered, and schools would close. It isn't as simple as the lights going off. Life as we know it would be altered dramatically.

In the worst-case scenario, there's a real risk of civil unrest and a high chance that martial law would be enforced. If things were to get this bad, everyone would be focused on surviving and keeping their families safe—at all costs. Even emergency workers and those we rely on to uphold the law would be forced to work for service rather than pay, and understandably, many would choose to prioritize their families. The services we rely on to protect us would be understaffed and strained in the face of rising crime levels, which is bound to happen if people become desperate.

I bring this up not to instill fear, and indeed, I would give anything for this never to happen. But I think being prepared means being aware of the worst eventualities and making sure you can survive no matter what happens outside.

REMEMBERING YOUR SURVIVAL PRIORITIES

I'm conscious that many of you will have read my previous book, *When Crisis Hits Suburbia*, and I want to avoid rehashing old ground. However, it's natural that there will be overlaps, and when we're thinking about survival there are 6 key priorities that you need to take care of. These are food, water, medicine, security, energy, and hygiene, and thriving in a grid-down situation means ensuring that these priorities are met. The areas we'll look at over the coming chapters will cover these necessities, so you don't need to worry, but I would advise keeping them in the back of your mind at all times. When you're forced to think outside of the box, it's important to stay focused on the most important details.

A grid-down situation would leave us without the things we take for granted for a longer period of time than a simple power outage. It could be short-term (think 4 to 6 weeks), or it could go on for much longer. While it may be less likely, and while we may hope that it never comes to this, we need to be prepared to cope if it happens. There's great peace of mind in that, I think, and I hope that by the end of this book, you'll share that peace of mind with me.

2

THE POWER'S OUT!

IMMEDIATE SHORT-TERM SOLUTIONS

The recent power outage was no problem for my family because we already had everything on hand to see us through. The kids came home from school the next day, however, with stories of classmates who had struggled more. One family, apparently, had no alternative lighting apart from the lights on their phones; another had been in the middle of cooking dinner and hadn't been able to finish the process. So I want to start with the basics and make sure we have the first moments of a grid-down situation or a very short-term power outage covered. From there, we can start thinking about how we can build on that in order to prepare for a more serious situation.

ESSENTIAL POWER OUTAGE SUPPLIES

I hope it never gets more serious than the occasional power outage, but I suspect that at the very least, we're going to see an increase in these over the coming years. Preparing for them is relatively simple, though, and even if you haven't thought about this before, you'll probably find that you already have a lot of what you need on hand.

Flashlights and Headlamps

The first place I'd start is with flashlights. It might seem obvious, but now that we rely on our phones so much, you'd be surprised by how many people no longer have them. I'd make sure you have something long-lasting that can withstand low temperatures and is waterproof. Think long-term: If you end up in a more serious situation due to extreme weather, you want to make sure all your gear can withstand the conditions. There are hundreds of options out there, but I'll give you a couple of good starting points. I have both of these, and I've only had good experiences with them so far.

Fenix PD36R: Waterproof, dustproof, and shock-resistant, this one lasts up to 115 hours. It needs charging though, so if the power was out for a long time, you'd need to be able to charge it from a backup power source.

Olight Warrior Mini 2 EDC Tactical Light: This one ranks well for durability. It's extremely waterproof and will last for about 164 hours. This model is battery-powered, but the battery can be recharged within the device.

I'd also recommend having at least one headlamp, but there's a good argument for everyone in the family having one. When you need to find your way around the house in the dark, having your hands free is a definite bonus, and if you're also dealing with the aftermath of a disaster, it's going to be essential. Again, there are hundreds of options on the market, but if you're not sure what to look for, this is what I have, and I can definitely recommend it.

Black Diamond ReVolt 350: Switched to low mode, this model has a 200-hour battery life, and enables you to see for over 260 feet. It has a night vision function, it's waterproof, and it has multiple settings for different purposes.

Food and Water

Government recommendations are to have enough food and water to keep each member of the household going for 72 hours. That means 1 gallon of water each per day for 3 full days. That's just for drinking though, and if the water isn't running, you'll need more than that for bathing and cooking. If you're starting from nothing though, these guidelines are a good place to begin, and it is likely that, for a short-term outage, you'll only need to get through a few hours.

When it comes to food, there are whole books you could write on the subject (I should know: I've written one!), but the short story is that if the power's out for more than a few hours, you're going to want to avoid opening the refrigerator as much as possible, and if it goes on for longer than that, you want to make sure you have food that won't spoil. Take a look at my last book, *The Prepper's Pantry* for a more comprehensive look at food stocking and storage. If you have pets, remember you'll need food for them too.

As for keeping food fresh short-term, I find it helpful to think of a power outage as being like a camping trip. If you think of it as camping from home, it's pretty easy to think about the kind of supplies you might want, and one of those things is a cooler. If your fridge is out of action, that'll ensure that your milk and other staples stay fresher for longer.

First Aid and Medication

The chances of someone getting injured aren't much more likely in a short-term power outage than they are in your normal life, but you should really have a first aid kit on hand anyway. You just never know. We'll take a closer look at medical care in Chapter Eight, but at the very least, make sure you have a basic first aid kit in your house. I'd also recommend having a stock of any prescription medications your family needs. Short term, it's probably not an issue, but if that power outage turns out to be something bigger, you're going to want these.

Alternative Lighting

Flashlights and headlamps will only get you so far. If the power's out even for just an evening, you don't want to have to sit around all night holding a flashlight. I'd recommend having a few battery-operated lanterns. You could also use oil lanterns or candle lanterns, or you could have a mix of all 3. Personally, we have all of them, although the candle lanterns, I must confess, are mostly because my wife likes to have them around anyway. She likes to hang them in the garden on a summer's evening, and she's not wrong: It makes the whole place look magical. If you could use a little help with choosing battery-operated lanterns, here's my favorite. I only have one of these at the moment, but I'd definitely consider getting a couple more.

Streamlight Super Siege: This is a bit extra in terms of the features it offers, but if it came to a long-term outage, I'd say it's worth the investment. It will last for 36 hours on the lowest setting and includes red LEDs for night vision. It has a rechargeable battery, so you'd need backup power long-term, and it's waterproof, so it will survive harsh weather. In fact, it even floats, so if you were to find yourself in a flood situation, it's possibly the best option you could have.

They might feel a bit retro in comparison, but I'd recommend having a good supply of candles too. Obviously, you'd need them for candle lanterns anyway, but they're a good extra for lighting rooms at night. Be careful about the candles you buy though. Don't bother with fancy dinner candles. They burn quickly, and you'll go through them fast. Go for an emergency candle—you can get them to last for up to 115 hours. Bear in mind that you'll need a good supply of lighters and matches too, especially if you'll also be lighting gas stoves for cooking.

Power

Even for a short-term power outage, you're going to want to have spare batteries on hand. That flashlight is useless if the batteries die halfway through the outage. I have a list of all the different types of batteries I need for specific emergency items so that I can be sure I have enough in stock. If any of your devices require a screwdriver to get into the battery compartment, keep this nearby so you can easily execute a battery change if needed. I'd recommend having portable phone chargers too. Make sure they're always fully charged so that if the power does go out for an evening, you still have access to at least one phone. A longer-term problem might be a different matter, but short term, you'll still have internet access, and having your phone will mean you can access information about the situation and contact anyone you need to. That said, I'd recommend having a weather radio in your emergency kit too. That way, you can still access updates if all else fails. You can get battery-operated ones, solar-powered ones, and hand-crank ones, and many double up as chargers, so they're well worth the investment.

Cooking

As far as a short-term problem goes, again, think camping. A camping stove is a good idea, even if the power's only out for a night. Remember my son's friend whose family didn't have a way to finish cooking the evening meal? If they'd had a camping stove, they wouldn't have had a problem. Remember you'll also want to have a couple of backup gas canisters on hand, and you'll need the appropriate cookware to use with your stove. I'm not going to go into a lot of detail about your options for camping stoves here, but we'll go deeper in Chapter Seven when we look at food and cooking. A thermos is a good idea too—you can't reheat anything in the microwave if the power's out, so a way to keep your food warm is a good idea, not only for ease but also for conserving power.

Bathroom Help

There are a couple of emergency items that not many people think of when it comes to short-term outages. Bear in mind that if your power's out, your toilet's not going to flush. Therefore, a bucket is a good idea. You can just avoid flushing some of the time, but not to put too fine a point on it, even in the space of an evening, there are times that you're going to want to flush, and if you have enough water in stock, you can use it for this if you have a bucket. You'll also want some hand sanitizer to cover you if your water's off.

Staying Warm, Cool, and Entertained

Whether you'll need to keep warm or keep cool when the power's off will depend on where you live, the time of year, and the reason for the power outage, but the chances are you could need provisions for either. For staying warm, make sure everyone in the family has an insulated sleeping bag, and keep a supply of cozy blankets on hand too. For staying cool, a battery-operated fan is a good idea, and you could even keep a supply of the old-fashioned manual type handy.

Lastly, remember that if the power's out, you've lost access to TV, video games, and web surfing. Especially if you have children, you want to have some power-free entertainment on hand. Books are a good option, but I also like the opportunity to bring the family together, particularly if people are uneasy or panicking. Board games, card games... Whatever you like. Just make sure you have something to while away the powerless hours.

WARM WEATHER POWER OUTAGE TIPS

If you live in a warm climate, or it's a warm time of year where you live, you'll need to factor this into your emergency planning. Your family's water needs are greater when it's warmer, so I'd up the one gallon each per day to two to be on the safe side. Think about the amount of heat generated by your light sources too. Candles, gas lanterns, and oil lamps will produce more heat than battery lanterns, and solar lamps are a good option too.

If you live in a warm region, you probably rely on air conditioning, and that won't be running if the power's out. To keep yourself cool, pay particular attention to hydration, drinking even if you're not feeling thirsty. Be cautious about alcohol and caffeine, as they dehydrate you, and you end up eliminating more water than you gain.

Keep the air moving by opening windows in the morning and evening, ideally on either side of a room to create a through draft. Keep them closed during the middle of the day though: At the hottest part of the day, opening the windows will only bring warm air inside. Make use of battery-powered or solar fans to keep the air circulating, and consider positioning one by the window to push warm air out and draw cooler air in. Even if you have the fan in the middle of the room, keeping the windows open will help you maintain a cross breeze. A final tip for keeping a room cool, which was given to me by a friend in the Philippines: Try hanging a damp towel in front of your fan. Easy DIY cooling system!

Wear light, comfortable clothes around the house, and when night falls, if you find it's too hot to sleep, try dampening your top sheet. You don't want to sleep with damp fabric against your skin, but if you use a top sheet, it will draw the heat out and help you sleep more comfortably.

When it comes to food, it might be a good idea to have supplies that don't require much, if any, cooking. The more cooking you need to do, the more you're going to heat your home. For a short-term outage, when you still have plenty of fresh food on hand or it's easy to get out for supplies, consider grilling outdoors to keep all the extra heat outside of the house.

As for your frozen and refrigerated provisions, unfortunately, they're going to warm up and spoil much more quickly in warm conditions. If you have backup power, you can keep your fridge and freezer running, but if not, you can prepare to keep food fresher for longer by filling empty spaces in the freezer with jugs or bags of water. This will help to stabilize the temperature and give your stocks a little extra life. Just be sure to leave enough room in the containers for the water to expand as it freezes. Another alternative is to get hold of some dry ice if you can, which will keep you going a little longer.

If you're without power for more than a couple of days, your frozen goods will start to perish. Eat the most sensitive things first (your kids won't be averse to helping out with the ice cream). If you need to save meat, fruits, or vegetables, you can set about preserving them. There's plenty of guidance for this in *The Prepper's Pantry*.

COLD WEATHER POWER OUTAGE TIPS

On the opposite side of the coin, if you live in a colder region, you're probably used to relying on central heating, and this won't be available to you if the power goes down. The first thing I'd recommend is to secure your property as much as you can to prevent it from losing heat. Common entry points for cold air are around the kitchen extraction fan and dryer vent, the gaps around windows and doors, the fireplace and chimney, the vents around the water heater and furnace, and any external wall outlets. You can reduce heat loss in these areas by sealing the leaks around the windows and doors with painter's tape, and stuffing gaps with rolled-up towels. You can also insulate the windows without sacrificing light by covering them with clear plastic sheeting.

With heat loss kept to a minimum, you can then begin to create microclimates in your home so that you have one area that's warmer than the rest of the house. One idea is to set up an indoor tent. It's slightly off-the-wall, I agree, but the added insulation is surprisingly effective, especially when you have several bodies in there creating heat. Alternatively, you could build a blanket fort. Get the kids involved in that one—they'll love it! To conserve fuel and encourage the microclimate ethos, try to keep most of your family's activity to one room. You can block drafts under the door with rolled-up blankets, and warm the room with a wood stove or alternative heat source (we'll look more closely at that in Chapter Four).

Clothing-wise, think layers. You want a base layer first, which will wick moisture away from the skin. Synthetic fabrics are a good choice for this. Follow this with a middle layer, which will add insulation and help your body retain heat. Flannel shirts and woolen sweaters are good choices. Top it all off with an outer layer, which is more important if you're going to be outside and exposed to the weather, but which will add extra warmth if you're struggling to maintain your body temperature indoors. A jacket or a thick hoodie are good options. Dress warmly from the moment you get up, and remember to cover your head to prevent heat loss, and protect your extremities (think gloves and thick socks). You can warm yourself up from the inside out too. Drink warm fluids and eat warming foods. As long as you have backup cooking options, this shouldn't be a problem.

Movement is also good for warming you up. A 20-minute exercise session can keep you warm for an hour, and you don't need to make it a formal workout. Play with the kids, dance, do jumping jacks… Do anything you like as long as you're moving and bringing up your body temperature.

Of course, you won't want to be on the move all day. In the evening, snuggle up in blankets and sleeping bags, sharing body heat with your family. Hot water bottles and brick warmers are a good idea too.

Lastly, when you're building your emergency stockpile, you'll want to pay particular attention to fuel. Make sure you have enough wood, gas, or whatever else you'll burn when the power's off to see you through at least a few days.

These tips will see you through a short-term outage and get you started in the immediate moments of a grid-down scenario. However, a full knock to the grid could take much longer to recover from, so we now need to build on from here, starting with a plan of action.

GRID-DOWN ACTION PLAN

I'd recommend writing an action plan or a checklist to make sure you cover all the important things if the grid does go down. Of course, this will look a little different for everyone, as your family's requirements and the power you normally rely on will be different, but I can give you a bit of guidance to get you started. I'm just providing you with a checklist at this point, but don't worry: We'll cover all the details throughout the coming chapters.

Day One

- Locate all members of your family, and get everyone home
- Investigate what caused the outage
- Go food shopping
- Fill up water bottles
- Turn the water off at the meter
- Set up your backup power sources
- Deal with frozen and refrigerated food (transfer what you can to coolers)
- Set up the kitchen
- Set up toileting and hand-washing stations
- Set up alternative heating/cooling equipment
- Get the kids to eat up the ice cream!

Next Few Days

- Preserve frozen foods
- Move woodpile to a secure, dry place
- Secure your property
- Disconnect your property from public utilities
- Liaise with the local community

After the First Few Days

- If you have a garden, get to work on food production
- Drain your indoor pipes to prevent freezing (if necessary)
- Set up a temporary fridge outdoors (i.e., use the shed)
- Get hold of any provisions you're still lacking (e.g., more blankets)

Of course, your list could look quite different to this depending on what you need to take care of in your own home, but I'd definitely recommend having a checklist of some sort. It's easy to panic in an emergency, and a clear plan will keep you focused and make sure you're covering all bases.

Your action plan, however, will be much more effective if you have things in place to see you through a longer-term problem, and that's what we'll start looking at in the next chapter.

TAKE ACTION: CHECKLISTS AND PLANS

At the end of each of the coming chapters, I'm going to give you a practical thing you can do now to help you prepare for the worst. In this case, it makes sense to start with that action plan. So here's your mission: Make yourself a checklist to cover all the essential short-term equipment we've discussed in this chapter, and create your action plan for the first few days of a long-term crisis.

3

A CLOSER LOOK AT OFF-GRID POWER

Before we go any further, let me come clean: I don't live completely off the grid. I still rely on municipal suppliers, but I'm getting closer to a point where I could survive without them if I needed to. And that's becoming increasingly less unusual. A growing number of people are choosing to live off-grid for economic, environmental, and political reasons—and not just preppers. For anyone who wants to be fully prepared for disaster, off-grid options should be a consideration, even if only as additional sources of power. It's always a good idea to have some kind of backup for short-term power outages but if the grid went down completely, having an independent system would mean your family could thrive despite the challenges.

Living off-grid simply means that your home is completely energy-independent. You supply your own power with renewable energy. If you thought growing your own vegetables was satisfying, wait until you try powering a heater with solar energy you've collected yourself! It's important to say at this point that whole books could be written not only on independent energy systems but on each one alone. My aim here is to give you an overview of the options and look at what can be done to prepare a grid-reliant home for a grid-down situation.

A QUICK NOTE ON GOING FULLY OFF-GRID

If you were choosing to live off-grid permanently, you would need to consider your home and your specific needs before deciding on a system. First, you'd need to consider the type of property you live in and its size. To put it simply, the smaller your property, the easier it will be to source enough energy to power it. If you live on a houseboat, or you have a motor home or a bungalow, you could well find that going fully off-grid is a plausible option for you. If you live in a big house, however, you may want to consider downsizing if your aim is to be fully independent.

Where your property is located also makes a difference. Sourcing your own energy is possible in both urban and rural areas, but it's much easier in a rural area because you're more likely to have space for turbines, solar panels, or generators. Also, your neighbors are less likely to complain, and while that might seem like a small point, it's not insignificant.

Lastly, you're going to want to think about regional climate. This will determine the best source of energy for your home. If you live in an area where you get a lot of sunshine, solar power is an obvious choice, while if you get a lot of wind, wind power might be a better idea.

Make sure you consider all these factors if you think a fully off-grid lifestyle might be the direction you want to head in.

OFF-GRID POWER OPTIONS

When it comes to sourcing your own energy, you have a number of options at your disposal. I think it's useful to bear in mind that it's not necessarily a choice you have to make, and you may well find that the best solution for you is to use multiple sources.

Solar Energy

Solar is probably what most people think of when they think of off-grid energy sources, and you can certainly gather a lot of power this way. Boiled down to basics, this involves photovoltaic solar panels and an inverter, which converts the sun's energy into electricity, which is then stored in batteries for later use. The whole system doesn't require much maintenance once you have it set up. However, as yet, it's not particularly cost-effective, and how much power you can produce does depend on your climate. That said, there are now government incentives available in many areas, and you can often sell excess power back to the grid; the chances of it becoming more affordable in the near future are increasing.

Solar panels aren't your only way to harness the sun's energy either. You can make a big difference to your use of energy simply by using specific pieces of solar equipment. You can use solar water heaters, solar cookers, solar lights, solar batteries… Every small change makes a difference.

Wind Energy

It's easy to think of wind power and imagine off-shore wind farms, but it's possible to get much smaller wind turbines for residential use. These are only really an option for powering a whole home if you have a smaller space and live somewhere with high wind speeds. All this said, you do still require significant space to have a wind turbine on your property. The US Department of Energy says in its *Small Wind Guidebook* that a turbine able to generate 5–15 kW of electricity each month would be needed to power the typical home (which uses, on average, 830 kWh a month). To look at an example from the middle of that range, a 10 kW turbine comes mounted on a 100-foot tower, and has a rotor diameter of about 23 feet. You would need to have space to accommodate this safely, and without bothering your neighbors. It's also worth bearing in mind that wind turbines need more maintenance and have more things likely to go wrong with them than solar panels. Wind power also tends to be less reliable: A sudden still day, and you can end up producing no electricity at all. Again, many areas offer government rebates and the option to sell excess power back to the grid, so there are definite plus sides if you can make it work for you.

Geothermal Energy

Geothermal energy is a far less common solution, but it's worth knowing about. The theory behind it is that because the temperature of the Earth (below the frost line) has a constant temperature of 50°F, we can make use of its natural energy to maintain the temperature of our living environment. The way it works is by pumping water to a geothermal unit through underground piping. This then uses the water to cool or heat the air in the home, circulating it around the space through ducts. These systems are usually quite expensive to install, but the amount you save in heating and cooling costs is significant. Of course, the limitation of a geothermal system is that it's only useful for heating and cooling, and while the benefits are substantial, you will need to use other power sources too.

Microhydro Energy

Microhydro energy sounds like it might be a relatively new phenomenon, but watermills are one of the oldest ways to harvest natural energy there is. They rely on turbines catching on moving water, which spins the rotor in order to power a generator. The term "micro" simply comes from doing it on a smaller scale than a traditional watermill. The problem is that unless you live near a river or stream, a water turbine won't work for you. That said, if you do happen to have a stream running through your property, it's a very cost-effective option. Provided that stream doesn't run dry, you can run it every hour of every day, producing a lot of energy for a prolonged period of time. Because it's such a consistent way of producing electricity, you don't need as many batteries for storage. Like wind turbines, however, it's worth bearing in mind that a microhydro system will require a fair amount of maintenance.

Biogas

Biogas is produced when organic matter (think food scraps or animal waste) is broken down in an oxygen-free environment. It can then be used to generate electricity, heat water, or power vehicles. What this means is that if you generate enough food and garden waste, you can use it to produce electricity; all you'll need is a biodigester and a compatible generator. I can't say I've ever used a system like this, but I hear that it's surprisingly easy, although you're unlikely to be able to generate enough power for all your needs. For cooking or heating, though, it could be a good choice for someone with a lot of garden waste.

Generators

So far, we've looked at renewable energy, and from an environmental point of view, this is definitely the way to go. However, even if your aim is to reduce your reliance on fossil fuels, there's a high chance that it'll take you a while to become completely renewable. When you're thinking about ways to add off-grid options to your home for an emergency, the generators commonly used to power log cabins and the like are a good option. And the good news is that some of these rely on renewable energy too. In fact, if you can, I'd say that your best option is to use renewable energy, even for a generator, for the simple reason that if the grid does go down, you're probably going to have a hard time getting hold of diesel or gas.

The first generator we know of was invented by Michael Faraday in 1831. It was a simple device that worked by using a bar magnet to produce an electrical current in a coiled wire. Eventually, this discovery led to the creation of the Faraday disc, which is commonly cited as the first electromagnetic generator. Since those early days, technology has developed significantly, and there are now a number of generator options available to us.

Standby Generators

Standby generators work automatically, but otherwise, they're basically the same as gas generators, which we'll look at in a moment. They have a larger tank (so they're less portable), and can usually provide enough power to see you through 48 hours. What's great about standby generators is that they usually have an automatic transfer function, which means they leap into action as soon as the main electricity supply cuts out. They are, however, very expensive, and they're not affordable to many people. They also require a fair bit of maintenance if you want to make sure they'll catch you in an emergency, which, of course, you do.

Gasoline Generators

Gas generators are the most common types of generator, and they're very user-friendly. They're also relatively cheap and are often portable, which is why they're so commonly used to power log cabins. That said, the more power you want to generate, the bigger the generator will need to be, so for powering your home, a portable model probably isn't your best bet. It's also worth bearing in mind that they're quite noisy, and they produce higher emissions than other types of generators.

Diesel Generators

Diesel generators use a combination of an electric generator and a diesel engine, which requires diesel fuel. They have low maintenance needs and tend to be more energy-efficient than gas generators, without costing much more. They do, however, emit a large amount of harmful gas, and they don't do well in wet conditions. If the grid goes down due to flooding, a diesel generator may not be the helpful companion you were hoping for.

Natural Gas Generators

Natural gas generators use either liquified petroleum or propane to run, and they're very fuel-efficient. They can be stored underground if you wish, which perhaps gives you more options in terms of what else you can use your land for. They have low emission rates, and the fuel is cheaper than fossil fuels. So are the maintenance costs compared to other generators, so this is a good value option. That said, they are expensive to install, and they don't always do well in very cold weather.

Portable Generators

Portable generators usually run on gas or diesel, and they're specifically designed to produce a short-term power supply. Of course, this is the main problem with relying on one as a backup power source: It won't keep you going very long, and you won't be able to power much with it. That said, they're great for a short-term power outage and could be a good addition to a much bigger arsenal. A word of warning though: The emission rates are high, and they shouldn't be used in enclosed spaces.

Solar Generators

As you might expect, solar generators capture the sun's energy and turn it into electricity. They usually have solar panels for harvesting and batteries for storage. Since you'll be using the sun, there are no fuel costs with this type of generator, and you won't need to worry about emissions. The downside is that solar generators are pretty expensive, so the initial outlay is significant. They also require a lot of maintenance, and they tend not to be all that durable.

Inverter Generators

Inverter generators contain an alternator, which produces alternating current (AC) power. This is then converted into direct current (DC) power, which is then inverted back again. They're quiet, and much more fuel-efficient than diesel or gas generators. But perhaps their greatest advantage is that they provide a safe source of power for sensitive devices like phones and tablets. Despite their fuel efficiency, though, inverter generators are quite expensive, and they're costly to install. They also won't be enough to power a large property, and although it doesn't tend to be that expensive, regular maintenance is necessary.

Hydrogen Generators

Hydrogen generators are a comparatively new development, and unlike water turbines, you don't need to live by a stream to run them. They have quite a high power output, and they're easy to run, but they're not as easy to get hold of as we might like, and they're often expensive. They also don't do well in very cold conditions as the water used to fill them can freeze, rendering the whole thing useless, and potentially causing a fault in the generator. It's worth knowing about them, but I'd say they're one to keep an eye on in the future.

Maintaining Your Generator

Every type of generator has a different set of maintenance requirements, but there are a few general guidelines that apply to all models. No matter what type of generator you choose, you'll need to regularly check the cooling system and keep a close eye on the coolant levels. Filters will need an annual clean, and you'll want to check the batteries regularly. Finally, if you don't intend to use your generator on a regular basis, it's important to give it a test run periodically. The last thing you want is to haul your generator out when the grid goes down, only to find that the electrolyte levels in the batteries are wrong.

STORING ELECTRICITY

Generating power isn't the only thing you need to think about; you also need to consider how you're going to store it. If you're using solar, you'll only be generating power during the daylight hours, and if you want to power the lights after dark, you're going to need some electricity stored up. You have 3 main options here: battery storage, heat storage, and inverters (which we discussed in the previous section).

Battery Storage

Whether your power's coming from solar, wind, or water, batteries are a good option for storing renewable energy. The size of battery you need depends on both your energy use and the size of your energy system, but the good news is that any advice you get when investing in a new system will include battery storage recommendations. A well-maintained battery bank can last for at least 5 years, but you will need to replace each battery several times during the course of your system's life.

Heat Storage

There are two variations of heat storage systems: thermal and battery. Thermal storage units are basically heavily insulated water tanks. They can provide hot water and store heat from multiple sources for later use. They generally hold between 54 and 110 gallons, but you can get bigger ones. Heat batteries, meanwhile, store the heat or electricity generated by renewable systems in liquid form, converting them back into a solid as needed. They generally take up less space than a thermal system and don't degrade as easily as standard batteries.

PREPARING AN ON-GRID PROPERTY FOR AN OFF-GRID SITUATION

Of course, the ideal backup system entirely depends on personal preference, your family's energy needs, and details relating to your property and location. However, unless you live in a place that gets little sun, my recommendation for a suburban house currently dependent on the grid is to opt for a backup solar system, or at least to use solar as part of your energy generation system. It's a clean source of power, it's quiet, and you need no additional source of fuel. Maintenance is low, and the uses are diverse. I'd supplement this with a gas or natural gas generator so that you have options when sunlight is in short supply.

Before committing to anything, you're going to want to estimate your energy use. To do that, multiply the power consumption of each appliance by the number of hours you expect to use it. So, for example, a 20 W television, expected to be used for 3 hours, will need 20 x 3 = 60 Wh of power. Once you've estimated the energy needs for each appliance, total the results to give you your total energy consumption figure.

Unless you really know what you're doing, I'd suggest you get a professional in to install and set up a backup solar system, but if you're dead set on doing it yourself, read trustworthy guides, and bear in mind that you need to accommodate solar panels, a charge control, a battery bank, and an inverter. For your gas generator, you will need the generator itself, plenty of fuel (and a way to store it), spare parts in case something goes wrong, and some heavy-duty extension cords.

In our house, we currently have a backup solar system and a propane generator, but I have to say, I'm seriously considering making the move to make us function completely off the grid full time. That said, I'm confident that if you have the right knowledge and backup in place, a regular suburban house connected to the grid could survive a grid-down scenario.

TAKE ACTION: DIY EMERGENCY SOLAR PANEL BATTERY CHARGER

I always like a little DIY action. There's something satisfying about creating a solution you know you can dig out in an emergency. You'll need to have made it (or at least have sourced the materials) before the grid goes down though. The chances of being able to get the supplies you need once disaster strikes are slim.

Here's how you can make your own solar panel backup to charge any 12-volt battery.

What You Need

- 2 x 100-watt solar panels
- 2 x metal hinges

- Self-tapping metal screws
- Wiring harness
- Zip ties
- 20 feet of lead wire
- 4-foot battery leads
- Alligator clips
- Charge controller

The Mission

Step 1

Connect the 2 solar panels with the metal hinges and screws so that they'll fold together, with the wires protected inside and the solar panels exposed.

Step 2

Unite the panels by attaching the wiring harness. Secure all the wires and the harness with zip ties.

Step 3

Add alligator clips to the ends of the battery leads so you can easily connect your charger to a battery. Keep these leads as short as possible to minimize energy loss.

Step 4

Start with the battery leads. Connect the black lead first to the negative output terminal on your charge controller and then to the negative terminal on your battery. Repeat the process with the red lead and attach it to the positive terminals.

Step 5

Once the battery leads are attached, connect the solar panel lead wires to the charge controller. Once again, start with the negative lead wire.

Step 6

Using the manual that came with your charge controller as a guide, adjust the settings to suit the kind of battery you want to charge.

Step 7

To charge, position your solar battery charger in direct sunlight. You may need to reposition the panels throughout the day.

4

LONGER-TERM SOLUTIONS

HEATING AND COOLING

We'll begin this chapter by looking at whole-house systems, but most of the solutions we'll be looking at are for homes that don't have an independent energy system. If you're already self-sufficient in energy (and use a renewable source), you'll be able to power your home if the grid goes down, and your heating and cooling systems will function as usual.

WHOLE-HOUSE SYSTEMS

The majority of you are probably looking for backup solutions, but I think it's worth taking a brief look at whole-house systems so you know what's available in case you're thinking about a bigger overhaul.

Passive Solar Design

Passive solar design simply means using the sun's energy to heat or cool your house through exposure to sunlight. Whenever the sun is shining on your property, the materials it's made of either reflect, absorb, or transmit the radiation. The sun's heat, meanwhile, causes a predictable movement in the air. These facts make it possible for us to design homes that work with the sun to heat and cool themselves. The real beauty of this is that because it works on a design level, it doesn't involve electrical devices or technical components—or at least, it doesn't have to.

There are 5 main elements at work in passive solar design. The first is an aperture, essentially a large window to allow sunlight into the building. To be effective, it should face no further than 30° away from true south, free of shade between 9 a.m. and 3 p.m. The second element is the absorber, an exposed dark surface such as a floor, masonry wall, or water container, which should be in the direct path of the light. This will absorb the sunlight as heat. Below this is the third element, thermal mass, which is made up of materials that will retain the heat. The fourth element is distribution, the means by which solar heat is circulated around the building, transferring through convection, conduction, and radiation. The final element is control, achieved through roof overhangs to shade the aperture during hot spells, electronic sensor devices, vents, and dampers to control heat flow, awnings, and blinds.

Geothermal Heating and Cooling Systems

Much like passive solar design, geothermal heating and cooling systems rely on building design to minimize electricity consumption, using insulation and layout to make the most of the sun's natural heat and the cooling effects of shade. Geothermal systems are often integrated with power from renewable sources, but they're powerful tools in their own right. The earth is a natural thermal insulator, and as we've seen, once you get below the frost line, the temperature remains constant no matter what the weather's doing above ground. Geothermal heating and cooling systems use this to their advantage and draw on this constant temperature to maintain the climate within a building.

A system like this is made up of two key components: a heat pump coming from the ground and a transfer system composed of underground pipes. These pipes contain a solution of water and antifreeze, which will absorb or radiate heat depending on the conditions. This sort of system takes an active approach but you can also take a passive approach to geothermal temperature control… and the chances are, if you have a basement, you're already doing it. The basement of a house will be cooler than the rest of the building during hotter seasons, and this is why they're so useful for storage. Conversely, if your power's out during the winter, you may find that it's the warmest place to be. This is a good tip if you want to see geothermal temperature control in action without redesigning your whole house!

Solar Powered Radiant Heat Floor

Radiant floor heating relies on either tubing heated by water or electric heat coils running under the floor. The heat that rises from the flooring then radiates through the space, warming everything it comes into contact with. This keeps the temperature constant throughout the room, rather than being concentrated in one area. While it may seem like a fairly new approach to temperature control, it's actually very old: The Ancient Romans heated their buildings with underfloor water pipes. Although it does require energy, it's a much more economical approach to heating than a central heating system powered by a furnace, and it can be done off-grid using solar or other renewable sources to provide electricity or heat water.

Biomass Boiler

Much like a traditional gas boiler, a biomass boiler is able to provide a home's heating and hot water. They tend to use wood pellets, but you can use firewood in them, which would be your best option in an emergency situation. If you install a biomass boiler now, you may be able to get some of the cost subsidized by the government (they're included in the incentives program), and since they're reliable and consistent, they make for a good, sustainable way of heating your home. Nonetheless, the upfront costs are considerable, and biomass boilers are quite large, so you'll need to account for the space one will take up. They're fairly labor-intensive, although you can reduce your workload by installing a silo to feed wood into the boiler. Bear in mind that a boiler like this will still need regular maintenance and cleaning.

Solar Chimney

A solar chimney regulates a property's temperature while simultaneously providing ventilation. They're basically hollow containers connecting the inside and outside of the building, and they're an economical way of regulating temperature. The chimney is coated with a black material, which reduces the amount of sunlight reflected back off the chimney, absorbing heat at the same time. In the northern hemisphere, the chimney is usually situated on a south-facing wall in order to get the most sun. Solar radiation hits the chimney, heating the air inside it, and vents at the top of the chimney allow the space to be closed, forcing the warm air back down into the building. As the air cools, the chimney pulls it back in, reheating it inside the enclosure.

Meanwhile, cooling is achieved through vents. While the vent at the top of the chimney can be opened to allow warm air to escape and cooler air to enter, there's also a second vent at the opposite end of the property, which serves as an opening to the outside air, allowing for further ventilation. Although the sun's radiation continues to hit the chimney and be warmed inside it, the chimney vent allows it to escape as cooler air is pulled in.

BACKUP SYSTEMS FOR GRID-RELIANT HOMES

Many of us will continue to rely on the grid for at least some of our energy. Nonetheless, we need to be sure that we can carry our families through tougher times without it. With that in mind, let's take a look at heating and cooling backup plans so that if your supply is cut, you can still keep your family safe and comfortable.

Heating

Preparing Your Home

Even if you're not planning on overhauling your heating system, if you live in a colder region it would be wise to prepare your property for the worst. The bonus of this is that you can reduce your heating costs significantly, even if there's never an emergency to navigate. Start by checking your attic space and adding extra insulation if necessary. Then check your windows and doors: Do they have tight seals? Can you feel a draft coming in around the edges? Are they contributing to the energy efficiency of your home? We recently replaced the windows in our living room, and it's incredible how much difference it has made to the temperature. I'd also suggest thick, heavy curtains, which will not only help you maintain the warmth in the evening when they're shut but will also reduce any draft that is coming in around the window frames.

However, even the most well-insulated house requires extra heat in the winter, and if you find yourself cut off from the grid, it's crucial that you have some backup heating options in place.

Wood Stove

If you have a wood-burning stove, you already have an off-grid backup in place. We have one, and I admit it was originally installed with a power outage in mind but it's actually just a joy to have anyway. If you don't plan to have one permanently, you can install a wood stove on a temporary basis, as long as you have a chimney pipe and a convenient window. Position the stove near to the window, and remove a pane of glass to run the chimney through. You can close the space around the chimney with plywood to keep the warm air in and the cold air out. A word of warning though: If you're planning on installing a temporary wood stove, you're going to want to make sure you get one that uses wood rather than pellets. Many stoves on the market now are fueled by wood pellets, and they're more energy-efficient, but they can't be used with regular firewood. So, as soon as you run out of pellets, your stove is useless. With a regular wood-burning stove, you can source your own firewood no matter what happens to the grid.

Kerosene/Propane Heater

The only real difference between a kerosene and a propane heater is the fuel it burns. Both are an effective way to heat a single room, radiating heat from each side, much like a wood-burning stove. The fuel is loaded into a tank and can be ignited either automatically or manually, depending on the model. Most heaters are portable, which means you can easily move them between rooms, and when there isn't an emergency, they're a great extra heat source to take on a camping trip.

Whether you opt for kerosene or propane is really a matter of choice, although it's worth noting that propane is cheaper and cleaner burning. Many models tend to burn for longer than their kerosene counterparts too. Whichever you choose, though, remember that you'll need to have a good supply of fuel in stock to see you through a crisis. Both can be stored for a fairly long time, but again, propane comes out on top: It will last indefinitely, while kerosene will only last for about 5 years.

I've had a few portable heaters over the years, but the Portable Buddy Heater is my favorite—it has the power to heat up to 225 square feet. You can get 6 hours of low heat out of a 1 pound propane cylinder, or 3 if you want it turned up high.

Gas Catalytic Heater

Arguably, gas catalytic heaters have the upper hand over both kerosene and propane heaters because you don't need to worry about fuel storage, and they don't require a flame to be ignited. They contain a ceramic element, which is filled with natural gas or liquid propane gas, and radiates heat as it burns. If you're wondering how they work, think back to science class: Catalytic combustion occurs when the gas comes into contact with oxygen, producing heat, water, and carbon dioxide.

The great advantage of this type of heater is that you don't need electricity or a stock of natural gas—providing, of course, that you can get to a natural gas pumping station. Of course, should the power be cut for any length of time due to an extreme weather event, it could be that the pipes at the pumping station are damaged, in which case, your heater won't be of much use to you unless you have a stock of liquid propane to use as an alternative. Natural gas does have an indefinite shelf life, but you can't really store it at home because a household tank can't cope with the pressure required to keep it in a liquid state.

Compost Water Heater

If you have a garden, you're going to want to try this. Think of your compost pile and how it steams when you turn it: Compost gets hot while it's decomposing, and you can use that to your advantage. A hose is coiled inside the compost pile, carrying water through it, which is heated by the decomposition process. You might not think that would be enough to generate much heat, but you'd be surprised: Compost can reach up to around 160°F, which is about the same as the average conventional water heater.

You're probably not going to be able to heat a room with this without a significant amount of work, but what you can do is heat water for a hot shower, and that's going to be something you'll be really glad of if you get cut off from the grid. I know, you're dying to try it. I'm one step ahead of you: We'll take a look at how to make one at the end of the chapter.

Urban Igloo

The urban igloo is really just an extension of creating microclimates. It's kind of like the ultimate blanket fort, and you can probably create one without needing anything you don't already have at home. You want to place a mattress beneath a dining table, and then drape thick blankets or rugs over the top so that they hang down the sides to make a tent. You want them to reach the floor, but be careful to leave a gap in one corner so you don't end up with an igloo full of condensation. Just as with a tent or a blanket fort, the more bodies you have inside, the warmer you'll be.

If the igloo experience doesn't appeal to you or you can't face lugging a mattress downstairs, remember you can insulate a room by hanging blankets over doorways. You can get even more from this approach by using a rescue blanket.

Wrapping Up Warm

We discussed clothing in Chapter One, so I won't go over it all again. However, I will remind you that the more you can do to keep your body warm, the less you'll need to worry about heating the room. Remember those layers, cover your head, and make sure everyone has a sleeping bag to snuggle up in during the evening.

Cooling

If you live in a warmer region, or the power supply is cut off during the summer, your concern won't be keeping warm: It'll be keeping cool. There's plenty you can do without the grid to help you here, though.

Preparing Your Home

The best thing you can do in advance is to minimize solar gain on your property, which you can do by increasing the shade covering your house. Planting trees is a long-term game plan, but it's still worth doing if you have the space. Alternatively, you can use awnings to create shade on your walls. Inside, you can use blinds and curtains, or you could consider adding reflective window coatings. You can mimic the effects of a reflective window coating during a crisis by covering the windows with aluminum foil.

Lastly, you want to be able to create a through-draft in your home as far as possible, so look at your current ventilation options and see if you could add further window openings or vents.

Lifestyle Changes

Although there are fewer things you can do to prepare your home in advance than there are for keeping it warm, you can make a few lifestyle changes that will help you out if you find yourself suddenly without power.

During hot weather, it's tempting to keep the windows open permanently, but this is actually a false economy. During the hottest part of the day, all that will happen is that you'll get more heat indoors. Keep them shut during the middle of the day, and open from the evening onward. You also want to make sure you have window shades on every window and shut them during the hottest part of the day. Of course, only you know your property. If a window isn't in the path of direct sunlight at any point during the day, you won't need to shade it.

The next thing you can do is pay attention to keeping your own body cool. My kids discovered one summer that if they spray each other with water and then stand in front of the fan, they can not only have a great water fight, but they can also cool themselves off after running around. I have to hand it to them: It's a great idea, and I've been known to do it myself on a hot day. You can also buy special neckties filled with polymer crystals. You soak them in water and tie them around your neck, and the effect is a soothing coolness throughout your whole body. And, of course, there's your clothing choice. Aim for lightweight fabric, and if you're going to be out in the sun, keep your skin covered, no matter how tempting it might be to rip everything off.

Lastly, think about the amount of heat your household generates throughout the day. If you plan to use a stove or oven, try to do it in the morning before the heat gets up, and while you still have the windows open. Think about cooking methods that generate less heat (slow cookers, for example), or consider cooking outdoors.

Off-Grid Air Conditioning

First of all, unless you live somewhere where the temperature makes air conditioning essential, bear in mind that it uses a lot of power and you may not want to make it a priority. However, I'm aware that in some regions, it can be absolutely unbearable without it, so let's take a look at your options.

A regular air conditioning unit is fairly likely to overload your energy system. They use a ton of energy. You're going to want a much smaller model, such as a mini split unit or a freestanding unit, which you can power using a generator or any other backup power source you're using. What I'd suggest doing is planning its use strategically, particularly if you'll be using batteries that need recharging. Use the morning to charge them, and only when the heat gets unbearable in the afternoon, plug in the air conditioning unit. Once it's cool enough to open the windows again, turn it back off.

Solar Fans

Powered directly by the sun, a solar fan comes with a solar panel, either connected remotely or mounted onto the fan itself. If you connect the panel to a battery pack as well as to the fan, you'll be able to run it even during the night or on overcast days. They are a bit more expensive than regular electric fans, but if you think about how much you'll save in energy costs, it probably evens out over time. Year-round air conditioning isn't necessary where I live, so for me, cooling is really only something I have to think about during the summer, and I have a solar fan. I don't claim to know what's best here, and to an extent, it depends on your needs, but I can tell you that we have a Cowin Solar Fan System, and it does the job nicely. It also has a USB charge port and a built-in LED light, which are good little bonuses.

Your heating and cooling requirements depend entirely on where you live, but they're always going to be important. Keeping warm or cool enough is vital to comfort, but it can also be crucial to survival in more extreme climates. Whatever your household's needs, make sure you've assessed them thoroughly and have the right backup in place before disaster strikes.

TAKE ACTION: DIY COMPOST WATER HEATER

You kind of have to, right?! The good news is, it's very easy, especially if you're already used to making your own compost. You'll need a flexible tube of at least 300 feet (an irrigation pipe will work well), and enough space to accommodate a heap with a 6-foot diameter. You'll also want to stock up on hay, as you'll need to insulate the pile once it's complete.

The trick is to start with a foundation of twigs and sticks before you start adding anything else. Aim to extend this a little further than the edge of the main pile, as this will promote good airflow. In order to accommodate the pipe, you're going to need a fairly big compost pile, and (as with any compost pile) you'll need both nitrogen and carbon to generate heat.

Begin with a 2-inch carbon layer (this is your "brown" waste, so think dry leaves, straw, cardboard, and eggshells). On top of this, add an equal layer of nitrogen (this is your "green" waste, so that's grass clippings, young leaves, and fruit and vegetable waste). Now coil your pipe on top of the upper layer, wet the pile well, and repeat the carbon and nitrogen layering. Press everything down tightly and dampen it again, before coiling the next section of pipe and repeating the whole process. You want to make sure that at least a foot of the pipe extends out from the compost pile. Finish up by insulating it with hay.

After that, it's simply a case of setting up a water source. While the grid's still running, this could be an outdoor

LONGER-TERM SOLUTIONS | 63

faucet, but in an off-grid situation, you'll want to use a water tank. All you need to do then is link it up to a showerhead, and a lovely warm outdoor shower is in your future.

5

LONGER-TERM SOLUTIONS

LIGHTING

If you have an independent energy system, you'll be able to keep your lights working even if the main grid goes dark. However, if you're totally reliant on the grid or you want to conserve your energy, you'll need backup solutions to see you through a full grid-down scenario. We'll take a look at your options in a moment, but before we do, a quick word on security: If the worst happens, there's a chance that people will become desperate for resources. If your home clearly shows signs that it has precious resources like fuel for lighting, there's a risk that it could become a target for theft. So while I don't want you to panic about this, I do think it's worth mentioning that if you're tempted to light up your house like a Christmas tree, make sure you have blackout blinds up. It's worth doing for heat conservation anyway.

BACKUP LIGHTING SOLUTIONS

Oil Lamps and Lanterns

I mentioned our garden lanterns earlier, but the truth is, they won't necessarily be the best if the grid goes down as a result of extreme weather. Luckily, I do have another lantern: a hurricane lantern. These are designed to stay lit even in strong winds, and although those garden lanterns are a great asset, I'd recommend getting hold of at least one hurricane lantern too.

Mine is a Feuerhand Storm Lantern, and I can't recommend it enough. Its tank holds over half a pint of fuel, and it will burn happily for about 20 hours. It hangs well from a hook or a tree branch, and it can withstand some serious weather. I tried using it with paraffin, which is probably the cheapest kind of fuel you could use for lanterns like this, but quite honestly, I can't stand the smell, so I prefer to use clear lamp oil. It's more expensive, but, for me at least, it's worth it.

If the grid goes down because of an earthquake or a hurricane, however—something which may cause leaks in the gas mains or destabilize the ground—you'd be best off avoiding flammable lighting like this at all. A hurricane lantern is obviously fine for hurricanes, but be mindful of the conditions when you think about lighting lamps.

Oil lamps and lanterns have a distinct advantage when you want to stay warm, in that they also produce heat (and if you want to harness the power of this even further, you can stick some aluminum foil on a wall behind the lamp to reflect the heat back into the room). If you live in a hot climate, however, you might find that some of the other backup solutions will suit you better. You don't necessarily want to be bringing extra heat into the house if you're struggling to keep cool.

If you're considering oil lamps and lanterns, bear in mind that size matters. While a smaller lamp may be useful for carrying around with you, larger models will have wider wicks, and will therefore produce more light. Personally, I'd focus on larger lamps, and keep your flashlight for carrying around with you. It's safer anyway. You'll also need to make sure you stock up on fuel and all the relevant wicks. Most lamps will take paraffin, clear lamp oil, or kerosene, and you can also burn citronella, which has the added bonus of keeping insects away in the summer.

Bear in mind that whether they contain candles or oil, lamps and lanterns are fire risks, so make sure you keep them away from clothing, soft furnishings, and other flammable items. I'd also recommend keeping a fire extinguisher in your house. Hopefully, you'll never need it, but why take the risk?

Propane Lanterns

Propane lanterns are also a good consideration. They run on one-pound propane cylinders, and much like oil lamps, they also generate heat. They will need to be kept away from flammable items, and should only be used in well-ventilated areas. There is some risk of carbon monoxide poisoning, so make sure you have a carbon monoxide detector in your home. You'll need to make sure you have a good stock of propane too. Remember that propane lasts indefinitely, so there's no reason not to keep a good amount in stock.

Candles

Some garden lanterns are designed for candles, and of course, you can also light your living area with naked candles in an emergency. I wouldn't want to rely on them, but I definitely think anyone who wants to be prepared should have some in stock for emergencies. Apart from anything else, they're going to be your best bet if we find ourselves in a grid-down situation due to EMP because of their lack of electrical components.

Look for thick candles like church candles, or candles set in jars. These burn for longer and are less likely to fall over. Your best bet, however, is an emergency candle like the SDS Liquid Oil Candle. It's not a traditional candle, in that it burns liquid paraffin instead of solid wax, but it's still sold as a candle, and it has a burn time of around 115 hours, which is far more than a traditional candle. If you're looking at traditional solid candles, look for emergency options with a burn time of at least 36 hours, but bear in mind that most of these can't be reused.

With traditional candles, the fact that they can be reused is a definite bonus, despite their shorter burn time. If you keep fresh wicks in stock, you can melt down the leftover wax to make new candles. Keep jars on hand to keep them in: The more you can protect the flame, the safer your family will be. Again, though, a fire extinguisher wouldn't be a bad idea.

LED Lanterns

Moving away from the more old-school options but sticking with the lantern theme, LED lanterns are a good option. These can light whole rooms, and they're pretty energy efficient, with a good run time. If you live in a hotter region, this will be a better option for you than an oil or propane lantern, as they run cooler than their traditional counterparts. The other advantage they have is that they don't come with the same fire risk, and you don't have to worry about storing oil or propane. That said, you will need a stock of batteries, or a way of recharging rechargeable models (although some lanterns come with built-in solar panels to sidestep this issue).

I have a Streamlight Siege X in my bug out bag, which is quite small compared to a lot of lanterns. It's a great little lantern for a portable kit, but if you're looking for something for the home, you might prefer a bigger model.

Solar Lights

Solar lights are a great option for outdoor lighting, and they've come a long way in recent years. We have a set lining the path up to our front door, and they really do make a difference in the evening. They don't produce loads of light but they're good for illuminating walkways. If you opt for motion-activated ones (for instance, mounted on your garage), this also provides you with a bit of a security boost, even if the grid is down.

You can use solar lights indoors as well, of course, and in an emergency situation, they might be a good option for placing in hallways and on the stairs—areas where you need to be able to see where you're going but don't need light for anything more. Pro tip: Leave them out in the sun during the day, and in the evening, bring them indoors and push the spikes into Styrofoam blocks to keep them the right way up. Then you can put them wherever you like.

Battery-Operated Lighting

The most obvious type of battery-operated lighting is the flashlight, but you have a few other options at your disposal too. You can get stick-on lights, which are useful if you want something you can easily move about, and again, these are a good option for hallways and the like. They don't tend to give off a lot of light, but they have a soft glow so they're good for areas in which you don't need bright lighting. They usually have a Velcro attachment, allowing you to fit them just about anywhere. Remember to check what batteries they need and add a good amount to your stockpile.

I wouldn't want to rely solely on battery-operated lights, simply because at some point, you're going to run out of batteries. I'd prioritize things you can recharge or stock a good amount of fuel for. That said, flashlights and headlamps are an absolute must, in my opinion. Refer back to Chapter Two for my advice on these.

What we didn't talk about earlier, however, was the everyday carry (EDC) flashlight. I'd really recommend everyone in the family has one of these in their pocket or handbag. It will mean you'll all have something with you the moment the power goes out. You could opt for much better models, but on the grounds that I wanted to make sure we all had something for the immediate problem, I've opted for a more budget-friendly route for my family. We have Maglite XL50s, which are strong and reliable, despite not being as bright as other models. You'll need to stock some AAA batteries for these.

Chemical Light Sticks

You're most likely to see a glow stick at a festival these days, but they're not a bad idea to keep on hand for an emergency, and like solar lights, they can be good in those high-traffic areas like hallways. I think maybe my favorite thing about them, though, is that they'll make the whole experience a bit more fun and a bit less scary for the kids. Some of them will actually carry on glowing for about 12 hours. They might not be the most environmentally-friendly option, but they're fun; reliable for a short time; and a handy, easy-to-store extra to have on hand.

Lighting is always important, particularly on shorter days. The good news is that all these solutions are simple and easy to stock up on in advance. I'd recommend having a number of different options available to see you through both a short-term and longer-term crisis. This way, no matter what the catalyst for the grid going down is, you'll know you have lighting options that will work.

TAKE ACTION: DIY EMERGENCY LIGHT

Regardless of all the lighting options there are out there, I can't resist a good DIY light, and if it involves food, all the better! Any well-stocked pantry should have a supply of oily fish, and if yours includes tinned sardines, there's a bonus lighting project you can embark on.

This will only work with sardines packed in oil, but once you've enjoyed your sandwich, keep the oil and the tin, and make your own fishy oil lamp (yes, it does smell a little, I'll be honest). Simply add a natural fiber wick to the oil in the tin. Once it's completely soaked, light the end, and you'll be surprised by how long that little lamp will burn.

If you'd prefer a tastier-smelling project, collect your excess bacon fat in a jar until you have enough to turn into a candle. Simply coat a natural fiber wick in fat, push it right down to the bottom of the jar, and voila: a delicious-smelling DIY candle. Word of warning though: I've tried this, and it drives the family crazy if you're not also going to offer them a bacon sandwich!

6

LONGER-TERM SOLUTIONS

WATER FILTRATION AND STORAGE

I'm lucky enough to have never been in a situation where I haven't had access to water, but during our recent power outage, I realized that in the event of a serious grid-down emergency, it wouldn't just be the electricity and gas we'd lose: It would be water too. So I've reassessed my stockpiles and started thinking more seriously about what we'd do if we lost access to running water.

WHY WATER IS A PRIORITY IF THE GRID GOES DOWN

If millions of people are affected by a large-scale power outage, it won't be long before the water supply is affected. We don't think about it much, but the running water in our homes is made possible by timers, valves, pumps, and substations, and when they're no longer able to provide enough water pressure to keep the water flowing, it's all going to stop. We can only live about 3 days without water, so making sure you have it is going to be a top priority in a grid-down situation.

The first thing to remember is that you need more water than you probably think you do. Drinking water is clearly a priority but you'll also need water to meet your family's hygiene needs, for washing dishes, for doing laundry, and for cooking. We looked at your short-term water needs earlier in the book, but if we're looking at a longer-term crisis, you're going to need between 20 and 30 gallons of water for every member of the household per month. I'm of the point of view that it's always best to err on the side of caution, so I'd estimate your needs nearer the higher end of the spectrum. That means a family of 4 would need about 360 gallons of water to see them through 3 months… and for that reason, you'll need to think carefully about storage. But don't worry: We'll get to that shortly.

WHAT YOU CAN DO IN ADVANCE OF A CRISIS

Just as you can make your home crisis-ready in terms of heating or cooling, you can prepare for an event that leaves you without water.

If you're a gardener, you probably already harvest your own water. If you're not, you should know that having a garden isn't the only reason you might want to consider doing so. If the water you collect is to be fit for human consumption, it will need to be purified (which we'll look at further down the chapter), but there are some household tasks (flushing the toilet, for example) for which this isn't necessary.

To collect rainwater, you need 5 basic elements: a catchment surface (like your roof); a way to direct the rainwater to your collection system (the gutters and downspouts on your property); a filter to keep debris out of the water; a lidded barrel to collect it; and a faucet to release it from the barrel. This should be installed low on the barrel, and ideally, you want to include a way of directing overflow (a lot of people use a hose connected to a backup barrel for this). The good news is that as you want to install this well in advance of an emergency, you can get a complete system from your garden or hardware store.

The other thing you can do well in advance is stock up on bottled water. This will only last you for a short time, but I would aim to store enough to keep your family going for the first couple of weeks of a disaster. It will keep indefinitely if you store it in a cool dry place. Keep it out of direct sunlight, and aim not to store it in contact with a cement floor or wall (this can transfer chemicals into the water). To avoid leakage, avoid stacking water containers too high, and rotate your stock to make sure it's all in good condition (single-use plastic deteriorates over time). Tempting as it may be to fill old containers with tap water, remember that juice, milk, soda, and water bottles aren't designed to be reused. Most of them contain polyethylene terephthalate (PET), and they can leach chemicals into the water if they're reused.

WATER STORAGE OPTIONS

Beyond your initial supply of bottled water, you're going to need to think about how you're going to store water for a longer period in such a way that you can replenish it as necessary. Before we get to my recommendations for this, a word of caution: Avoid gallon jugs. They're comparatively cheap, but you'll quickly find that they're a hindrance to your whole storage system because you can't stack them. They can also be quite flimsy, and all it takes is for one to be caught on something, and you have water all over the floor and one less gallon in your stash. There are other options that are much more reliable and easy to store.

Portable Water Storage Containers

A better alternative is portable water containers, which typically hold between 5 and 7 gallons of water. You can get larger ones, but the heavier they are, the less portable they become, and the harder it will be to take water from them. A good option is the Reliance Aquatainer. With a 7 gallon capacity, it's sturdy, easy to store, and has a spigot for easy use. It also has a liquid level indicator, which is a useful bonus. I've seen these in Walmart, and they're not all that expensive, so they're easy to get hold of and stock up on in advance. For me, the spigot really is a game-changer. We use these when we go camping, and it works a bit like a wine box: You can just leave it on a camping table and use it as necessary. There's no wastage, and even the clumsiest child can use it independently.

I would aim to store enough water to see your family through two months in containers like these. The added advantage of using them, even if you also have a tank or a barrel, is that you can easily take them with you if you need to evacuate your home.

When you're using containers like this, you're going to want to refill them every six months or so, discarding the old water and rinsing them well. Without doing this, you run the risk of bacteria breeding in your water, and that's the last thing you want in an emergency situation.

Storage Barrels and Tanks

It does require you to have a bit more space, but if you have the luxury, a water tank or barrel is a good idea. I can't say they're cheap, but they do allow you to store a large amount of water for a considerable amount of time. They come in a range of sizes, so if you have a garage or a basement, you should be able to clear a big enough corner for one. You can store between 50 and 250 gallons of water this way.

For the average suburban family, a water cistern is an unrealistic option, but it's worth mentioning anyway. These tanks will hold several thousand gallons of water and are usually buried beneath the ground. Many people link them up to their rainwater harvesting system. If you do consider this route, however, it's important to make sure you choose a cistern made of food-grade materials and don't buy one that has previously been used for chemical storage.

Cistern, barrel, or tank, you'll have to take an extra precaution with storing water in this volume: You'll need to treat it in order to prevent bacterial growth. You can buy water treatment drops (Water Preserver is a trustworthy brand)— just follow the instructions on the bottle. We'll also look at some other purification methods further down the chapter.

Aqua Pods and WaterBOBs

You could also consider something like an Aqua Pod or a WaterBOB, which are essentially plastic bladders you put in the bath and fill from the faucet. As they fill with water, they mold to the shape of the bathtub, keeping your water supply safe and secure. Of course, you could just put the plug in and fill the bath before the water cuts out, and if you don't have a device like this, it's still worth doing. But the advantage of these products is that they'll protect your supply from bacteria and any unpleasant extras that might be lingering in the bathtub. A WaterBOB will hold 100 gallons of water and keep it fresh for around 16 weeks; an Aqua Pod will take 65 gallons, keeping it fresh for about 8 weeks.

Containers like this are designed for single-use, so once you've used your supply, you can't use them again. That said, you probably wouldn't need to: They're designed to be filled from the faucet, and once that's no longer an option, you won't have any use for it again. Don't be tempted to keep them to reuse in the future though: Bacteria will grow inside them, and they won't be safe.

Personally, I'd recommend having something like this so you can make the most of your bathroom faucet as soon as you realize there's a problem. It's an easy way to top up your supply straight away, and it's more hygienic than filling the bathtub without any kind of protective container.

IF THE GRID GOES DOWN: WHAT TO DO IMMEDIATELY

When the grid goes down, the water supply hasn't got long. The first thing to do is to collect as much water from the faucets as you can. If you have a WaterBOB or an Aqua Pod, now's the time to fill it. If you don't, put the plug in the bath, and fill it anyway. Put buckets at the bottom of your gutter downspouts to collect any extra rainwater that might come your way, and lay a piece of tarpaulin outside to collect groundwater (you can angle this so it drains into a bucket too). Fill any empty storage containers from the sink faucets, and fill bowls and buckets too. The water you collect in these won't keep for as long, but you can use it for your immediate needs. The mission at this stage is simply to collect as much water as possible before the system runs dry.

THE WATER YOU SHOULD NEVER DRINK

Once you've been living without power for a while and you're beginning to go through your water stocks, you're going to have to think about sourcing more water. However, before we get to that, it's important to bear in mind that not all water is safe for drinking. Some of these things may seem obvious, but if you're panicking, it's easy to forget the basics, so I don't think it's wise for me to assume that anything's too obvious to mention.

Avoid water from the toilet cistern and bowl, the radiators, your pool, or any water beds you may have. All of this water could be contaminated, and shouldn't be used without treatment. You should also avoid drinking floodwater or water from a well unless it has been declared safe. This is worth noting because in the event of a natural disaster, well water that may previously have been deemed safe could be contaminated. Don't trust it unless it has been tested and given the all-clear. Finally, if you live near the ocean, don't be tempted to drink the saltwater without distilling it first.

SOURCING WATER FROM THE WILD

I say "wild," but there's water hiding from you all over the place, not just in natural bodies of water.

Your first source is, of course, rainwater, and if you've installed a water barrel, you'll already have been collecting it before disaster strikes. It can contain contaminants, however, so you'll need to filter and purify it. If you don't have a rainwater harvesting system, you can still collect rainwater in buckets.

Your hot water tank is also a source of emergency water and probably contains around 30 gallons. To drain the water, you'll need to turn off the supply and the power (even if neither of these things is working). If yours is a gas heater, switch the thermostat to the Pilot setting. The drain valve will be near the bottom of the heater. Connect this to a garden hose, and then turn on a hot water faucet nearby. Put the other end of the hose into a bucket before opening the valve. I'd recommend gathering several buckets before you start because you'll definitely need more than one. That said, you don't necessarily need to drain the whole tank at once—you can always close off the valve and drain the rest later. You may notice some mineral deposits once you get to the end of the water, but these aren't harmful and you can easily filter them out.

The next place to look for water is in your neighborhood. Streams, ponds, rivers, lakes... All of this depends on where you live, of course, but unless you live in the desert, you're likely to have some water nearby. This is where those water storage containers will really come into their own but bear in mind that you'll need to be able to carry whatever you collect. If you have a handcart or a wheelbarrow, this might be a good way of being able to carry several containers further.

Treating Water

Any water you do collect will need to be treated before it's safe to drink. Your first option is filtering. I use a Big Berkey Water Filter, mostly because of its shelf life: Each element will filter around 3,000 gallons. We often take it camping with us because it's powerful enough to purify stream water, and it's made of steel, so it's easy to transport without damaging it. There are plenty of other brands out there though, so you have options. Just make sure you have a supply of filters on hand. Whichever system you use, strain the larger debris away before you run the water through it in order to keep your filter clean and running for longer.

You can mimic the effects of a water filter by using natural filters. If you add a layer of sand to the bottom of a straining container, followed by layers of charcoal and rocks, you can run your water through it to minimize the bacteria levels. Bear in mind, however, that this will not get rid of giardia if it is present.

Alternatively, you could boil your water, which will kill any bacteria lurking inside it. Simply bring it to the boil and allow it to continue for 10 minutes or so, before leaving it to cool. It won't be the tastiest water you've ever drunk, but it will be safe… and you can always make tea with it to enhance the flavor.

You can also get UV pens designed to kill water-borne bacteria. Again, you'll want to strain any debris off first. I can't vouch for these as I've never tried one personally, but I do know people who've used them on camping trips and say they work well.

Chlorine bleach is another alternative, but you need to be careful. It's technically carcinogenic and can lead to poisoning, but if you're out of other options, it can be a useful last resort. Avoid scented bleach or bleach with added chemicals, and double-check the expiry date first (you might be surprised to know that it's only effective for 6 months). Don't use pool chlorine: It's much stronger than domestic bleach, and this is why you shouldn't drink the water in your pool. You'll need just 8 drops of bleach for every gallon of water, but again, strain off any debris first. Shake your container well, and leave it for 30 minutes before using it.

I hold my hands up and admit that I'm a little nervous of using chlorine bleach myself. I'd do it if I had no other option, but if I was going to use chlorination, I'd prefer to use chlorine dioxide tablets. They kill many different viruses and bacteria (including giardia, which chlorine bleach won't), and they're easy to use: All you need to do is add the tablets to the water—just follow the instructions on the packet. You can also get the same thing in liquid form, the only difference being that you add drops rather than tablets.

Alternatively, you could opt for distillation. This requires a bit more planning and equipment, but if you want to follow that route, you can always set yourself up in advance. To distill water, you require a heat source, a heat-resistant container, a condenser, and another container to collect the distilled water. You'll also need a tube (made of food-grade materials) to transport the steam from the first container, through the condenser, and into the second container. You can actually buy countertop distillers for around $200, which might be your best bet if you're willing to make the investment.

CONSERVING WATER

No matter how good your storage and collection plan is, you want to be mindful of how much water you're using, and conserve what you can. This doesn't mean drinking less than you need, but you can be mindful of what you eat in order to reduce unnecessary thirst. Try to avoid salty foods if water is becoming scarce, as these will make you more thirsty. Bear in mind that the human body does need sodium though, so don't go overboard; just rein in your potato chip obsession. We'll look at laundry and dishwashing specifically a little later, but this is definitely an area in which you can conserve water. Wait until you have a good load before you contemplate using precious water for it. You could even opt for disposable cups and plates to minimize the number of dishes that need washing.

If there's one thing I want you to take away from this chapter, it's this: It would be wise to calculate how much water you're going to need to get your family through at least a month without water, ideally 3 months. It will probably be more than you expect, so make those calculations now—and don't forget to account for your pets.

TAKE ACTION: CALCULATE YOUR FAMILY'S WATER NEEDS

Remember the golden rule: 1 gallon per person per day. So, to calculate your family's water needs, you can use the following equation:

Water requirements = (1 gallon) x (number of people) x (number of days)

This will give you your family's drinking and sanitation requirements, but you'll also need to add on water for cooking and pets. As a guideline, most dogs need about 1 ounce of water per pound of body weight every day. You'll also need to account for your regional climate: If you live somewhere hotter, you're going to need more water.

7

LONGER-TERM SOLUTIONS

FOOD AND COOKING

The best advice I can give you when it comes to cooking when the power's out is to practice. Being prepared means being prepared with your skills and knowledge as much as it does with your supplies. So when I say the best thing you can do is practice, what I mean is, you need to practice alternative cooking methods *before* disaster strikes. At least, you do if you want to avoid culinary disasters, and let me tell you, I've learned this the hard way. Just ask my kids about the first time I tried to roast a shoulder of lamb on the campfire…

It would be best to prepare to cook both indoors and outdoors. Cooking outside is safer for some methods, and if you live in a warm region, you're going to want to keep the extra heat inside to a minimum. But it may be that the weather is too bad for you to cook outdoors, which means you need to be prepared to cook inside too. Of course, you won't necessarily need to practice every method of cooking there is, but it would be wise to have skills to cover a few approaches.

OFF-GRID COOKING OPTIONS

The first thing I would say is that the best cooking method depends entirely on what it is you're cooking, and that's why it's a good idea to be familiar with a few approaches. It will also mean you'll need to have a few different types of fuel on hand to use with whichever devices you'll be cooking on, so bear this in mind when you're taking an inventory of your supplies.

Camping Stove

There are two main routes you can go down with camping stoves: gas stoves and alcohol stoves. Gas stoves are typically fueled by canisters of propane, butane, or isobutene, and a few models allow you multiple options. If you only have a small stove for camping, it might be worth getting something that connects to a larger cylinder for long-term disaster preparedness. Word of warning though: Not all camping stoves are certified for indoor use, and you'll always need to ensure that you have good ventilation, even with those that are. We have a butane stove that has been certified for use indoors, and I've tested it out at home as well as for camping. It fits neatly on the kitchen counter, and it almost feels like cooking on a regular stove. What I would say, though, is that butane cylinders aren't cheap, and these stoves burn through a lot, particularly if you'll be doing long, slow cooking. They'd be great for a short-term outage, but you'll want something else up your sleeve to cover a longer crisis.

The other type of camping stove is an alcohol stove, which typically burns alcohol, pure methanol alcohol, or pure ethanol. A lot of people seem to prefer alcohol stoves to gas stoves, but you definitely want to get your practice in. It takes a bit of perseverance to get the hang of heat control, and I can't say I've mastered it myself.

There is an alternative route with camping stoves too: portable wood stoves, which actually require very little wood. I've never used one (I'm a big fan of a campfire), but I have friends who swear by them. They work by trapping the heat so you can cook with little fuel, and have a built-in pot stand. They're sort of a halfway house between camping stoves and wood stoves.

Wood Stove

If you're heating your home with a wood stove anyway, you have the added option of using it for cooking. Bear in mind that all wood stoves should be properly installed with adequate ventilation—this isn't just something you can add on a whim for cooking purposes.

If you do decide to cook on your wood stove, you can basically cook anything you would usually cook on your regular stove, but you'll need to come to grips with controlling the heat. This is simply a case of getting to know your stove. Start by finding out where it gets hottest: This will be where you can cook food quickly. As you move further away from this "sweet spot," your food will cook at a slower rate. You can also control the temperature by adjusting how you build the fire. If you opt for several thinner logs in place of one large one, they'll burn more quickly and generate more heat.

Campfire

A wood stove is your indoor fire option. If you don't have one or you'd prefer to cook outside, a campfire is totally an option, as long as the weather is onside and you have suitable space for a firepit. As you'll know if you've ever tried to embrace your inner caveman on a camping trip, however, campfire cooking is a skill. I've burned many a pan of beans over an open fire, let me tell you.

Before you build your firepit, you want to check the wind direction to make sure that the smoke won't be blowing toward where you're planning to eat. With this established and a good spot chosen, you'll need to dig a pit and mark a perimeter around it with stones. Dig further down in the center, which will make the fire less likely to escape.

Your next step is choosing firewood. I would recommend stocking up on kindling in advance because it saves you searching for dry twigs, which can be tricky in damp conditions. Otherwise, this is the first thing you'll need to do, as well as searching for larger pieces of wood. Look for broken branches and deadwood. If you cut branches directly from trees, they'll contain too much moisture to burn well. If you have a choice, go for hardwoods like ash, oak, or birch, rather than softwoods like spruce or pine. Softwoods get going quickly, but they don't burn for as long and don't allow you as much control when you're cooking.

You then want to lay your firewood, and there are several ways you can approach this. Personally, I'm a fan of the tepee style, which works with a tepee-like structure to allow air circulation and concentrate the flame. I've always found this method to be reliable, and it's easy to construct. Start by sticking a forked branch into the ground as a center pole, and then stack your wood up against it to form a tepee shape. Remember to leave a gap for adding and lighting the kindling.

Once you have your fire burning, you want to let it blaze for a little while before you start cooking. As it burns, it will produce embers, and it's these (rather than flames) that you'll need to cook over. Spread the embers out, being careful not to poke them so much they die out, and let the fire keep burning. Your goal is to have a bed of embers and a roaring fire from which you can keep topping it up.

We'll look more closely at the cooking equipment you'll need further down the chapter, but it's worth mentioning that you'll want a grilling rack to place over the embers. You can also wrap your food in foil and place the packages directly in the embers to cook. Again, this is something you want to practice before disaster strikes because it can take some trial and error to get it right.

Reflector Oven

You can take your campfire cooking a step further by building a reflector oven. You'll just need a piece of sheet metal and a cookie sheet or grill pan to put inside. Fold the sheet metal in half to make the main body, and then cut two right-angled triangles to make the sides, along with some tabs to interlock the pieces. I'd recommend using proper metal tools for this, but you can just use some garden snips if you're careful. Then it's simply a case of putting it together and integrating it into your campfire, placing it beside the glowing embers. You'll probably need to place some stones behind it to make it stand up properly. The idea is that it uses radiant energy from the fire to cook the food inside it, so you'll need to keep drawing embers from the fire to keep it at a constant temperature. You can actually bake cakes and pies like this, but you'll definitely need to practice.

Earth Oven

Alternatively, you could set up your backyard for outdoor cooking with an earth oven. This is relatively easy to construct yourself with a little elbow grease, but you'll want to do it well in advance of any disaster so you know you have it as an option as soon as you need it. You'll also want to get hold of some masonry sand for best results. Start by preparing a base: You can either build directly onto the ground, or you can build it up to a more convenient height by using logs, rocks, or concrete blocks.

Aim for a floor size of between 20 and 30 inches, and create it by laying bricks on a level bed of sand about 6 inches deep. Make sure any bricks you use are free from old mortar and make sure they're pressed into the sand firmly to create a surface as flat as possible. What you want to do next is pile moist sand on top of the bricks and flatten it down, creating a dome shape between 16 and 20 inches high. You'll need a bit of math next: Measure the sand form and multiply its height by 0.63 to work out the height of your oven door.

You then want to find some good mud from beneath the topsoil in your backyard. This should contain clay, which will hold your oven together. It should feel a bit greasy and be sticky to the touch. If you're unable to find this in your backyard, you can always collect some from a riverbank or a construction site. Mix 1 part clay soil into 3 parts masonry sand, and add water until a cement-like consistency is reached (this will take some muscle!). Before you go further, you want to test the strength of your mixture by making a tight ball and dropping it from a height. If it cracks, you want to add more water. Once you have a strong, firm mixture, you can start building your oven.

Cover the sand dome with smooth, wet newspaper to stop the walls from sticking. Now add a 3-inch layer of mud, and pack it solidly against the sand base. You might find it helpful to use a board for this. Allow this layer to dry before adding another layer. You could even cover this with plaster for an extra finish once the final layer has dried. Bear in mind that this is a slow process: Drying could take up to a week. Once the mud can be touched without denting, it has dried sufficiently.

Once the outside of the oven is built and dried, you can remove the sand dome, but before you do that, make a mark in the mud where the doorway should be (use the measurement you took earlier). Remove the sand, and smooth out the doorway with a spoon or a stone.

To make the door, cut out a template that will fit the opening, and use this to craft a door out of the clay mixture. It doesn't need to fit perfectly because you can always cover it with a damp towel, which will help with the cooking process and prevent the door from charring.

If you've got this far, it's worth the extra effort to make a covering for your oven. In wet weather, it will become damp, and this can extend cooking time significantly. Just be sure to leave enough room around the oven to allow good air circulation: Think roof rather than snug covering.

Finally, your oven is ready to use. Build a fire inside, allowing smoke to escape through the doorway. Fire it for around 3 hours (or until the black soot at the top has disappeared), and then pull out the coals. Put your food inside, and close the door. This is a great little garden project anyway, I think, disaster or no disaster. Once you've got your practice in, you'll be well equipped to make pizza and bread al fresco any time you like.

Thermal Oven

This seems like a logical point to turn our attention toward alternative ovens. We'll start with the hay box or thermal oven, which is essentially a box that traps heat for long, slow cooking. It's not one to use for a quick evening meal, but if you plan in advance, it provides a good opportunity for conserving fuel. It's also one of the very few cooking options that you don't have to monitor the whole time, and it's a great method for cooking stews or other meals that need to be simmered for a good chunk of time. It's pretty easy to make a DIY thermal oven. You'll need an insulated box such as an old cooler, or a shoebox lined with aluminum foil or old clothing. A lidded saucepan or casserole dish is then placed inside the oven, and the box (if you take the traditional hay box approach) is surrounded with hay for further insulation. You could even make your own box out of wood and insulate it with polystyrene and cardboard if you're skilled in this area. A well-made thermal oven like this won't require the extra hay.

To cook with a thermal oven, you'll need to start your food off over another heat source. Let's say you were making a stew: You would cook all your ingredients as usual, and bring your meal to the boil. You would then remove it from the heat and put it into your thermal oven, where it would continue cooking without additional fuel for a further 8–12 hours. I've tried making stews this way, and I have to say, the results can be quite mind-blowing.

You can also buy commercial thermal cookers. The Wonder Oven is a popular choice.

Tealight Oven

I like to talk about the "tealight oven" as opposed to the Home Emergency Radiant Cooking (HERC) oven because it sounds so much more relatable, but they're the same thing. I was astounded the first time I came across these. If you've ever used a tealight in a candle holder, you'll know that they don't give off a lot of heat on their own. However, if you shelter them in an enclosed space, that space will trap heat and create an oven effect. It's another slow one though, and you'll need several hours to cook an ordinary oven recipe in one, but it's a good alternative to be aware of.

You can buy a specially designed HERC oven, or you can make your own using tealights. To reach a high enough temperature for cooking, you'll need about 12 tealights. Remove the elements and plug from an old toaster oven, and drill some holes in the back. Line the bottom of the oven with tealights, and if you can, attach a piece of baking stone to the top. It should still work fine without this, but you stand a better chance of your food cooking evenly with the stone in place. Because there are flames involved, you'll want to cook on the upper rack rather than the lower one, or you run the risk of your food burning.

Solar Cooking

An alternative outdoor oven option is a solar oven, which you could buy or you could make DIY-style. What's great about this is that you don't need to use up any of your fuel stocks, but it's most effective when the UV Index is above 7. It's a relatively slow cooking method, but it allows the food to retain its moisture, so it offers good results. One brand I hear recommended time and time again is Global Sun Ovens, so if you're thinking of buying one, check them out. If you can afford it, buying one is probably a good idea simply because of the size and stability offered by a professionally built one. However, you can make a small-scale version with a clean pizza box if you're interested in exploring.

Start by drawing a square within 1 inch of the edges of the box lid. Cut out 3 sides of this square with a knife, and crease the uncut side to make a flap. Next, cut out a piece of aluminum foil to cover the internal side of the flap, pressing it down tightly and securing it with tape. Now line the bottom of the box with black paper. Cut 2 squares of plastic wrap the same size as the top part of the box, and secure this to the inside edges of the window. You want this to be airtight. Stuff the sides of the box with rolled-up newspaper as insulation, making sure that the lid will still close.

You won't be able to cook a lot with a DIY oven like this, but it'll do in a pinch, and it's a fun project to do with the kids. It'll work best when the sun is at its highest, so between 11 a.m. and 2 p.m. is your best bet. Simply put a dish inside, angle the reflective flap toward the sun, and you're good to go. The black paper inside the oven will absorb energy from the sun, and the warm air will stay inside because of the plastic wrap.

Portable Solar Power Stations

With the exception of wood stoves and camping stoves, most of your alternative cooking methods limit you to cooking outdoors, but there is one more option for indoor cooking. You could use a portable power station (or use your generator, if you have one) to run your stove. However, these can be quite pricey, and you'll need to make sure that they're designed to power energy-guzzling appliances like electric stoves before you buy one. The advantage of a portable solar power station over a generator is that you can charge them outdoors in the sun and then bring them in fully charged. Of course, opting for something like this gives you plenty of other options besides cooking too.

Barbecue Grill

I don't want to explain your barbecue grill to you here, but I do want to bring it up because barbecuing is an excellent option (weather conditions permitting) in a power outage. Plus, it's likely to be something you've already had a lot of practice with. Just make sure you have a good supply of charcoal, and you'll be able to cook outdoors without the use of any more complicated equipment.

I've chosen what I think are the most realistic cooking options to discuss here, but search around online, and you'll find dozens of alternative cooking methods. If you feel like going further down the rabbit hole, check out hobo stoves, wick stoves, and buddy burners. At the very least, there's a lot of educational fun to be had with the family discussing cooking methods and trying out DIY projects.

OFF-GRID COOKING ESSENTIALS

I often speak to people who think they're fully prepared in the cooking department, confident in their knowledge that they have some solid alternatives to grid-reliant cooking up their sleeves. But, what many people don't realize is that alternative cooking methods require alternative equipment. If you're cooking over an open fire, your cheap non-stick frying pan is quickly going to become useless.

First off, let's look at what you definitely want to know you have at home, starting with aluminum foil. Foil has played a role in a few of the DIY projects we've mentioned but it's also a really good resource. As well as keeping food fresher for longer, you can use it for open-fire cooking and for making emergency containers if necessary. It may seem obvious, but the next thing you definitely want to have is a good can opener… possibly two in case anything goes wrong with your first one. You should have a lot of cans in your pantry: Make sure you can get into them! You'll want a bottle opener, pot holders and oven mitts, and wooden spoons. It might seem strange to draw attention to wooden spoons, but if you're used to cooking with plastic utensils, you may find yourself in melted plastic hell if you don't have a backup option for some of these cooking methods. Lastly, you'll need to think about your pots and pans: Nearly all the methods we've looked at require them to come into contact with an open flame and that's very different from cooking on an electric burner.

Durable Cookware

First, for any open-flame cooking, be that over a campfire, over the embers of your wood-burning stove, or on the barbecue, you're going to need a grill. You can get these in various sizes, so make sure you get something that's big enough for your family's needs but small enough to suit your heat source. I have a couple of camping grill grates from Redcamp which are made of stainless steel and about as easy to clean as a grill can ever be. Any brand will be fine, though: Just make sure it's durable and certified as safe for use with food. I also have a campfire grill, which is a much better option for an open fire. It's conveniently foldable and it stands over the flames like a table so you can easily set a pan of water over it without worrying about putting your fire out.

With the grill covered, you want to turn your attention to cookware. Your main goal is durability, so I'd recommend cast iron, stainless steel, or aluminum. They all have their advantages and disadvantages, and I think ultimately, I'd recommend having a bit of everything if you can. It just gives you more flexibility in terms of the types of food you can cook and how. Stainless steel has the advantage of being easy to use and it's great for using over moderate heat. It's not as good for cooking over an open fire where the temperature is high, though, and it's hard to clean the outside of a stainless steel pan. Aluminum isn't great for very high temperatures either but it does have the very definite bonus of heating up quickly, so used over a camp stove, it can help you conserve fuel. Cast iron is renowned for its weight and durability and I'd say this is really your best option for open-fire cooking. If you want to keep costs to a minimum, skip the aluminum and focus on cast iron for open flames and stainless steel for less intensive cooking.

FUELING THE FIRE

Many of these cooking methods require fire, so stocking up on fuel and fire-lighting tools should be a solid part of your preparation plan. This is part of the reason it's so important to decide what cooking methods you plan to turn to in advance and practice using them. You need to know exactly what stocks you need so that you can be confident that you really do have an emergency backup option.

Exactly what you need to stock up on depends, of course, on what devices you need to fuel. But regardless of the details, I'd recommend having plenty of matches and lighters on hand. These will always be useful and I'm not sure it's possible to have too many. That said, I'm a firm believer that the best thing you can stock up on is knowledge, and knowing what to do if you run out of matches or lighter fluid is a peace of mind I know I want to have. So, let's make sure you know how to get a fire going even if your stocks dry up.

Emergency Fire Lighting

There are four primary ways you can start a fire without matches: friction, sparks, the sun, or chemicals. I mention chemicals only so that you're aware of all the options but I'm not going to look at that too closely here. I don't like the idea of stocking potentially hazardous materials if I don't have to and you can easily start a fire without resorting to using them.

There are multiple ways to use friction, sparks, and sunlight but here we'll just look at one solid option for each approach.

Friction

While friction may be the first thing that comes to mind when you think of starting a fire, it's actually one of the most difficult approaches. Using a hand drill is probably the simplest option available to you but this can be tricky in wet conditions. Begin by cutting a V-shape in a piece of board and making a small depression beside it. Place a bit of bark beneath the notch in order to catch the ember when it lights. You'll now need a spindle about 2 feet in length. Place this in the depression, and roll it between your hands while moving them up and down the spindle with speed and pressure. Keep going until the end of the spindle glows red and an ember is created. Now tap the board to knock the ember onto the piece of bark, and then use it to spark a bundle of tinder. This will quickly go out if left alone, however, so you'll need to blow on it to generate a flame.

Sparks

To use sparks to start a fire, flint and steel is probably the most straightforward method. You can actually buy kits to save you searching for the right materials, which might be a worthwhile investment if you're not used to the process. I've used these, and I have to say they're easier than trying to use found objects. The spark is created when the hard flint is struck with the relatively soft steel.

Begin by holding a piece of hard rock (the flint) between your forefinger and thumb, allowing the sharp edge to stick out a couple of inches. Next, you'll need to lay some char cloth against the flint. Use the steel to strike the flint using a quick wrist movement. You'll need to do this a few times but you will find that sparks will begin to fly at the char cloth fairly quickly. Once it begins to glow, you can transfer it to a pre-prepared nest of tinder and then wrap the nest with the char cloth. Again, you'll need to blow on it to get a flame going. You could also add dry twigs and grass to encourage it along. Once you have a steady flame, you can transfer the bundle to your fireplace, which should already be laid with logs.

Sun

Harnessing the power of the sun to start a fire works by concentrating a sunbeam onto a particular material but it's only really an option in bright, clear weather. The most obvious way to do this is to use a magnifying glass, preferably one that will allow you to rotate it rather than one with a handle. This will give you greater control and allow you to change your angle as necessary. Lay your tinder on the ground, and use the magnifying glass to direct the sunlight onto it. Keep the angle steady, and slowly you should begin to see smoke rising from the tinder nest. As soon as that happens, it's time to blow on it until you have a flame.

FUEL CONSERVATION TECHNIQUES

No matter how much fuel you've stocked up on, you're going to need to use it wisely to make sure it lasts for as long as possible. Mostly, what this comes down to is mindful cooking, by which I mean paying close attention to how you're cooking each food. This begins by using the right equipment for the job. If your wood stove is already burning to heat the house, this is a logical place to boil your water as it won't require using any additional fuel. On the other hand, if all you want to do is boil that pan of water and the stove isn't being used for another purpose, you'd be better off using your camping stove. Think about what fuel you're already using and consider whether you can also use it for cooking. If not, ask yourself which is the best tool for the job.

When you're cooking, aim to cover your food as often as possible. This prevents heat loss by keeping the steam in the pan and cooking its contents more quickly. Of course, there are times when keeping the steam in the pan isn't going to work for the type of meal you're cooking, so use your discretion. Another trick is to cut your food into smaller pieces in order to speed up the cooking process. Think of cooking a jacket potato in the oven versus frying small pieces of potato over a burner: If you have an open fire going anyway, baking potatoes in foil packages is a good use of fuel; if not, you'll use less fuel if you opt for small chunks of potato fried over a camp stove.

Of course, a few of the cooking techniques we looked at also lend themselves naturally to fuel conservation. Any time you can use solar energy for cooking you're essentially getting free fuel, and if you turn to thermal cooking, you'll be using no fuel beyond what is required to get the dish started. One method we didn't look at, however, was pressure cooking. This is often seen as quite an old-fashioned way of cooking but in a grid-down situation, it will really come into its own. If you want to cook dried beans, for example, a pressure cooker will allow you to do this in just a little more time than it takes to warm up a pan of cooked beans. As a result, you'll make significant savings in fuel—particularly if you then finish those beans off using thermal cooking techniques.

GRID-DOWN COOKING SAFETY

It's easy to focus on the ways you can cook as normally as possible in the event of a power outage without giving a second thought to safety. But this will need to be at the forefront of your mind as normal safety mechanisms won't be in place, and you'll often be working with dangerous tools and substances.

The main thing is really just to be aware of the hazards. If you're using gas, carbon monoxide is always a risk so it's important to have a detector. Any open flame is also a danger. It's obvious, but it's something the whole family needs to be aware of. Make sure the kids know to stay a safe distance from the fire and make sure everyone knows how to use a fire extinguisher. My attitude has always been to get the kids involved in everything. That way, you teach them the skills while also building a natural awareness of safety. Obviously, you want to keep very little ones away from the cooking action but once they're old enough, I think the best way to keep them safe is to let them understand what you're doing, how you're doing it, and how you're making sure you're doing it safely.

SOURCING FOOD

I'm assuming that you're coming to this book with a lot of things already in place for an emergency situation, and that includes a well-stocked pantry. If you still need more information on this, have a look at my last book, *The Prepper's Pantry*. One thing I'd like to add here, though, is that it's a good idea to stock up on some foods that don't require cooking. This will help you conserve fuel, and it means you'll always have an option if everything doesn't go to plan with your cooking arrangements.

Hopefully, your stocks will see you through the length of the disaster, but the reality is, if the grid goes down in a big way, we just don't know what the future's going to look like. I want to look at a few other ways of procuring food for that reason, but bear in mind that whole books can be written on this and you'll definitely need to do further research.

Gardening

The reason your pantry is so important during a grid-down situation is that food supplies are going to be hit hard. If you have the space to grow your own food, I'd say that's really the best thing you can do to ensure your family has a steady supply of nutritious food. Of course, you can't account for every disaster, and if the reason the power's out is due to extreme weather, the chances are your garden's going to take a knock. But getting a vegetable garden started now is going to serve you well in most situations, so if you have the space, I'd say it's definitely worth researching and adding to your project list.

Keeping Livestock

Keeping livestock isn't a possibility for everyone and if you live in an urban or suburban area, there may well be zoning laws preventing it. Space is also an issue for many people. Nonetheless, protein is an important dietary requirement, and animals and animal products provide it in abundance, so if it's an option for you, it's worth considering. Chickens, ducks, rabbits, and goats are all good options but you'll need to do your research carefully and make sure you know what you're doing before you get started. Animal welfare is crucial, and you'll need to know how to recognize signs of sickness and make sure you know what to do about them. You'll also need to learn skills in butchery and safe meat preparation. I'm certainly not suggesting it's an easy task, or even one that will suit everyone, but if you have the space and time to invest in the project, it would be a great asset in a grid-down situation.

Hunting

If you're not able to keep your own animals, it doesn't mean that fresh meat isn't available to you, but again, you're going to need to train up well in advance of an emergency. If you're already a seasoned hunter, you're one step ahead of the game, but bear in mind that hunting in a grid-down situation could look a little different from what you're used to. You may not have gas to fuel your car, so bringing a deer home might be challenging. You may need a little more knowledge about the habitats and behaviors of your prey. You may even need to resort to some unusual animals: Trapping animals like raccoons, rats, and beavers could become necessary in an extreme survival situation.

It's also crucial to keep safety in mind. If you live in a densely populated area, this is probably still going to be the case in an emergency, so shooting ducks at the local pond isn't necessarily a safe choice. If you do intend to add hunting to your skill set, I'd recommend taking a survivalist hunting course to make sure you know exactly how to hunt safely and exactly what equipment you need to have on hand.

Foraging

It blows my mind that we don't forage more. There's so much food around us that we're often not even aware of. The problem is, some plants are highly nutritious but others are poisonous, so foraging is a risky business if you don't know what you're looking for. I think a book on edible plant identification is an incredibly worthwhile investment for any household that wants to be prepared for the worst. We have a couple and we've actually had some brilliant family days out searching for food in the wild and then coming up with ways to use it.

Foraging can be split into two main categories: urban foraging and wilderness foraging. Wilderness foraging is probably the kind you naturally think of: searching for foods that are readily available in the wild. Your best bet is to buy a book and get to know what grows near where you live. Everything from crabapples and pine nuts to berries and mushrooms is a possibility.

When it comes to urban foraging, this comes down to what's available in your city. Community gardens are an obvious source of fresh food but beyond that, you need to tune into your apocalypse movie mindset. Think abandoned grocery stores, restaurants, vehicles, and dumpsters. It's a bit grim perhaps, and hopefully not something you'll ever have to resort to, but I find there's a bit of comfort in thinking through all of these possibilities and knowing where you can turn in an emergency.

Your pantry is a crucial part of your survival plan but it's of limited use if you don't know how to use it. That means making sure you have alternative cooking methods ready to go as soon as they become necessary… and it means practicing all to a proficient level.

TAKE ACTION: MAKE A CROSSBOW

I did think twice about including this section but in the end, I decided that if you're not a seasoned hunter, having the skills to make a DIY crossbow would be a definite bonus, and I know you'll have fun with this one.

A crossbow is essentially a hunting weapon made up of a horizontal bow attached to a stick (known as the stock). It is used to shoot bolts at a target, and if you have good aim, it's an efficient way of making a catch.

What You Need

- Pine wood, 2-inch thickness
- Pine wood, 1-inch thickness
- Nylon string
- Varnish or wood stain
- Wood glue
- 36-inch length of 1-inch PVC pipe
- 2 x wood screws
- 2 x pulleys
- Wire tires
- Nylon string
- Duct tape
- Nails
- Foam padding
- Dowels (if you want to make your own bolts)

The Mission

Step 1

Begin with a 2-inch x 2-inch pine board that is approximately 38 inches long. This will make your stock. Gripping this in your hands while pressing one end to your shoulder, find a comfortable size for your bow. Mark this length and saw off the excess wood.

Step 2

Lift the wood up into a crossbow position again, pressing one end to your shoulder as you did before. Now make a mark on the top surface of the wood where it would feel comfortable to have a handle and trigger. On top of this mark, draw a rectangle around 4 x 1 inches in size.

Step 3

Taking care not to split the wood, gouge out the rectangular area with a drill, a chisel and a wood rasp until you have a clean hole. Smooth the surrounding area with sandpaper. This is your trigger hole.

Step 4

Now make a groove about ⅛-inch long by the front of the trigger hole using a chisel. Sand the area well. This is where the string will lie across the trigger hole.

Step 5

The next step is to make a groove to hold the bolt, which will reach from the trigger hole to the end of the wood. On the opposite end of the wood from the string groove, make a mark in the center. Now mark the center of the end of the trigger hole at the end furthest away from the string groove. Join your two marks with a straight line, and then use a hammer, chisel, and drill to make a channel around ¼ inch deep. Sand this area well.

Step 6

You now need to make a grip that you can use when you're shooting. You'll need a second piece of wood for this, cut to a length of 8 inches. Glue this to the bottom of the stock and allow it to dry thoroughly.

Step 7

Varnish the stock, or use a wood stain to protect it from the weather.

Step 8

To make the bow, you'll need a 36-inch length of 1-inch PVC pipe. Cut a groove into either end of this large enough to hold a small wood screw.

Step 9

Now put a small wood screw into each grove and attach a pulley to each one with wire ties.

Step 10

Fasten one end of a piece of nylon string to the screw on the left-hand side of the pipe, and then loop the opposite end around the pulley on the right-hand side. Now bring the string back to loop around the left-hand pulley, before taking it back to the right-hand side and tying it to the wood screw. A quick word of caution here: Be careful not to pull the string taut when you wrap it around each pulley, otherwise you won't be able to pull it and operate the crossbow. The string should now be running across the pipe 3 times, and it should be secure but not tight. You can test this by pulling on the string. If the pipe flexes, the tightness is correct. Otherwise, you'll need to rethread the pulleys.

Step 11

Return to the stock, and use a chisel to carve out a groove that the pipe will fit into snugly. It should have no space to slide around.

LONGER-TERM SOLUTIONS | 113

Step 12

The bow will now need to be attached to the stock with the strings in the right place. Attach the pipe to the stock securely with duct tape. Make sure that there is only one string on top of the wood (this is the firing string). The other two strings should be underneath the wood.

Step 13

Test the bow by drawing back the firing string and securing it in the string groove you made earlier. If it won't stay in place, you'll need to make the notch deeper.

Step 14

Sketch out a rough L-shape on a new piece of pine wood, ideally about 1 inch thick. This will be your trigger system. The bottom line that makes the L should be a little smaller than the rectangular hole in the stock. Cut out the L-shape and sand it until the edges are smooth.

Step 15

Carve a channel, about ⅛ inch long, across the shortest side of your L-shape using a chisel.

Step 16

In the center of the L's corner, drill a hole big enough to hold a nail. This is how the trigger will be fixed to the stock.

Step 17

Your aim is to fix the trigger to the stock so that when it's pulled, it will push the string out of its groove. Place the trigger in the rectangular hole so that the L is pointing forward and the groove is facing upward. It should have space to move without touching the back of the trigger hole. Hammer a nail into the stock, holding the trigger in place.

Step 18

Ensure a smooth firing action by sanding the trigger down thoroughly.

Step 19

You're now going to make a handle so you can hold your crossbow steady while you pull the trigger. Cut an 8-inch piece of pine wood into a rough handle shape and refine it by sanding it down.

118 | SURVIVE AND THRIVE 2-IN-1 COLLECTION

Step 20

Glue the handle onto the stock behind the trigger. Leave this to dry completely and then strengthen the join with nails.

Step 21

In order to make the crossbow more comfortable to use, pad the end that will press against your shoulder with foam and secure this with duct tape.

Step 22

You can always buy bolts from a hardware store, but you could also make your own using dowels. To do this, cut dowels down to fit the channel on the crossbow, making notches at the ends to grip the string.

Step 23

You now need to test your crossbow, so set up a target and find a safe space to try it out. It could fire bolts to a distance of 100 feet so make sure you test it somewhere with lots of space.

It's Time to Channel Your Inner Athlete!

If you aren't going all the way, why go at all?

— JOE NAMATH

Athletes can tell us a lot about survival. There's something about the competitiveness of pro sports, the utter determination, strength, and resilience you need to make it to the top, that mirrors the attitude you need to survive an emergency.

I'd hazard a guess that some of the people best equipped to thrive in a grid-down emergency are elite athletes. I'm pretty sure Joe Namath is going to be fine... and not least because he knows what it means to be part of a team.

When I think about that quote, I don't think about football... I think about preparedness.

If you aren't going all the way, why go at all?

If you're preparing your home for a disaster, why stop short of preparing for a grid-down situation? I know I had to look at my own plan carefully... I hadn't gone all the way. And, truth be told, I still haven't – and I won't have until I know I've done everything possible to get this information out there.

So I want to take a sliver of inspiration from Joe... and I want to bring you along for the ride. I want us, together, to go all the way. To make this journey really worth it, we have to bring as many people along as possible. It's not just about my family surviving. It's not just about your family surviving. It's about the whole team.

And I'm going to need your help.

In order to get this information to as many people as possible, we're going to need to spread the word. It's not enough for us to be the athletes; we have to be the coach and the cheerleaders as well.

So here's what I'm asking: Would you be willing to leave an honest review of this book on Amazon?

Every review will bring our community one step closer to what they're looking for.

When we work together, we truly can go all the way… and I can't thank you enough for joining forces with me.

We're healthy; we're strong; we're prepared… Let's make sure we all stay that way!

8

LONGER-TERM SOLUTIONS

MEDICAL CARE

I could devote a whole book to medical care, so I'd like to start out by making the disclaimer that this chapter is designed to give you the basics. I have to admit, when I was researching it, I realized that my own stockpile was somewhat lacking in the emergency health department. I had medicine and first aid covered, but I'd neglected to include useful ingredients that could be used for first aid in an emergency. Needless to say, I've remedied this now and it is my hope that by the end of this chapter, you'll have a better understanding of what you need to have in your home to ensure peace of mind in an emergency.

I covered basic medical and first aid supplies in my first book, *When Crisis Hits Suburbia*, so I'm going to assume that you have the basics covered. That way, I won't have to repeat things you already know. However, for those of you who are just getting started, the *Take Action* section at the end of this chapter is a first aid kit checklist—so don't worry if this is still all a bit new to you.

MINIMIZING RISK

Before we get to essential supplies, let's take a step back and look at how you can minimize risk in the first place. There are four main categories that we can split this process into preventative medicine, infection control, injury prevention, and disease management.

Preventative Medicine

Crisis or not, the health of our families is always at the forefront of our minds and we have a duty to make sure we're making lifestyle choices that support our physical and mental health. That means a good diet and regular exercise, and it means keeping up with medical and dental appointments. Of course, if the grid goes down, those appointments might not be possible but by staying on top of your health now, you run less risk of these being necessary during an emergency. What you can also do is make sure your pantry is stocked with nutritious long-life foods that will provide you with all the nutrients you need to stay healthy and strong no matter what's going on outside.

Infection Control

The next layer of reducing risk is to keep infection at bay as far as possible. The best way you can do this is to make sure the whole family is washing their hands, not just regularly but often. If the causal agent behind grid disruption is a pandemic, use what you learned when Covid-19 broke out in 2020: If you go out, wear a face covering and wash your hands as soon as you come back home. Keep a safe distance from others and if you suspect that you or someone in your family has been infected, keep everyone at home.

Infection control is still important even when there isn't a pandemic at work. In any crisis, we'll be collectively producing a lot of waste that may not be disposed of in the usual way. This provides the ideal breeding conditions for bacteria, so be mindful of managing waste safely (we'll look at this more closely in the next chapter) and keep washing your hands often.

Injury Prevention

Infection isn't the only risk to your health: Injury is also a possibility and in a grid-down crisis, getting medical attention is probably going to be very difficult. Taking active steps to reduce the risk of injury is, therefore, vital. What this mostly comes down to is being aware of everything in your environment and the risks they pose. In an emergency situation, avoid areas where you're more likely to run into danger and avoid being out on your own after dark. Do your best to avoid confrontation, and if you're out and about and sense that tempers are rising, abandon your mission and head home.

At home, you want to make sure you take extra steps to protect your family's safety around emergency backup plans for heating, lighting, and cooking. Make sure you have key safety equipment like fire extinguishers and carbon monoxide detectors, and make sure your walkways are lit well enough that you can see where you're going as you're navigating your property.

Disease Management

If you live with a chronic disease, part of being prepared is to plan for how you intend to manage it in an emergency scenario. Physicians will usually write prescriptions for 90 days if you ask them, and this is worth doing so that you have essential medications in backup. You'll also want to stock up on any foods, supplements, or alternative medicines you rely on for the management of your condition. If you generally attend physiotherapy appointments, make sure you're aware of the exercises you can safely do at home if this service becomes unavailable to you.

MEDICINE TO STOCK UP ON

Stockpiling medicine is a little more sensitive than stockpiling food. Although most foods have a limited shelf life and you have to think about this when you're stocking your pantry, you can generally build up a bigger supply than you can with medicine. Most medicines have a relatively short shelf life, and it's important to aim not to use them past their expiry dates (although you can afford a bit of flexibility when you have no other option).

Building Your Stockpile

The best way to start is to think about the needs of every member of your household. Consider whether anyone in your family has allergies to any pharmaceutical products. Does any member of the family have a chronic condition that needs to be accounted for? How about seasonal allergies? Acute pain? You want to consider your family's daily needs and not just possible emergencies. When I did this for my family, I made a spreadsheet to make sure I could track everyone properly. I'm a big fan of spreadsheets but a word of caution: If you're the same, make sure you have a hard copy of all vital information. Those spreadsheets won't bring you peace of mind in a grid-down situation if you can't log onto your computer.

The next thing to think about is quantity. You'll need to plan for the worst and figure out the amount of medication you'll need to take care of your family, and then add a little more to be on the safe side or share with others as necessary. Stocking over-the-counter medication is fairly easy: You can probably keep enough to last for a good couple of years. But with prescription medication, while your doctor may be willing to write a script for a longer supply, you're unlikely to be able to get more than enough for a few months. And of course, you can't just buy all your supplies and forget about them: You'll need to re-stock every few years to make sure that you're only keeping medicine within its expiration date.

Medicine Shelf Life

I would always recommend paying attention to expiration dates and making sure your stockpile is as fresh as possible. That said, in an emergency situation, it's helpful to know how safe some of those older medications are. When they're stored properly, many medications are still very effective for a good five years after their expiration date. They will, however, lose potency with time, so the older a medication is, the less effective it will be. Liquid medicines are also likely to deteriorate more quickly than those in tablet form. If you find yourself in an emergency situation with only medication that is past its date, make a judgment based on its appearance. If it's still the same color and it hasn't visibly deteriorated, it's most likely safe to take. If tablets stick to each other, are chipped or cracked, or are softer or harder than they should be, give them a miss. Of course, it *is* a risk, and not one I would take unless it was essential.

Storing Medicine Safely

The best way to ensure that your medicines are still safe to use even if they're a little past their expiration dates is to store them properly. That means keeping them in a cool, dark place, out of the reach of sunlight. You might think the medicine cabinet in your bathroom would be the best spot but it's actually a fairly bad idea, especially for long-term storage: The humidity and heat in your bathroom aren't good for medicines. Storing your medical supplies in the same place that you store your food is a good idea, as long as you can still keep them safely away from children. And a little extra security measure: Consider locking prescription meds in a safe. In an emergency situation, those drugs are going to be very valuable, and not just to those who need them for medical conditions.

Essential Medicines for Your Store Cupboard

I can't tell you exactly what your medical supplies should look like: This will be very personal to your family's unique needs and that's why thinking it through carefully is so important. What I can do, however, is provide you with some hints for a strong foundation. There are probably a few things that it would be good to have in an emergency that you don't already have in your first aid kit.

Pain medication/fever reducer: Over-the-counter pain relief is useful for a whole range of potential issues, including fatigued muscles, headaches, and minor injuries, so it makes sense to have plenty on hand. Acetaminophen is a good choice for treating both pain and fever, while ibuprofen and aspirin also work to reduce inflammation. Bear in mind, however, that children shouldn't take aspirin. I'd opt for a liquid medicine for younger children but remember that this won't keep for as long as tablets.

Anti-diarrheal: Not many people keep an anti-diarrheal medication in their regular medicine cabinet but you won't necessarily be able to run out at the last minute if the grid goes down, and diarrhea is not what you want to contend with in an emergency, not least because it can lead to dehydration. You've got two options here: a thickening mixture to absorb water or an antispasmodic to slow down activity in your lower intestine. Loperamide is a good option for this.

Oral rehydration solution: I'm including this here because if someone does have diarrhea and becomes dehydrated, an oral rehydration solution is a helpful tool. You don't need to buy this though: You can make your own by dissolving 1 teaspoon of salt and 7 teaspoons of sugar in a pint and a half of boiling water and allowing it to cool.

Constipation relief: At the other end of the spectrum is constipation, which is a risk if your food stocks dwindle and you struggle to get enough fiber. It can also be a problem if your diet changes slightly or if you're stressed, and both of these things are highly possible in a grid-down situation. An osmotic laxative like Polyethylene Glycol 3350 is a good choice, as well as glycerin suppositories for quick relief.

Antibiotics: In the case of a bacterial infection, you'll want to have antibiotics on hand (either in tablet form or as a topical cream) if you can get hold of them, but you'll need a prescription, which may be tricky if you don't have an immediate need. Hopefully, they won't be necessary, but it's possible that you'll cut yourself at some point, and the last thing you want is to have no way of treating it if it becomes infected. Remember that antibiotics don't have any effect on viruses though, so they're useless for colds, the flu, and the majority of sore throats and coughs.

Colloidal silver: I'm mentioning colloidal silver because many preppers firmly believe it's a necessity, but there's a lot of debate around it, so read up carefully to decide if it's right for you. It's a strong natural antibacterial, antibiotic, antiviral, and antifungal treatment, and can soothe everything from burns to boils. It doesn't require a prescription, which is why so many people favor stocking it, and it may be a good alternative to fall back on in an emergency.

Cough drops: I don't really know what I can say about cough drops, apart from, "Get some!" They're cheap enough and a cough is irritating at the best of times.

Antihistamines and anti-itch cream: An over-the-counter antihistamine is a good idea to have on hand to fight the symptoms of seasonal allergies, itching, respiratory infections, and hives. Diphenhydramine is a good option and it has the added bonus of reducing anxiety and relieving insomnia, both of which are perhaps a bit more likely in a grid-down situation. A topical anti-itch cream is a good idea too.

Ammonia inhalant: Basically a fancy way of saying "smelling salts," an ammonia inhalant is designed to revive people who have fainted. Hopefully, you won't need it but having some on hand will bring you peace of mind.

Specialty drugs for specific risks: We've discussed the importance of stocking up on prescription medications but it may also be a good idea to think of the potential crises that could cause a grid-down situation and stock medication for these scenarios too. There are two main areas I'd look at here: a nuclear event and a pandemic. If there was a nuclear disaster, radiation would be a risk, so potassium iodide tablets are a good measure to take. These will prevent radiation from being absorbed by your thyroid gland. The specifics of a pandemic cannot, of course, be predicted but you can stock a couple of antiviral medications that may help. You will need prescriptions for these, but if you're able to get hold of them, oseltamivir or zanamivir (used for the treatment of influenza) are a good idea.

NATURAL MEDICINE

Although some medicines may be usable after they've passed their official expiry date, medication does have a shelf life and we have no idea how long a potential disaster could go on for. That makes some knowledge of herbal remedies essential, in my opinion, and there's a whole world of possibility out there when you open yourself up to it. I have to admit, since I started looking into natural remedies myself, I've got the bug for it. You'll find whole books out there dedicated to herbal remedies. All I've done here is compile a list of some of the ones I think may be most useful in an emergency situation. Some of these are stock cupboard staples; others you may want to grow at home or find in supplement form from a health food store.

Aloe vera: This spiky little plant has huge healing powers, especially when it comes to treating skin and burns. It's also helpful for the digestive system and immune health. You can grow it at home or you can buy it as an essential oil.

Echinacea: Echinacea stimulates the production of white blood cells and increases your ability to fight infection. It's great for the common cold, a sore throat, or bronchitis, and it also has anti-inflammatory properties which can help with arthritis. To ease a sore throat, add around 15 drops of essential oil to a cup of water and use it for gargling.

Elderberry: As well as making a mighty delicious cordial, elderberry is helpful to the immune system and has been shown to be effective against avian and swine flus. You can grow it and use the berries or you can buy capsules.

Honey: Is there a better way to start the day than with a hot piece of toast loaded with honey? Even better when you find out how powerful honey is. If you can resist eating it and use it as a topical application instead, it has skin rejuvenating and antibacterial properties. And when you eat it, it has huge benefits for your gut health. The only thing is, a lot of the honey on the shelves is very processed, so to get the most beneficial product you'll need to spend a bit more and opt for natural, raw, organic honey that hasn't been pasteurized. Ideally, you want Manuka honey, which is thought to be the most healing, but this can be very expensive.

Peppermint oil: A cup of peppermint tea can help with soothing cramps and muscle spasms, it can ease a headache, and it can be used to help with sinus infections. You can also use it externally for pain relief by applying it to a damp washcloth and laying it over the affected area.

Apple cider vinegar: If you have an apple tree you can make your own apple cider vinegar, but it's readily available in most stores if not. It's great as an energy booster and it can help with digestive problems, as well as having topical applications for first aid.

Salt: The chances are you already have plenty of salt in your pantry, but were you aware of its healing properties? It plays an important role in balancing your electrolytes and therefore supporting muscle function. It also helps with digestion and aids in recovery when you're sick. And as if that wasn't enough, it has dental benefits and antibacterial properties, making it a good addition to a gargling solution for sore throats.

Garlic: Garlic is loaded with goodness and has strong antibiotic and antiviral properties. When ingested, it's very good for gut health and soothing oral infections but it has topical applications too. A crushed clove of garlic spread onto a piece of gauze and applied to a painful area is surprisingly helpful. It can reduce joint pain, as well as soothing earaches and toothaches.

Coconut oil: Coconut oil has huge nutritional benefits when ingested but it also has oral benefits when used as a mouthwash, and it can be used topically to improve dry skin conditions. If you're planning on making balms or ointments using other natural ingredients, it makes the perfect base.

Cayenne pepper: This is a powerful tool in the fight against disease prevention, and surprisingly enough, it also has healing powers when applied topically to a wound. If you suffer from arthritis, you can dilute cayenne extract in dimethyl sulfoxide (DMSO) and use it as a topical treatment. Added to hot water, it can also help with digestive issues or it can be added to a gargling solution to soothe a sore throat.

Chamomile: If you've ever had trouble sleeping you've probably tried a comforting mug of chamomile tea before bed, and there's a reason it works. It's a mild sedative, and it can help to calm the mind and body. It can also help with indigestion, menstrual cramps, and morning sickness. Soaked flowers can also be used in a warm compress to soothe ear infections and eye problems.

Dandelion: A highly misunderstood plant, dandelion has a number of health benefits. It can reduce cholesterol levels and stabilize blood sugar, and it can also reduce the symptoms of gout. The chances are you already have plenty in your backyard, even if you aren't intentionally trying to grow it.

St. John's wort: Another plant that grows abundantly in the wild, St. John's wort has antibacterial and anti-inflammatory properties and can soothe wounds when applied topically. It can also be used to treat hemorrhoids, relieve joint pain, and reduce anxiety and fatigue.

Marigold: If you're a gardener, marigold is a helpful companion plant, and if you're growing it for this reason you have a wealth of bonus health benefits up your sleeve. It can be used on the chest along with peppermint to reduce a fever, and it can be steeped in water and combined with apple cider vinegar to make a tonic to be applied topically for inflammation relief. It also has healing properties when applied to an open wound.

Thyme: Apart from being delicious, thyme is a powerful little herb. It can help with gastric problems, soothe a sore throat, and be added to tea to treat a fever. It also has benefits to the nervous system and can help to soothe a headache. When used topically, it's useful for treating skin conditions like eczema and psoriasis and can also be used to treat burns and infections.

Sage: Sage has antiseptic properties and can be used to improve oral health. A sage bath will also help to bring down a fever and sage tea will soothe stomach problems and ease flu symptoms.

Nettles: I'm not sure if there's a more maligned plant than the stinging nettle, but as much as it hurts to brush up against one when you're out walking, this is a plant with some powerful properties. Nettle tea can be an effective solution for reducing allergy symptoms, and, bizarre as it may seem, it can also treat skin conditions. It can relieve joint and muscle aches and increase immune function, and it has benefits to urinary and prostate health.

A basic knowledge of herbal medicine, a well-stocked medicine cabinet, and some essential first aid skills are all going to be essential in a grid-down crisis. If you're not confident in your first aid skills, now's the time to enroll in a basic first aid course. I make sure I refresh my knowledge regularly, and I've made sure my whole family knows the basics too. If the grid goes down, medical help may not be readily available, so it's up to us to do what we can to protect our families.

TAKE ACTION: EMERGENCY FIRST AID KIT CHECKLIST

Besides your medications and herbal backups, you want to make sure you have all the essential first aid tools in stock. I covered this in *When Crisis Hits Suburbia*, but I've made this checklist a little more comprehensive. Use this list to make sure your first aid kit is up to scratch.

- ☐ Medical tape
- ☐ Nitrile gloves
- ☐ Rolled gauze
- ☐ Gauze pads
- ☐ Trauma shears
- ☐ Liquid bandage
- ☐ Moleskin
- ☐ Abdominal gauze pads
- ☐ Butterfly bandages
- ☐ Chest seals
- ☐ Z-fold gauze
- ☐ Coban roll
- ☐ Pressure dressing
- ☐ Band-Aids
- ☐ Styptic powder
- ☐ Tourniquets
- ☐ Splints
- ☐ Tweezers
- ☐ ACE bandages
- ☐ Rubbing alcohol
- ☐ Peroxide
- ☐ Saline eye drops
- ☐ Irrigation syringe
- ☐ Plastic wrap
- ☐ Safety pins
- ☐ Emergency blankets
- ☐ Thread and needle stored in isopropyl alcohol

9

LONGER-TERM SOLUTIONS

SANITATION AND HYGIENE

As we saw in the last chapter, prevention is one of the best ways to make sure your family stays healthy in an emergency, and a big part of prevention is maintaining hygiene and sanitation without the support of the grid. Perhaps you remember the 2010 earthquake in Haiti: It was followed by an outbreak of cholera which resulted in a huge number of deaths. This is exactly the sort of thing we want to avoid, so we need to make sure we know how we're going to deal with personal hygiene and waste in the event of an emergency.

ESSENTIAL SANITATION SUPPLIES

Let's start with the supplies you're going to need in your stockpile. I'd recommend stocking enough supplies to last a year, so first you'll need to calculate how much of everything you use. This is easier than it sounds: Just scribble the date on every new package you open, and when you finish it, make a note of how long it lasted. Every household is different, so you might have things you want to add or remove from this list, but this is what I'd recommend as a basic starting point:

- Toilet paper
- Reusable washcloths (emergency toilet paper)
- Cleansing bottle (makeshift bidet)
- Baby wipes (for cleaning up without water)
- Soap
- Hand sanitizer
- Shampoo
- Toothpaste
- Toothbrushes
- Dental floss
- Deodorant
- Dishwashing liquid
- Laundry detergent
- Disinfectant
- Disposable gloves
- Feminine hygiene products
- Garbage bags
- Diapers (if applicable)
- Quicklime (for toilet safety)
- Appropriate chemicals to keep chemical toilet running (if applicable)
- Rodent poison/traps
- Insect repellents

TOILETING

It's not the most pleasant thing to think about, but it's one of the most important things to get right in an emergency situation. Every member of your household generates about 5 gallons of human waste per week. If you have no running water, disposing of it is going to be an issue, and if it's not managed properly, it can pose a danger to your family's health. While urine is relatively safe, feces can spread disease, so it must be managed correctly in order to prevent odor, disease, and illness.

Flushing with Water

When You Have a Septic System

If you have your own septic system, you have an advantage if the grid goes down. As long as you have access to water, be that water you've stored or water you've collected, you'll be able to flush your toilet. You'll simply need to fill the cistern until the water hits the float and then flush as normal. Alternatively, you could pour a 2-gallon bucket of water into the toilet bowl, which will trigger it to flush on its own. Word of advice though: Your water is precious, so don't flush unless you really have to. A friend of mine likes to say, "If it's yellow, let it mellow," which I think is great advice in this situation. There's no harm in a few people using the toilet before you flush if it's only urine. Even if you do have a septic system, however, I'd recommend coming up with a contingency plan, just in case something goes wrong or you run low on water.

When You're on a Sewer Line

Most septic systems have been replaced now and the majority of households are connected to a sewer line. What you'll need to do if this applies to you is check that the sewer main hasn't gone down. If it has, avoid flushing your toilet—this will protect your plumbing from backing up and stop sewage from coming up into your sinks and toilets. If there's no problem with the sewer line, however, you can top up your cistern with water and flush as though you were on a septic system—as long as you have enough water to do so.

Alternative Toilet Options

Regardless of whether you have a septic system or not, I would recommend having a backup plan that doesn't involve water at all. Water is going to be a precious resource in a grid-down situation, and personally, I'd be wary of using too much of it for the toilet. The good news is that you have plenty of options, but the best one for you will depend on whether you live in a rural or an urban environment.

Rural Settings

If you live in a rural area (or even a suburban one with plenty of space and privacy around your home), outdoor toileting is going to be a good option for you in a grid-down emergency.

Cat Hole

A cat hole is really better for a short-term crisis than it is for a long-term one but it's worth knowing about, and it will make a good temporary measure while you're sorting out a longer-term solution. It's not something you can do once and then use again and again though: You'll need to dig a new hole each time someone wants to use the toilet.

Use a trowel or a shovel to dig a hole about 8 inches deep and about 6 inches wide. Use the hole as a toilet, and bury your waste with the dirt you removed to make the hole. It's super easy but you should keep a few rules in mind before you start digging holes all over your backyard. Your cat hole site shouldn't be within 200 feet of a water source, and you should avoid digging your holes anywhere that water is visibly flowing. Aim to spread your cat holes out as far as possible and try to dig in an area that's exposed to a lot of sunlight to encourage decomposition.

Trench Latrine

In the event of a long-term crisis, a trench latrine is a better solution. It's essentially a giant version of a cat hole that can be used repeatedly. You'll need to follow the same rules as you do for cat holes, keeping it away from your water source or any flowing water and aiming for a sunny spot, if possible.

This time, you want to dig a trench around a foot deep, spanning a length of about 2 feet, and with a width of about 1 foot. I would take a bit of extra time to build some sort of privacy barrier too, which can be as simple as a piece of tarp or an old sheet stretched between stakes in the ground. Your family will be using the trench regularly, so flies and pests may be an issue. Keep them off your waste (and keep odor to a minimum) by covering it with quicklime or wood ash after each use. Once your trench is half full, add a layer of quicklime and then fill in the hole with soil. Build this up into a mound so that there's an extra foot of earth covering the surface. You'll then need to dig a new trench.

Deep Pit Latrine

A trench latrine is better than a never-ending string of cat holes in a longer-term emergency, but if the crisis goes on for a long time, a better option would be a deep pit latrine. Think of Roman toilets—the wooden seats placed over a deep pit. That's essentially what you're going for. You want to dig a hole about 6 feet deep, 2–6 feet long, and 2 feet wide. Make a seating area from whatever materials you have available, and construct some kind of shelter or privacy barrier as you would for a trench latrine. You'll still need to sprinkle quicklime or wood ash into the trench after each use, and the pit will need to be covered once it's full to within a foot of the surface, just as with a trench latrine. The good news is that when you dig your new trench, you won't need to make a new seating area—you can just reuse the original one. Make sure the new pit is the same size as the first one though, or you run the risk of the seat collapsing into the trench.

Urban Settings

If you live in the city or a densely populated suburban area, you probably don't have the land you'd need to dig latrines, so you'll need to consider other options. Luckily, there are a few ways around the problem.

Permanent Porta Potty

Even if you're not able to flush your toilet, you can still use it in an emergency; you'll just have to repurpose it a little. Start by turning off the water supply to the toilet and removing as much water as you can from the bowl, and then tape a double layer of heavy-duty trash bags to the bottom side of the toilet seat. After using the toilet, cover the waste with a layer of ash, quicklime, or sawdust to control odors. Once the bag is ⅔ full, add a generous amount of quicklime, tie the bag up, and replace the lining in the toilet. Keep the lid down when the toilet's not in use but bear in mind that odor will still be a problem when you can't flush. Combat this by covering the whole toilet with a 30-gallon trash bag when it's not in use.

Bucket

Okay, so it's not glamorous, but a bucket makes a perfectly serviceable toilet if you double-line it with heavy-duty trash bags. To make it more sanitary, mix a cup of liquid bleach with 2 quarts of water and add this to the lining, adding a bit more bleach after each use. Don't let the bag get over a third full before changing the bag. You can either perch on the rim of the bucket, or you can remove the toilet seat from your toilet and use this over your bucket. You can actually buy toilet seat covers especially made to fit 5-gallon buckets, so that's an option too. If the smell is a concern, you can get toilet deodorants to control the odor.

Chemical Toilet

The advantage of chemical toilets is that you can flush after every use, they reduce the risk of disease spreading, and the chemicals help with odor control. They have a removable bucket so you can dispose of the waste safely, but if you opt for one of these, you'll need to make sure that your stockpile has enough of the right chemicals to keep you going through an emergency.

Commode

Anywhere that sells medical supplies will sell bedside commodes and they're really useful in an emergency. They have an easy-to-empty bucket and they often have an adjustable seat height. You'll need to use liners with them, which typically come with an odor neutralizer, decaying catalyst, and gelling agent to reduce the risk of disease and control odors.

Composting Toilets

You might see these called biological toilets, waterless toilets, or dry toilets, but they all amount to the same thing. They convert human waste into soil or fertilizer by allowing the organic matter to break down into its essential minerals. Word to the wise, though: You can't use the resulting compost on your vegetable garden. You only want to use it on land where you're not growing food. Composting toilets are a more expensive option but they're certainly one to consider, and they're perhaps the best option when it comes to minimizing odor.

PERSONAL HYGIENE

Frequent handwashing is one of the most important things your family will need to do to keep healthy during a grid-down crisis. Make sure you do this before every meal, after each time you use the toilet, and after doing any other manual task. Water conservation is important but it's still possible to be clean and comfortable, even when you have to be mindful of water use.

Keeping Clean without Running Water

The most important thing to keep in mind is that your purified water should be used for drinking, cooking, and doing the dishes before it is used for anything else. Any water you do decide to use for washing can be recycled for other purposes, such as flushing the toilet or watering plants. If you live near a stream, river, or lake, you have access to free washing water. If you do this, however, make sure you use biodegradable soap (which you can also use for washing in the rain).

If you don't have access to rivers and lakes, and it doesn't rain regularly where you live, you still have options. You could use a spray bottle to minimize the amount of water you're using, or you could use damp washcloths and sponges, baby wipes, or a sanitizing lotion. Just make sure you have all these things in stock and make sure you have a dedicated area reserved for sanitation. If you're at home, your bathroom will still probably be your best option, but if you have more than one bathroom and you'll be using an indoor toileting system, I'd suggest using one bathroom for washing and one for going to the toilet.

Alternative Bathing Solutions

While minimal-water sponge baths and river bathing are adequate enough to maintain personal hygiene, if the grid is down for any length of time, you will want a more comfortable option, and there are some make-shift bathing options you have at your disposal.

Gravity Solar Showers

A surprisingly cheap option is a gravity solar shower, which essentially works when you warm water up in the sun and then use it for showering. A black shower bag is left to sit in the sun for a few hours and a showerhead is then used to shower in the usual way. Most of the gravity solar showers I've seen have a 5-gallon capacity which is probably about enough for two showers.

Pressure Tank Garden Sprayers

You could also use a pressure garden tank sprayer in a similar way: The tank is left in the sun to warm up (or you could heat your water separately and then fill the tank). These sprayers have various kinds of nozzles, but for showering your best option is to look at sporting stores. They often carry sprayers designed specifically for showering.

Tubs and Cowboy Baths

Baths will obviously use more water but you could go old school and use the same water for the whole family. This is how baths were traditionally used among ordinary working folk. Remember that you'll need to heat your water first before filling the bath.

A less water-intensive version of this is the cowboy bath. For this, you heat the water and keep it in a bucket beside the bath, and then pour it over yourself while you're sitting in the tub.

WASTE MANAGEMENT

The final piece in the sanitation puzzle is waste management. With garbage collection being a standard part of daily life, it's easy to forget how much waste a household produces, but once collections stop, you'll soon see that it's significant. The problem is that garbage attracts pests and diseases, so you'll need to have a plan in place in case garbage collection comes to a halt.

Separating Waste

Start by separating your waste into things you can burn, wet trash, and recyclables like glass, plastic, and cans. If you leave these things mixed together, the wet trash will contaminate everything else, and wet trash breeds bacteria and attracts pests.

Reducing Bulk

You then want to make your trash as small as possible, which you can do by flattening boxes, squashing cans, and compacting whatever you can. You want to make sure you have plenty of high-quality trash bags on hand, and ideally, a few lidded trash cans.

Composting

If you have the space for one, composting is a good idea, even if you don't have a garden to fertilize, as it's a hygienic and efficient way of disposing of organic waste. You can compost kitchen scraps, shredded cardboard and paper, and yard waste, as well as manure from non-meat-eating animals. You want to set up your compost heap as far away from your house as you can because, as hygienic as it is, it will attract insects. If you don't have a compost bin, cover your compost heap with black tarp to speed up decomposition, and be sure to turn the pile regularly.

Burning Trash

Some garbage can be burned and although this may not generally be the most environmentally-friendly choice, it may be necessary in a grid-down situation—and it means you have free fuel for cooking. You can burn cardboard, paper, and packaging like cereal boxes and cook safely over the fire. And to really make the most of your resources, you can use the cooled ashes for odor control in your latrine (alternatively, these could be added to your compost heap). Make sure you know what can safely be burned though: Never burn Styrofoam, plastic, or other items that could release toxins.

Burying Trash

If the crisis goes on for a long period of time, it may become necessary to bury some of your garbage. If it comes to this, bury it as far away from your house as you can. You'll need to dig a hole about 4 feet deep and cover your trash with around 20 inches of soil (this will keep pests away). If you want to dig a hole and keep filling it before you're ready to cover it, lay a large piece of wood over the top, and weigh it down with rocks to keep pests out. If you're using the same hole for multiple bags of trash, I'd recommend layering it with quicklime or ash to keep odors to a minimum.

PEST CONTROL

No matter what care we take with our sanitation, it's important to keep pest control in mind at every stage. All the waste generated by your household is liable to attract pests and this can put your supplies at risk.

To prevent insect infestations, keep garbage disposal areas as clean and as far away from the house as possible, and try to avoid having areas of standing water as this encourages mosquitos. Keep lids on trash cans closed, cover food and crockery, and keep insect control devices like fly strips and fly swatters on hand. Make sure all your food is packaged carefully and stay on top of your laundry (we'll look at this in the next chapter).

Your other threat is rodents and keeping these guys away can be a little more challenging. I'd recommend storing some traps and poisons just in case. Keep your storage areas clean and make sure all your food supplies are packaged properly. Mylar bags can be tempting when you're storing food for an emergency but rodents can easily chew through these, so if you're using them, I'd recommend storing them in plastic buckets or boxes.

Sanitation and hygiene are crucial to safety in an emergency situation, and if the grid goes down, the ways this is usually handled will fall by the wayside. Make sure you have a plan in place to keep personal hygiene and waste management in check if the worst happens.

TAKE ACTION: DIY HAND SANITIZER

Although you'll still need to have the supplies to make it, you can make your own DIY hand sanitizer, and to me, hand sanitizer means peace of mind when the water's off. All you'll need are isopropyl alcohol, aloe vera gel, and tea tree oil. Combine 3 parts isopropyl alcohol with 1 part aloe vera gel, and add 3–5 drops of tea tree oil to improve the scent. You could use a different essential oil for this if you're not a fan of tea tree oil.

10

LONGER-TERM SOLUTIONS

LAUNDRY AND DISHWASHING

Laundry and dishwashing are really a part of sanitation and hygiene but I wanted to separate them to make it all a bit more manageable. Keeping your clothing and bedding clean, and making sure your kitchen hygiene is as close to your usual standards as possible, is important for your family's health and safety. We'll start with dishwashing, and the good news is that if you've ever been camping, you probably already know exactly what you need to do.

DISHWASHING

The lack of running water means you can't rely on your kitchen sink, so I think the best plan for a grid-down scenario is to use the three-sink dishwashing method used by campers, which is probably easiest done outdoors if the weather permits.

Essential Kit

Here's what you'll need to set up an efficient and hygienic dishwashing station.

- 3 buckets/dishwashing bowls/camping sinks
- Sponges/brushes/scouring pads (for washing)
- Chamois cloth (for drying quickly)
- Biodegradable dishwashing detergent
- Bleach or Steramine tablets
- Metal strainer

The System

Start by removing all solid food from your dishes and scraping off as much wet residue as you can. Heat enough water to half-fill all three buckets and cut this with cold water until you reach a comfortable washing temperature. Your aim is to create a washing sink, a rinsing sink, and a sanitizing sink. The washing sink should contain warm water and dishwashing soap, the rinsing sink should be filled only with warm water, and the sanitizing sink should contain warm water and your sanitizing agent (use 2 teaspoons of bleach or 1 Steramine tablet per gallon of water).

Begin with the cleanest dishes, washing each one in the wash sink before dunking it into the rinse sink to remove all suds. Then soak your dishes briefly in your sanitizing sink to ensure they're completely disinfected. It may be tempting to overlook this step, but it's particularly important if any of your dishes or utensils have come into contact with raw meat or fish.

You then want to towel-dry your dishes with your chamois cloth. Once everything is washed, consolidate your gray water into one bucket, and strain the food particles out with your metal strainer. The food waste will go in with your wet garbage, and the water can be disposed of. If you're able to use the drains, this can be poured directly down, but if everything's blocked, you'll need to throw your water away outside. Try to spread it over a large area in this case, and don't dispose of it within 200 feet of a water source.

LAUNDRY

Laundry is a little more challenging than dishwashing, but it's just as important. If you're able to connect it to a water supply, you can use your backup power source to run your washing machine, but washing machines take a considerable amount of power and water, so personally, I'm not sure that doing this is the wisest move. Luckily there are quite a few alternatives available to you, but the bad news is that they mostly involve a bit of elbow grease.

Manual Methods

We'll start off with the most labor-intensive options. These approaches to laundry don't require electricity and use minimal water and they're the methods used before the washing machine was invented. When I think about the inconvenience of doing laundry this way, I try to remind myself that this was what the generations before us had to do all the time. For all of these methods, the best bet is to make your own detergent, simply because commercial brands tend to leave you with a lot of suds, and they're going to be hard to rinse out without a machine. The good news is, that's an easy task: See the *Take Action* section at the end of the chapter for details.

Wash Basin and Washboard

The washboard method was used for centuries and while it's hard work, it's an effective way of getting clothes clean. Washboards were originally made from metal and wood, but nowadays you can get silicone ones too. You'll need one of these and three buckets of warm water: one for washing and two for rinsing. The idea is to apply soap to both the washboard and any large patches of dirt on the fabric. The clothes are then scrubbed up and down on the board until they're clean. Each garment must then be soaked in the first rinse bucket and rinsed thoroughly, before being transferred to the cleaner water in the third bucket for a final rinse. For particularly dirty garments, you may want to soak them overnight to boost the chance of removing any stains.

Bucket and Brush

The bucket and brush method is essentially the same kind of deal, but it involves scrubbing with a brush rather than against a washboard. Prepare a wash bucket with warm water and laundry soap. Immerse each garment thoroughly, soaking them for longer if necessary, and agitate them to mimic the motions of a washing machine. Then use a soft-bristled scrubbing brush to scrub the most soiled areas. As with the washboard method, each garment will then need to be rinsed thoroughly in two separate rinse buckets.

Plunger

I really like the plunger method because it's a little less back-breaking than the washboard or brush methods. You can buy plungers specifically designed for laundry (The EasyGo Washing Wand is a popular example), or you can just use an ordinary toilet plunger. The slight advantage of specifically-designed laundry plungers is that they have holes in them, which means the water is pushed out and sucked back through, resulting in a more thorough wash. You'll need a bucket filled with warm water and laundry soap, and the idea is to mimic the action of a washing machine by pushing and pulling the plunger to agitate the laundry for around 10 minutes. You'll then need to rinse it in your separate rinse buckets, or for particularly dirty items, you may want to let them soak overnight before rinsing.

Sailor's Method

The sailor's method is particularly useful for larger items like sheets and blankets. You'll need a heavy-duty trash bag (ideally black because the idea is to use the sun to warm the water) filled with water and laundry soap. The idea apparently comes from the way sailors would wash their clothes on voyages: The sun would warm the water and the movement of the ship would agitate the clothes. You don't have a ship to do this for you but you can get the same effect by pressing and moving the bag. Once you've agitated the laundry for around 10 minutes, you'll need to rinse it using the two-bucket method we've discussed.

Powerless Washing Machines

Before you get too excited, powerless alternatives to washing machines still require a fair amount of work, but they're a little less labor-intensive than the more old-fashioned methods.

A Wonder Washer is essentially a hand-cranked washing machine, designed to take around 5 pounds of laundry. You simply add your laundry load, fill up the machine with warm water and laundry detergent, and mix it using the built-in levers. One of the best things about these is that you don't need the extra buckets for rinsing because you can just drain the soapy water and then add clean water to rinse. Personally, I think one of these is well worth the investment, particularly if you think you might struggle with the more labor-intensive hand-wash methods (you'll still need to be able to turn the lever around 200 times though, so it's not as easy as putting a load on and making a cup of tea). There are other models that do the same kind of job as the Wonder Washer too—I've heard good things about the Avalon Bay Eco Wash and the Laundry POD, for example.

Powered Washing Machines

You have two options when it comes to using some of your power for laundry: the wringer washer and an energy-efficient regular washing machine.

Wringer Washer

Wringer washers were popular after the war, and work in a similar way to a regular washing machine. Many Amish families still use them with their diesel generators, and you'll be able to use one of these with any backup power source you're using. They have an accessory for wringing garments out after washing but you'll want to buy a separate spinner, as they tend not to be that efficient.

Energy-Efficient Washing Machines

If you do want to use a washing machine during a long-term grid-down crisis, you'd be better off with an energy-efficient washing machine. If you're intending to use a machine in an emergency, I'd recommend looking into the most energy-efficient appliances you can find so that they don't drain your power. The wringer washer will use less power than a standard energy-efficient washing machine but they do still require you to wring out the clothes, so you may prefer a completely hands-off approach. Even with the most energy-efficient model, however, this is only really an option for you if you have a strong source of backup power.

The Extra Steps

Unless you're able to use a machine, laundry is going to involve a few more steps than you're used to.

Rinsing

We've touched on rinsing in all of the manual methods, so you already know about the two-bucket rinse system. When you're doing this, you'll also need to agitate the laundry, just as you did at the washing stage. This will release the suds but you'll end up with suds in your water, which is why the second bucket is necessary. If you're opting for the plunger method, using the plunger to agitate the clothes will make rinsing easier. If you're using a Wonder Washer or similar device, you can simply refill it with clean water for rinsing after your initial wash. Just don't be tempted to skip this step.

Wringing

You don't necessarily need to wring out your load after rinsing, and there is a school of thought that says it's better not to as it can stretch the fabric. However, it does speed up the drying process considerably, so unless you have delicate items that are more likely to stretch, it's probably worth doing. You can wring each garment out by hand, but that will require a fair amount of effort, and it can get tedious by the time you get to your sixth shirt. An old-fashioned wringer where you turn the handle to press the water out of the clothes will be worth the investment if you don't fancy spending a whole day squeezing water out of clothes.

Drying

If you're used to drying your clothes in a machine, you'll need to change your plan if the grid goes down. Dryers use a considerable amount of energy, so it wouldn't be wise to plug a dryer in when power conservation is so important. Your best bet is to hang them on a line outside. Even in very cold weather, your laundry will dry eventually, but this can take a full day, so you may want to hang it on a drying rack in whichever room you're heating instead.

Tips for Taking the Torture Out of Laundry

There's no way around it: Laundry during a grid-down crisis is going to be more difficult than usual and I doubt any of us are going to love it. Here are a few hacks to keep the torture level to a minimum.

The first thing I'd suggest is making sure you shake out each garment before washing it. This will mean that your washing water stays cleaner for longer and avoids debris getting stuck to other items. To be honest, we do this at home anyway, mostly because my kids are incapable of putting a pair of pants in the laundry hamper without checking the pockets first, and it does help get rid of large pieces of dirt.

The next thing I'd suggest is soaking your laundry before you wash it, even if it isn't particularly soiled. Again, this will keep your washing water cleaner for longer, and it'll also mean that any dirty patches you haven't noticed will require less effort once you get to the washing stage. With manual methods, your hands will really thank you for any corners you can cut along the way.

I've mentioned warm water throughout this section, and I think that's probably the most effective approach. It's also more pleasant if you're washing by hand. That said, if you need to conserve energy, don't panic if you need to wash in cold water. Your laundry will still clean this way. There is one garment where heat is necessary though: underwear. For personal hygiene reasons, you want to make sure underwear is as clean as possible and the easiest way to achieve this is by boiling it. Place your undergarments in a pot of water and bring it to a boil over your fire or stove. Be very careful not to burn it though and don't put too many garments in at once. They should have room to float in the water without touching the sides.

I can't say I'm looking forward to doing laundry in a grid-down crisis, but there's no denying that it's a necessity. It'll take water and a lot more manpower than you're probably used to, but it will be possible to maintain high laundry standards without the grid.

TAKE ACTION: DIY LAUNDRY DETERGENT

Making your own detergent will make rinsing your clothes a lot easier than it would be with commercial soap. All you need to do is mix 1 cup each of borax, Fels-Naptha soap, and washing soda; scent the mixture with an essential oil (if you like); and seal it in an airtight container. You'll just need 1 teaspoon of detergent per 5 gallon wash.

11

LONGER-TERM SOLUTIONS

COMMUNICATION

If the grid goes down, it isn't just your computers that will go dark: It's your cell phone too. Communication is often overlooked when we think about preparedness, but being able to keep in touch with your loved ones and keep on top of changing information will be vital in an emergency situation, no matter what the cause.

During the initial stages of a power outage, cell phones should still work, at least for a few hours. Cell towers do rely on power, but most will have a backup system that will allow them to operate for a few extra hours. Landlines, however, might fare a little better. They are powered by the phone lines, which means that if the main grid goes down, they may still work. It's not a failsafe by any means, but if you've done away with your landline in favor of your cell phone, I'd think about getting it reconnected. It could make a huge difference in an emergency. Bear in mind, though, that if you opt for a cordless phone, these do still need power.

Nevertheless, extreme weather and other disasters can easily bring phone lines down, so you'll need some backup communication plans in place too.

GOTENNA

Being able to keep in touch with your family within the local area is probably the biggest communication priority, and the goTenna is a useful tool for this. When attached to a smartphone, it enables you to create a short-range network. This can span anything from half a mile to a few miles, but it largely depends on the terrain of the area. Even if the cell towers are down, a goTenna will allow you to call and text your family and local friends if someone needs to leave the group for whatever reason. They are quite pricey though, so you may prefer to use another option.

CB RADIOS

Citizens Band radios, or CB radios, are pretty easy to get hold of, but they have limitations. They're most frequently used by truckers for short-range communication, they're not that expensive, and you don't need a license to use them. Like the goTenna, they have a limited range, so while they'll be great for staying in touch with your family in the local area, they won't be so helpful if you need to go further afield. Not all that many people use them, so to make them worthwhile, you'd need to get one for every member of your household, and even then, you may not be able to tap into emergency station frequencies. That said, there's a low barrier to entry with the CB radio and if you know that other people in your area are using them, it could be a useful addition to your communication plan.

FRS/GMRS

Other options are Family Radio Service (FRS) or General Mobile Radio Service (GMRS) radios. Both kinds use UHF frequencies, which usually have a short range of around a mile. You don't need a license to operate an FRS radio, and you can have different conversations on one channel because of the privacy codes they're programmed with. Nevertheless, the short range again makes them better for a small group staying within a localized area.

GMRS radios are less accessible as you do need a license to use them, but they have a lot more power and a lot more uses. A license isn't all that expensive, and it remains valid for five years, but individuals have to be licensed separately. It is technically possible to run an unlicensed station, so if your license runs out, you could still potentially use your radio in an emergency when licensing laws are not a priority. Don't go into this with this in mind though: Always stay on the right side of the law and get any necessary permits. Using an unlicensed radio should only ever be a backup option in an emergency. The power range is much stronger than the FRS radio, and if you use a removable antenna and a repeater you can extend the range to around 30 miles (depending on the terrain). Some channels overlap with FRS frequencies, which means you can pick up a wider range of benefits with the GMRS radio.

SATELLITE PHONES

Satellite phones have a lot of potential in an emergency but they're not without their drawbacks, the main one being that they rely on satellites—so if the satellites stop working, so do the phones. They're also quite costly, not least because you need to pay for the service and the time you spend using it as well as for the phone itself. Nevertheless, they're a great option. The least expensive approach is to opt for a device that sends short text messages and is able to transmit your location. You can get satellite phones with much greater capabilities than this but the more your phone does, the higher the costs are. I have a Garmin Inreach Explorer and I'd definitely recommend it. Get your practice in on Twitter though: You can only send text messages up to 160 characters long, so you'll need to get used to being succinct. If you'd rather have a device that also allows voice communication, I've heard good things about the Inmarsat IsatPhone 2, which can make calls across the globe and will work in extreme weather conditions. I'm considering getting something more comprehensive like this, but they're expensive, so weigh your options carefully.

HAM RADIO

I'm not sure there are many communication devices as effective as ham radio, but this is something else you need a license for. I got my Federal Communications Commission (FCC) license not all that long ago and I'm really happy I did. Ham radio can reach far out of your local area, which is why they're so commonly used by search and rescue teams. Using one means you'll be able to keep updated on the crisis by tuning into emergency stations, and you'll also be able to stay in contact with your loved ones. Despite the requirement for a license, ham radio is actually more common than CB radio, so the chances of being able to contact people outside of your household are greater. They take a bit of practice, it has to be said, but if you're studying for your license anyway, you'll get that practice in. The barrier to entry is quite high because the licensing tests are quite science-based and you do need to study to acquire the necessary knowledge. I enjoyed it though, and if you can handle it, I'd still recommend getting a license. Expense-wise, there's quite a range with ham radios. The more you get into it, the more you're likely to spend on accessories and equipment, but at a basic level, you can access what you need to without spending too much.

WALKIE TALKIE

Walkie talkies have their limitations, but they're great for local use and they're dead simple, so they're great if you have children. No licenses are required and they're battery-operated, so as long as you have plenty of AA batteries in stock, you should be fine in an emergency. Like the CB radio, however, the range is very short, so you can only really use them in a localized area. That said, to keep in touch with family and neighbors over short distances, they're a great asset. We have them in our house and the kids like to use theirs when they're playing outside. I've always encouraged this on the grounds that it might make a real-life emergency a little less daunting for them.

POWERING COMMUNICATION

Whatever devices you intend to use, you'll need to factor in what you need to power them. Make sure that when you're taking an inventory of the batteries you need to stock up on, all communications devices are accounted for. A quick word on batteries though: They don't last forever and they lose power over time. Just because your devices have fresh batteries in them now, doesn't mean you can assume they'll still be fine in a year's time. Check your supplies regularly, and make sure you refresh them as needed. If you plan to use a solar charger, make sure this can connect to your communications devices or batteries.

It's easy to forget about communication in an emergency situation because we have such good communications in place in regular life, but if the grid goes down, keeping in contact with your family and local community is going to be invaluable. Having a way to access emergency stations and keep on top of updates is also going to be crucial. If you're considering ham radio, make sure you get a license and learn the skills in advance. Even if the license becomes irrelevant in a crisis, you'll need it to use and learn ham radio now, and that's something you'll need to do long before a disaster.

TAKE ACTION: KNOW THE EMERGENCY FREQUENCIES

Whatever radio system you're using, you're going to need to know what emergency stations to tune in to. This is by no means an exhaustive list of the emergency frequencies, and you'll definitely want to research the ones in your local area too. However, I suggest making a chart like the one below and printing it out to keep with your emergency devices so that you know you can always tune into emergency updates in a crisis.

RADIO	STATION	FREQUENCY
CB RADIO	PREPPER CB NETWORK (AM)	CHANNEL 3 (26.984 MHZ)
CB RADIO	THE AMERICAN PREPPERS NETWORK (TAPRN)	CHANNEL 4 (27.005 MHZ)
CB RADIO	UNIVERSAL CB EMERGENCY/REACT CHANNEL	CHANNEL 9 (27.065 MHZ)
CB RADIO	COMMONLY USED ON CAMPGROUNDS AND IN MARINE AREAS	CHANNEL 13 (27.115 MHZ)
CB RADIO	SURVIVALIST NETWORK	CHANNEL 36 (27.365 MHZ)
CB RADIO	PREPPER 37 USB	CHANNEL 37 (27.375 MHZ)
HAM RADIO	EMERGENCY FREQUENCY FOR NATIONWIDE NATIONAL GUARD	34.90
HAM RADIO	POLICE INTER-DEPARTMENT EMERGENCY COMMUNICATIONS	39.46
HAM RADIO	NATIONWIDE RED CROSS CHANNEL	47.42

HAM RADIO	FEMA* DISASTER RELIEF CHANNEL	138.225
HAM RADIO	EMERGENCY FIRE DEPARTMENT CHANNEL	154.265
HAM RADIO	POLICE INTER-DEPARTMENT EMERGENCY COMMUNICATIONS	39.46
HAM RADIO	NATIONWIDE RED CROSS CHANNEL	47.42
HAM RADIO	EMERGENCY FIRE DEPARTMENT CHANNEL	154.28
HAM RADIO	EMERGENCY FIRE DEPARTMENT CHANNEL	154.295
HAM RADIO	USED DURING SEARCH AND RESCUE	155.160
HAM RADIO	POLICE EMERGENCY COMMUNICATIONS	155.475
HAM RADIO	INTERNATIONAL MARITIME WEATHER UPDATES	156.75
HAM RADIO	NOAA**	162.40

HAM RADIO	NOAA	162.425
HAM RADIO	NOAA	162.45
HAM RADIO	NOAA	162.475
HAM RADIO	NOAA	162.50
HAM RADIO	NOAA	162.525
HAM RADIO	NOAA	162.55
HAM RADIO	NOAA	163.275
HAM RADIO	EMERGENCY COMMUNICATIONS FOR THE NATIONAL GUARD	163.4875
HAM RADIO	MILITARY NATIONAL DISASTER PREPAREDNESS	163.5125
HAM RADIO	FEDERAL GOVERNMENT CIVILIAN AGENCIES EMERGENCY AND DISASTER FREQUENCY	168.55

HAM RADIO	NATIONAL COMMUNICATIONS FREQUENCY FOR THE DEPARTMENT OF STATE	409.625
HAM RADIO	GENERAL MOBILE RADIO SERVICE EMERGENCY COMMUNICATIONS AND TRAVELER ASSISTANCE	462.675

*FEMA: FEDERAL EMERGENCY MANAGEMENT ASSOCIATION (FRONT LINE OF LARGE-SCALE DISASTER RESPONSE)

**NOAA: NATIONAL OCEANIC AND ATMOSPHERIC ADMINISTRATION (GOVERNMENT ADMINISTRATION FOR SENDING OUT EMERGENCY BROADCASTS)

You can download a printable version by scanning the QR code below.

12

LONGER-TERM SOLUTIONS

SECURITY

I covered security in *When Crisis Hits Suburbia*, so again, I'm mindful of repeating information. Nonetheless, it's worth recapping the three Ds of security: detect, deter, and defend. These are the three basic principles to work with when it comes to protecting your home, with defense being the final line of protection. Hopefully, if you have detection and deterrence in place, you'll never have to get to that stage. And when it comes to a grid-down emergency, the good news is that a lot of your measures don't need to rely on the grid anyway, so if you have all of this in place, you shouldn't need to worry about too much extra.

SEEING THROUGH THE EYES OF AN INTRUDER

If you're starting to think about security for the first time, I think the best approach is to look at your property through the eyes of an intruder. You can actually make this into a fun game with the whole family (my kids loved donning balaclavas and creeping around the house like ninjas for the afternoon!)

Start from the street around dusk when the light begins to wane. Think about what you can see through the windows. Are there valuables on display? Could someone watching the house see what was going on inside? Next, think about the landscape around your property. Are there places for someone to hide? Would it be easy for someone to hop the fence? Consider what you could do to make your home seem less appealing to intruders. If you're really getting into the spirit, you can challenge your kids to get into the house (without breaking anything) without using their key or any key codes you may have. I was sure my family wouldn't be able to get into our house. We have no key under the doormat or anything, and I was sure everything was secure, but my son was able to pry open a window that I didn't realize I'd left open—it was quite an eye-opener.

Take notes on any weak points you noticed and start thinking about what you can do to strengthen your property. Would more secure fencing be a good idea? Do you need to upgrade any windows or doors? Perhaps some net curtains would be a valuable asset for hiding the contents of your living room. It's amazing what insights you can get simply by viewing your home through the eyes of someone who might want to break into it.

OFF-GRID SECURITY

If you have intruder alarms or security cameras that rely on the grid, you may need to think more carefully about your non-grid reliant security, so it's worth reviewing a few key points here.

Layers of Protection

I think it's helpful to think of home security in layers, starting by making your property a less appealing target. Remember that your main priority is to protect the people who live in your home. After that, it's precious supplies and resources. Personal possessions are the last thing to worry about, although of course, you want to make sure they're safe too if you can. A quick word of warning though: You don't want your home to be so secure that escaping it is difficult. In an emergency, your family needs to be able to get out quickly and easily.

Start by thinking about the appearance of your home. Consider valuables that may be on view both inside and outside of the property. The more you can hide from view, the less attractive your home will be to intruders. Aim to blend in with your neighbors' properties, and try to make your home look secure without seeming like a fortress that could be protecting huge assets. You want to stay under the radar but still look secure enough that no one is tempted to break in just because it will be easy.

Barriers

Perhaps the best thing you can do to protect your property is to minimize the risk of an intruder getting to it in the first place. And a good way to do that is to create barriers—most likely in the form of fences. I know some people talk about making these fences hostile by using barbed wire or electrification but I have two thoughts that put me in the camp against doing this. First, although some of you may live in rural areas, there's a high chance that you live in the suburbs where this kind of defense simply isn't safe in regular life. Second, if you have children, your job is to protect them and make them feel safe, and if they're playing out next to an electrified fence, this isn't going to do that. And the icing on the cake is that if we find ourselves in a grid-down situation, that electrified fence is going to be pretty useless. Personally, I think a tall, solid fence is all most people need to provide an effective barrier. I think we need to find the balance between protecting our homes and living a full and peaceful life.

Alarms

If you have intruder alarms, it may be that they're currently reliant on the grid, so you'll need to think about what to do to mitigate this should the grid go down. The good news, however, is that you can switch to solar or wind energy to power your alarm system. Alarms have two benefits: First, they deter criminals as soon as they're triggered, and second, they alert you to the presence of an intruder. The even better news is that you can easily create an off-grid alternative that doesn't require power at all.

One of my favorite DIY alarm systems is the good old cans-on-a-wire setup, which simply involves stringing empty cans on a wire, close enough together that they'll rattle if they're knocked. This should be semi-hidden behind some foliage above ground level. The only problem with this is that high winds can trigger a false alarm. An electronic system is probably more reliable if you're able to hook it up to your alternative power source.

Lights

Lights work in a similar way to alarms to deter intruders, but they do rely on electricity. If you're generating power through wind or sun, you should be able to power some intruder lights; alternatively, you could power them through deep-cycle batteries. There are three approaches you can take to lighting: You can opt for an always-on approach, you can have them only on at certain times (i.e., only at night), or you can have them activated by movement. Movement-activated lights make for good deterrents but the problem is that they can just as easily be triggered by animals as they can by people, so they're not always a reliable alert. The added problem in an emergency is that if the reason the grid is down is due to extreme weather, they could easily be triggered or damaged by those conditions.

Dogs

We have three dogs, none of them trained solely as guard dogs, but they would still be a real asset if there was an intruder trying to break in. Most breeds don't require much training to want to protect their territory or their family, and even a good bark can be enough to deter intruders. In a grid-down event, the fact that dogs don't require electricity is a definite bonus—although there may be times you might wish you could power them down for an hour! If you're considering getting a dog, bear in mind that each animal you have is an extra mouth to feed, and weigh this carefully against the benefits to security.

Traps

I'm not of the mindset that having traps permanently set up around your property is a safe way to live, particularly if you have children or pets. Nonetheless, if we find ourselves in a crisis situation, there may come a time that setting up a few traps will be a good way of adding an extra layer of protection to your security system. If you're genuinely concerned about a threat to your property, you can set up snares using heavy-duty steel wire. These won't cause permanent harm to the intruder but they will make it difficult for them to get closer to your home or to escape if they get caught. The other advantage, of course, is that traps like this may also snare you some small game, which could be a valuable source of food. Double-check the zoning laws in your area before setting up any kind of trap. Small snares like this will probably be okay in most areas, but if you were considering something more serious like a bear trap, you may find that there are laws against this. At the very least, you'll need to display warning signs on your property.

Reinforced Doors

With deterrents in place, you can then move your attention to more localized barriers. A good starting point is to think about the strength of your doors. You can boost your security significantly simply by reinforcing the doors you already have in place, and this isn't as hard as it sounds. All you need to do is replace the short screws fixed into the strike plate with longer screws that can pass through the frame and screw into the stud—3-inch screws would be a good call for this. You can also replace any weak hinges with sturdier ones and install a deadbolt. You may also want to install a peephole so you can keep the door shut until you know who's behind it. If you have any glass panels in your door, these can be covered with grills to improve security. If you want to up your game even more, you can install a security bar or a door jammer. If you opt for a barricade bar, you have an added advantage if the emergency is due to a hurricane: They're great for strengthening your door against high winds.

If you wanted to replace your doors altogether, you could consider security doors (also known as storm doors). Not only do these make it harder for intruders to enter, but they also offer protection from extreme weather.

What we're mostly thinking about here is the standard outside door, but there's a high chance these aren't the only kind of doors you have. If you have sliding glass doors, you automatically have a weak spot in your security system. These can be very easy to open unless you put measures in place to strengthen them. There are a few things you can do to improve the situation, though. You can fit track locks in the base track, or double-bolt locks to prevent the doors from being lifted from their tracks. You could also add sliding locks at the top and bottom of each door. Of course, no matter how many locks you add, glass can always be broken, so you can't completely protect a glass door from intruders. You could consider applying security window film to the glass, though, which will provide a little extra protection.

Securing Windows

Windows are just as vulnerable as glass doors, and they can easily be pried open or broken. The simplest thing you can do is keep them locked when you're out, but you may want to consider some additional reinforcements. Window locks are fairly cheap and come suited for most window types. Be cautious about ones that require a key though because this could slow you down if you need to escape your home in a hurry. Opt instead for sash locks and window latches if possible. If you have horizontal sliding windows, you can improve their security by putting a wooden dowel inside the track. Beyond this, consider what windows allow you to do: They allow you to see out, and therefore, they allow others to see in. Keep your curtains drawn after dark and add blinds in the garage and hallways—areas where you may not be using curtains for comfort.

If you're considering bigger renovations, storm windows are an option. They provide insulation benefits too, which could be a big advantage if the grid goes down, and are helpful against strong winds. You could also consider installing roll-away shutters, but bear in mind that many of these require power. You could also add window grills or bars, but these could cause you problems if you need to exit in an emergency.

Securing Valuables

Hopefully, your deterrents and security measures will keep intruders safely outside, but in the event that someone does make it into your home, it's worth making sure your valuables are protected. One thing you can do is engrave valuable objects with your name and driver's license number, which will deter thieves from taking them. You can also think about where you store your valuables. Most thieves will look in the master bedroom, so consider less appealing places to store things of high value: places like the bathroom or linen closet. It's a good idea to store them inside something that also serves as a decoy too... For example, I've got some of my mother's silver stored in an old coffee tin and stacked in a cupboard. I'm fairly confident that if someone broke in, they'd never know it was even there. For sensitive items like documents, cash, prescription medications, or firearms, opt for a fireproof safe.

The reality, however, is that in an emergency situation, one of your most valuable resources is not your grandmother's jewelry, it's your food stocks. Keep your pantry locked, and if possible, make it look as little like food storage as you can.

The likelihood of someone breaking into your home is fairly low, and I certainly don't want you to panic about the safety of your supplies, but I do think it's worth taking measures to protect it—just in case the worst happens.

Firearms

I did touch on firearms briefly in *When Crisis Hits Suburbia*. They're a useful tool to have, both for hunting and for protecting your home, but I think that protecting your family is the most important thing. You're not prepared to lose a single member of your family; therefore, it's important not to operate as a household that's prepared to exchange gunfire. If you keep firearms, keep them safely locked away, and think of them not as a weapon but as a defense you can fall back on only if it is necessary... and also as a way to snag yourself a rabbit for the pot. The last thing I want to say is that if you do find that you need to use a gun to protect your property, bear in mind that your shot doesn't have to be lethal. You can keep someone out of your home without killing them. In fact, some people even switch their ammunition for rock salt, which is an old trick used by farmers to wound an intruder, allowing them to escape without any lasting damage.

The good thing about grid-down security is that it's really not that different from security with the power on. The only things you'll need to rethink are lights and alarms that are wired up to the grid. Everything else you're doing to secure your home is most likely going to be unaffected by a lack of power. That said, extreme weather events could interfere with some of your measures, so be careful to repair anything that is damaged by a flood or storm.

TAKE ACTION: PLAN YOUR ESCAPE ROUTES

To me, defending your home boils down to this: You want to keep your family safe. Therefore, I think a crucial part of security is having a clear idea of how to escape your home in an emergency, be that because of fire or because there's an intruder inside. Use the checklist below to come up with an emergency escape plan. Make sure everyone in the household is familiar with it, and practice it regularly to make sure everyone knows exactly what to do.

ESCAPE ROUTE CHECKLIST

- Identify at least two escape routes from each room in your home
- Clear access to all windows and doors that will be used in an escape
- For multiple-story homes, consider installing escape ladders
- If you have door and window keys, make sure everyone knows where they're kept and ensure that they're accessible in an emergency
- Identify the safest place in the home to hide if escape isn't possible
- Plan for how infants, elderly family members, and pets will be helped out in an emergency

- Come up with a meeting point a safe distance from your home
- Make sure your address is visible on the outside of your property (this will help first responders find you and your home if necessary)
- Practice the escape plan with the whole family (from each room in the house)

13

IN THE EVENT OF ECONOMIC COLLAPSE

A lot of people ask me about how to prepare for an economic collapse so I wanted to make sure we touched on this topic, but it's important to acknowledge that it could be a whole book in itself. The reality is that there's no way of knowing exactly what will happen if the grid goes down indefinitely, but we can take a few precautions to help us out if things take a turn for the worse.

WHAT'S VALUABLE NOW: CASH

We can only assume that cash will continue to be valuable, at least in the short-term, and it certainly makes little sense to assume that a crisis will mean it will no longer be important. I'd recommend having a supply of cash stashed away safely to see you through a short to medium-term grid-down situation. If the grid is down, ATMs won't work, card readers won't work, and you won't be able to pay for anything online. The banking networks will be down, and in all likelihood, the banks themselves will close. But cash will still have value, and you may need it.

If you need to bug out, you may still be able to buy food or gas, at least in the short-term, or you may be able to buy goods from another household. And if you're sheltering in place, cash could still be useful for buying supplies while they last. Electronic systems may be down, but while there's stock to sell, retailers will want to sell it, so cash is going to be important.

So that brings us to the question of how much cash to have on hand. I'd shoot for something in the region of $1,000–$2,000 to cover last-minute essentials. You should already have stocked your pantry and stored fuel and supplies to see you through a crisis, so unless you're planning on leaving the country (which could be impossible anyway), there really isn't a need for much more than this.

The other thing you'll need to think about is where you're going to store your cash. I think a locked safe somewhere in your home is a good idea: It's somewhere that you can also store important documents, firearms, and any other sensitive items that you don't want to fall into the wrong hands. Other people prefer objects with hidden compartments (like wall clocks or a hidden drawer in a trinket box). What I would say, however, is that it would be wise to store your cash in a waterproof pouch before you put it into any container. If you've been affected by flooding or other extreme weather events, this will help make sure your money's still of use to you.

IF CASH LOSES ITS VALUE

If we find ourselves in a long-term crisis, cash may well lose its value, and if this happens, bartering may become necessary. It's impossible to predict with any certainty what items will be of value if this happens but it's fairly safe to assume that all of your supplies will be highly sought-after items.

What I imagine may become currency in an emergency situation are things that are essential to living, luxury items, or items that act as substitutes for money. In the money substitution category, that might be things like semi-precious metals, silver, or precious stones—things of high value that can be exchanged for necessities. Luxury items might include alcohol, medicine, herbs and spices, sugar, and comfort items (anything from musical instruments to cosmetic products). Beyond this, anything you might need for survival will be of great value: water, food, candles, oil, matches and lighters, ammunition, seeds, salt, batteries, wood, livestock... Anything you might need to keep your family safe and healthy will be what's important to everyone else too.

So what does this mean for you? In terms of things that may eventually become a new form of currency, it means keeping these items safe and well-protected. Jewelry, furs, and any precious metals you have at home could one day be used in exchange for useful resources, so keep these safe. Everything else, you'll only really know about when you get there. If you have a surplus of propane, for example, but your family is short on batteries, you may be able to exchange with someone else to help keep both households stocked. It's another strong argument for conserving resources: Not only will they be essential to your day-to-day life; they might also be valuable currency.

BARTERING TIPS

We live in a currency-based economy, and the chances are you haven't had to do much bartering up to now. Bartering is simply a way of exchanging goods or services, which might involve agreeing to exchange a certain amount of gas for a set quantity of pasta (for example) or agreeing that your neighbor can share your vegetable patch in exchange for them allowing you to pick fruit from their apple trees.

Bartering does come with some risks, however, and therefore, it's best done with people you trust. The problem is, it requires you to disclose something about the supplies you have, and if the person you're talking to turns out to be untrustworthy, this could put your resources—and your home—at risk. This is particularly dangerous if you're trading with addictive substances like alcohol, prescription medications, or tobacco. In these instances, you may be dealing with someone who has an addiction, and this can bring with it extra dangers to your security and safety. The other danger is that trading too much of something you have in your supply closet could mean you don't have it for yourself when you need it later.

Being prepared to barter is a wise move, and a good way to do this is to find out what your friends and neighbors might need. Do they have a particular love of something that you have in abundance? Do you have skills that they lack that you could offer? I think skills are a great way to make trades if you do have to barter because you lose nothing but your time, and only stand to gain valuable additions to your stockpile. Everything from plumbing skills to gardening skills to massage skills could be valuable—so encourage your family to train up and explore their interests. My youngest son is a big animal lover (he once brought an injured duckling home to take care of), and I'm sure he'd be up for training a neighbor's dog in our backyard in exchange for supplies. Everyone's skills are valuable—no matter how young they are.

It's impossible to predict for certain what any future currency might be based on, but my gut feeling is that useful survival items will be the most desirable if currency loses its value. Make sure you have enough cash to see you through a short-term crisis but remember that bartering may become essential further down the line. My goal, however, is to make my family as self-reliant as possible so that we can reduce the chances of this being necessary.

TAKE ACTION: DIY DRY BAG

Keeping cash and other valuables safe is about more than security: It's also about protecting it from the environment, and in a serious emergency situation, it's quite likely that this will be necessary. You can make your own dry bag with fairly minimal skills—but who knows? Maybe those skills will be useful for bartering—take the opportunity to practice them!

What You Need

- Strong, waterproof fabric (e.g. Cordura fabric)
- Lighter/seam sealer
- Firm plastic (e.g., plastic from soda bottle)
- Webbing
- Side-release buckle (plastic)
- Polyester thread
- Sewing machine
- Clips to hold the fabric (use clips rather than pins because it's important that the bag doesn't have holes in it)

The Mission

Step 1

Measure and cut out an 8-inch circle on your fabric. The outer inch of this is for seam allowance. Then cut out a 22 x 26-inch rectangle (this will wrap around the circumference of the circle, with an additional inch for seam allowance).

Step 2

Sew the ends of your rectangle together with the fabric inside out, forming a tube. Next, sew the tube onto the circle of fabric, keeping the inside of the fabric facing the tube.

Step 3

Using a lighter or seam sealer, carefully melt the circumference of the base and the length of the body in order to melt the seam and form an airtight seal.

Step 4

Lie the bag down flat so that the seam is in the center and line the plastic up with the top edge of the bag. Cut this down to fit the edge. Now, fold down the top 2 inches of the bag and sew this down. Slide the plastic strip into the resulting pocket.

Step 5

The length of the top of the bag should now be 10 inches. Cut a length of webbing to 20 inches, and sew the side-release buckle on. You'll need part of the buckle at either end, with about 9.5 inches between the two pieces. Now, sew the webbing straps together so that it fits the top of the bag. Sew the strap to the bag on the side opposite the one with the plastic strip.

Step 6

Cut out a hole beneath each end of the buckle to allow it to slide through (your bag is still inside out—when the pieces slide through, they'll be on the outside of the bag).

Step 7

Turn the bag inside out and sew down the buckles on the outside. Roll down the plastic edge a few times to seal it and then clip the buckles together. This should keep your valuables safe from the weather.

CONCLUSION

I sincerely hope we're never in a situation so serious that the grid goes down for a significant length of time. However, there's no denying that it's a possibility, and I think it's important that we prepare for the worst. The more self-reliant you can make your home, the better off you'll be in any emergency situation. The ideal scenario would be to operate completely off the grid, but the reality is that this simply isn't an attainable goal for most families to reach quickly.

If you're new to the preparedness game, the first thing you'll need to do is make sure your pantry is fully stocked (my book, *The Prepper's Pantry*, will help with this), but bear in mind that an emergency situation is likely to take you off-grid, at least for a while. To be fully prepared, you're going to need to be able to cope without municipal power lines. Take an inventory of your current situation and look at what you need to improve on. All of this can be done one step at a time, so approach it methodically and don't panic if it seems like a lot. Every single thing you do to prepare your home for disaster brings you one step closer to the ultimate goal. Being prepared is a journey, and there's pleasure to be found in achieving each small goal.

It still concerns me that so few people are prepared for a grid-down scenario. The chances are this is what will happen in the event of any large-scale emergency. So I have two missions right now: One is to continue to improve my own homestead and take my family one step closer to complete self-reliance each day. And the other is to help other families to do the same. And that's where I'd like to ask you to help me. The more people we can share this information with the better… And how can we do that? We can spread the word. So, if you could spare just five minutes before you start building your earth oven or crafting your first crossbow, leaving a review on Amazon would be a massive help. Think of it as a kind of risk-free bartering: You'll get the satisfaction of sharing your opinion, and in exchange, they'll get their hands on the information they need. Alright, so it's a bit of a stretch, but we all have to help each other here—after all, this isn't the kind of education you get at school.

I'll leave you with one last thought: No matter what happens, stay healthy, stay strong, stay prepared!

Ted Riley

REFERENCES

Akart, B. (n.d.). *Hygiene sanitation for preppers.* Freedom Preppers. https://www.freedompreppers.com/hygiene-sanitation.htm

Ashworth, B. (2020, July 30). *How to DIY your own hand sanitizer.* Wired. https://www.wired.com/story/how-to-make-hand-sanitizer/

Barton, J. (2022, January 15). *Grid-down communication methods.* The Survival Corps. https://www.thesurvivalcorps.com/grid-down-communication-methods/

Berrie, T. (2020). *How to cook on a wood heat stove.* Our Tiny Homestead. https://www.ourtinyhomestead.com/woodstove-cooking.html

Blackout: What to do when the grid goes down. (2021, February 19). American Outdoor Guide. https://www.americanoutdoor.guide/prepping/blackout-what-to-do-when-the-grid-goes-down/

Bleach storage and expiration tips for preppers. (2021, March 11). happypreppers.com. https://www.happypreppers.com/bleach.html

Boechler, E., Hanania, J., Pletnyova, A., Stenhouse, K., Yyelland, B., & Donev, J. (2021, September 27). *Solar chimney.* Energy Education. https://energyeducation.ca/encyclopedia/Solar_chimney

Brady, H. (2018, August 28). *This man has lived off the grid for 20 years—Here's how.* National Geographic. https://www.nationalgeographic.co.uk/environment/2018/08/man-has-lived-grid-20-years-heres-how

Brown, B. (2021, November 22). *Grid down scenarios: How to survive a power grid attack.* The Prepping Guide. https://thepreppingguide.com/grid-down-scenario-causes/

Bryant, C. (2008, July 10). *How radiant floor heating works.* HowStuffWorks. https://home.howstuffworks.com/home-improvement/construction/materials/radiant-floor-heating.htm

Bug out cookware. (2015, August 12). Bug Out Bag Builder. https://www.bugoutbagbuilder.com/product-reviews/bug-out-cookware

Carter, B. (2014, October 28). *Prepper emergency lighting: The best options.* US Preppers. Be Prepared, Not Scared. https://uspreppers.com/prepper-emergency-lighting-the-best-options/

Centers, J. (2021, January 23). *Best emergency candles.* The Prepared. https://theprepared.com/gear/reviews/candles/

Cobb, J. (2014, November 14). *Using water heater water in an emergency*. The Survival Mom. https://thesurvivalmom.com/water-heater-emergency-water-supply/

Coffman, S. (2021, December 23). *5 ways to contact loved ones after the grid goes down*. Urban Survival Site. https://urbansurvivalsite.com/ways-contact-loved-ones-grid-goes/

Creekmore, M. D. (2019, October 21). *What are the best alternative heat sources to use during a power outage?* MDCreekmore.com. https://mdcreekmore.com/staying-warm-and-heating-your-home-during-a-long-term-grid-down-situation/

Denzer, K. (2002, October 1). *Build your own wood-fired earth oven*. Mother Earth News. https://www.motherearthnews.com/diy/build-your-own-wood-fired-earth-oven-zmaz02onzgoe/

Deziel, C. W. (2022, January 31). *What is a solar fan? (with pictures)*. WiseGeek. https://www.wise-geek.com/what-is-a-solar-fan.htm

Dodrill, T. (2021, December 21). *20 SHTF currency options better than gold*. Survival Sullivan. https://www.survivalsullivan.com/shtf-currency-options-better-gold/

Dunn, C. (2020, September 29). *Generating off-grid power: The 4 best ways*. Treehugger. https://www.treehugger.com/generating-off-grid-power-the-four-best-ways-4858714

8 different types of generators for your off-the-grid cabin. (2021, August 20). Architecture Lab. https://www.architecturelab.net/types-of-generators/

Engels, J. (2017, January 16). *How to make a hot water heater with compost*. One Green Planet. https://www.onegreen

planet.org/lifestyle/hot-water-heater-with-compost/

5 effective ways to heat your home during a power outage. (2020, September 28). The Prepping Guide. https://theprepping guide.com/heat-your-home-during-power-outage/

Fortey, I. (2020, August 23). *How to make a dry bag.* Boat Safe. https://www.boatsafe.com/how-to-make-a-dry-bag/

Garen, J. R. (2021, December 21). *Emergency lighting solutions for preppers.* DIY Prepper. https://www.diyprepper.com/emergency-lighting-solutions-for-preppers/

Garen, J. R. (2021, December 21). *How do preppers store water? Storage ideas and solutions.* DIY Prepper. https://www.diyprepper.com/prepper-water-storage/

Geothermal energy: Mother Nature's HVAC. (2020, January 29). American Outdoor Guide. https://www.americanoutdoor.guide/survival-gear/survival-gear-guides/geothermal-energy-101/

Hart, N. (2020, August 27). *How to make a solar panel emergency backup system.* Dengarden. https://dengarden.com/safety/How-To-Make-A-Solar-Panel-Emergency-Backup-System

Hart, S. (2016, January 15). *Hurricane lantern old school preppers light.* UK Preppers Guide. https://www.ukpreppersguide.co.uk/hurricane-lantern-old-school-preppers-light/

Heating and cooling an off-grid home. (2021, June 25). Survival Realty. https://www.survivalrealty.com/2021/06/25/heating-and-cooling-an-off-grid-home/?utm_source=rss&utm_medium=rss&utm_campaign=heating-and-cooling-an-off-grid-home

Heddings, J. (2019, September 9). *The best emergency/camping LED lanterns*. Review Geek. https://www.reviewgeek.com/20642/the-best-emergency-camping-led-lanterns/

Henry, P. (2013, February 26). *Where there is no kitchen: Cooking when the grid goes down*. The Prepper Journal. https://theprepperjournal.com/2013/02/26/where-there-is-no-kitchen-cooking-when-the-grid-goes-down/

Henry, P. (2013, September 7). *Medicine to stock up on for when there is no doctor*. The Prepper Journal. https://theprepperjournal.com/2015/09/07/medicine-to-stock-up-on/

Henry, P. (2013, November 8). *Do you have water if the grid goes down?* The Prepper Journal. https://theprepperjournal.com/2013/11/08/water-if-the-grid-goes-down/

Henry, P. (2015, April 28). *How much cash should you have if the grid goes down?* The Prepper Journal. https://theprepperjournal.com/2015/04/28/how-much-cash-should-you-have-if-the-grid-goes-down/

Herbst, C. (2022, January 27). *17 power outage supplies you need in case of an emergency*. Taste of Home. https://www.tasteofhome.com/collection/power-outage-supplies/

How do propane heaters work. (2022, January 16). Home Air Guides. https://homeairguides.com/how-do-propane-heaters-work

Howell, B. (2021, October 26). *A step-by-step guide to going off-grid*. The Eco Experts. https://www.theecoexperts.co.uk/blog/going-off-grid

How to make a crossbow. (2020, July 25). wikiHow. Retrieved February 10, 2022, from https://www.wikihow.com/Make-a-Crossbow

REFERENCES

How to make a solar oven. (2022). Education.com. https://www.education.com/science-fair/article/design-solar-cooker/

How to plan your emergency escape route. (n.d.). First Alert. https://www.firstalert.com/on/demandware.store/Sites-firstalert-Site/default/Content-Show?cid=escape-plan

How to wash dishes while camping. (2019, October 26). Fresh Off The Grid. https://www.freshoffthegrid.com/washing-dishes-while-camping/

James, J. (2021, December 30). *4 steps to building the best fire pits in survival shelters.* Survival Freedom. https://survivalfreedom.com/building-the-best-fire-pits-in-survival-situations-based-on-shelter-type/

Johnson, J. (2018, August 31). *4 ways to wash clothes on your off-grid homestead.* Down to Earth Homesteaders. https://downtoearthhomesteaders.com/4-ways-to-wash-clothes-on-your-off-grid-homestead/

Jones, K. (2018, August 11). *Prepping for basic emergency sanitation.* The Provident Prepper. https://theprovidentprepper.org/prepping-for-basic-emergency-sanitation/

Jones, K. (2019, April 9). *The prepper's guide to securing your home.* The Provident Prepper. https://theprovidentprepper.org/the-preppers-guide-to-securing-your-home/

Jones, K. (2019, July 10). *Prepper home pharmacy: The best medications to stockpile.* The Provident Prepper. https://theprovidentprepper.org/prepper-home-pharmacy-the-best-medications-to-stockpile/

Jones, K. (2019, October 18). *A wise prepper's guide to bartering skills and supplies.* The Provident Prepper. https://theprovi

dentprepper.org/a-wise-preppers-guide-to-bartering-skills-and-supplies/

Jones, K. (2019, December 5). *30 day grid-down cooking challenge—Lessons learned and fuel usage.* The Provident Prepper. https://theprovidentprepper.org/30-day-grid-down-cooking-challenge-lessons-learned-and-fuel-usage/

Jones, K. (2020, October 23). *6 lifesaving tips to keep warm during a winter power outage.* The Provident Prepper. https://theprovidentprepper.org/6-lifesaving-tips-to-keep-warm-during-a-winter-power-outage/

Jones, K. (2021, August 7). *7 lifesaving tips to help you survive a summer power outage.* The Provident Prepper. https://theprovidentprepper.org/7-lifesaving-tips-to-help-you-survive-a-summer-power-outage/

Jones, K., & Jones, J. (n.d.). *Emergency heating—Recommended products.* The Provident Prepper. https://theprovidentprepper.org/recommended-products/emergency-heating-recommended-products/

Jones, M. (2021, March 22). *Camp cooking: How to cook over a campfire.* advnture.com. https://www.advnture.com/how-to/cook-over-a-campfire

Kenneth. (2020, March 4). *Preparing for grid down: My step-by-step to-do list.* The Provident Prepper. https://theprovidentprepper.org/preparing-for-grid-down-my-step-by-step-to-do-list/

Lampert, E. (2019, May 22). *Off-grid power systems: 7 main types and the safety components you'll need.* Green Building Canada. https://greenbuildingcanada.ca/2019/off-grid-living/

Larsen, J. (2020, August 11). *How much water should a dog drink?* PetMD. https://www.petmd.com/dog/nutrition/evr_dg_the_importance_of_water

MacWelch, T. (2016, February 3). *How to build your own reflecting oven for camping or survival situations.* Outdoor Life. https://www.outdoorlife.com/blogs/survivalist/how-build-your-own-reflecting-oven-camping-or-survival-situations/

Margene. (2021, January 26). *DIY cooking without electricity.* DIY Preparedness. https://diypreparedness.net/diy-cooking-without-electricity/

McCafferty, E. (2019, July 17). *Keep your house cool without air conditioning.* Accidental Hippies. https://www.accidentalhippies.com/house-cool-without-air-conditioning/

McCoy, S. (2021, December 16). *The best flashlights of 2022.* GearJunkie. https://gearjunkie.com/outdoor/hiking/best-flashlights

McLean, J. (n.d.). *The most effective off grid home heating methods.* Thermal Earth. https://www.thermalearth.co.uk/blog/most-effective-off-grid-home-heating-methods

MissouriVillian. (2011, September 21). *7 methods of primitive fire starting.* Instructables. https://www.instructables.com/7-Methods-of-Primitive-Fire-Starting/

"Mountain Man" John. (2015, June 10). *Distilling—An overlooked survival skill.* Intrepid Outdoors. https://intrepidoutdoors.com/distilling-overlooked-survival-skill/

Muhjesbude, M. (n.d.). *10 must have alternative remedies for preppers.* https://www.survivopedia.com/must-have-alternative-remedies-for-preppers/

National Academies of Sciences, Engineering, and Medicine. (2017). *Enhancing the resilience of the nation's electricity system.* National Academies Press. https://doi.org/10.17226/24836

Natural herbs and plants for medicine and illness that you should be storing. (2019, February 20). UK Preppers Guide. https://www.ukpreppersguide.co.uk/natural-herbs-and-plants-for-medicine-and-illness-that-you-should-be-storing/

Nicholas O. (2014, October 21). *4 life-saving ways to communicate when the power is out.* Off The Grid News. https://www.offthegridnews.com/extreme-survival/4-life-saving-ways-to-communicate-when-the-power-is-out/

Oetken, N. (2017, November 5). *How to communicate when the grid goes down.* Outdoor Revival. https://www.outdoorrevival.com/instant-articles/communicate-grid-goes.html?chrome=1

Off grid. (2022, February 10). Energy Saving Trust. https://energysavingtrust.org.uk/advice/off-grid/

Planning an escape. (2021, July 2). NI Direct. https://www.nidirect.gov.uk/articles/planning-escape

Rader, T. (2019, June 15). *IFAK first aid kit list.* The Prepared. https://theprepared.com/bug-out-bags/guides/first-aid-kit-list/

Ramey, J. (2021, May 7). *Best headlamps for prepping.* The Prepared. https://theprepared.com/gear/reviews/headlamps/

Ready, J. (2020, June 19). *9 quick and efficient ways to wash clothes without electricity.* Ready Lifestyle. https://readylifestyle.com/how-to-wash-clothes-without-electricity/

Rejba, A. (2022, January 11). *9 methods to start a fire without matches or lighter.* The Smart Survivalist Blog. https://www.thesmartsurvivalist.com/9-methods-to-start-a-fire-without-matches-or-lighter/

Rhoades, J. (2021, July 23). *Using rain barrels: Learn about collecting rainwater for gardening.* Gardening Know How. https://www.gardeningknowhow.com/garden-how-to/watering/collecting-rainwater.htm

Rich M. (2015, September 30). *The 7 most important survival skills when the grid's down.* Off The Grid News. https://www.offthegridnews.com/extreme-survival/the-7-most-important-survival-skills-when-the-grids-down/

Rich M. (2016, January 12). *3 emergency heat sources when the power's out.* Off The Grid News. https://www.offthegridnews.com/grid-threats/3-emergency-heat-sources-when-the-powers-out/

Riley, T. (2021). *When crisis hits suburbia: A modern-day prepping guide to effectively bug in and protect your family home in a societal collapse.*

Should you get a kerosene or propane portable heater? (2020, October 28). Mi-T-M Blog. https://www.mitm.com/blog/get-kerosene-propane-portable-heater/

Siler, W. (2015, May 20). *How to build the only five campfires you'll ever need.* Gizmodo. https://gizmodo.com/how-to-build-the-only-five-campfires-you-ll-ever-need-1705895804

Stewart, C. (2021, June 1). *Power's out and in a pinch? How to create 5 makeshift urban survival lights.* The Art of Manliness. https://www.artofmanliness.com/skills/outdoor-survival/

powers-out-and-in-a-pinch-how-to-create-5-makeshift-urban-survival-lights/

Storing energy. (2022, February 10). Energy Saving Trust. https://energysavingtrust.org.uk/advice/storing-energy/

Storing salt for survival. (2021, February 1). happypreppers.com. https://www.happypreppers.com/salt.html

Superfood for survival | How to make stinging nettle tea. (2020, April 5). UK Preppers Guide. https://www.ukpreppersguide.co.uk/superfood-for-survival-how-to-make-stinging-nettle-tea/

Survival medicine for grid down survival. (n.d.). Family Survival Planning. https://www.familysurvivalplanning.com/survival-medicine.html

Survival sanitation: How to deal with human waste. (2019, February 25). The Prepper Journal. https://theprepperjournal.com/2014/03/17/how-to-deal-with-human-waste/

Tate, A. (2020, December 27). *Emergency radio frequencies preppers must know.* SHTF Blog. https://www.shtfblog.com/emergency-radio-frequencies-preppers-must-know/

Tips for basic backup power in a power outage or a SHTF situation. (2021, November 16). The Village Prepper. https://thevillageprepper.com/tips-for-basic-backup-power-in-a-power-outage-or-a-shtf-situation/

Top 7 emergency light sources for preppers. (2022, February 9). The City Dark. https://thecitydark.com/top-7-emergency-light-sources-for-preppers/

12 must have items for an emergency power out. (2019, October 1). Magic Valley Electric. https://www.electricteam.com/

blog/2019/october/12-must-have-items-for-an-emergency-power-out/

Vuković, D. (2021, May 27). *22 ways to cook without electricity when the grid fails.* Primal Survivor. https://www.primalsurvivor.net/ways-cook-without-electricity/

Vuković, D. (2021, August 30). *Essential survival lights and lighting: 9 options for disaster preparedness.* Primal Survivor. https://www.primalsurvivor.net/survival-lighting/

Walter, J. (2018, August 6). *Foraging for food in a winter survival situation.* Super Prepper. https://www.superprepper.com/foraging-for-food-in-a-winter-survival-situation/

WaterBob vs AquaPod: Bathtub storage made easy. (2021, June 3). Primal Survivor. https://www.primalsurvivor.net/waterbob-vs-aquapod/

Water survival guide. (2021, March 31). happypreppers.com. https://www.happypreppers.com/water.html

What is biogas? (n.d.). National Grid Group. https://www.nationalgrid.com/stories/energy-explained/what-is-biogas

Why is propane stored in household tanks but natural gas is not. (2019, August 22). Dependable LP Gas Company. https://www.dependablelpgas.com/why-is-propane-stored-in-household-tanks-but-natural-gas-is-not/

Williams College. (n.d.). *Passive solar design.* Sustainability. https://sustainability.williams.edu/green-building-basics/passive-solar-design/

WINDExchange. (n.d.). *Small wind guidebook.* US Department of Energy. https://windexchange.energy.gov/small-wind-guidebook

THE BUG OUT BOOK

TAKE NO CHANCES AND PREPARE YOUR BUG OUT PLAN NOW TO THRIVE IN THE WORST CASE SCENARIO WHEN BUGGING OUT IS YOUR ONLY OPTION

INTRODUCTION

"The time to repair the roof is when the sun is shining."

— JOHN F. KENNEDY

Reluctant as I am to start a new book with such a depressing statistic, I think this is an important one for us to be aware of as we embark on this journey together: The number of natural disasters across the world is ten times what it was in the 1960s. Changes to the climate have increased the chances of natural disasters caused by the weather, and we're likely to see even more floods, storms, droughts, and wildfires as the years go by. This makes being prepared not just a sensible decision but an essential one.

As you'll know if you've read my previous books, I'm a big believer in bugging in—sheltering at home safe in the knowledge that you have everything you need to survive on hand.

That said, there are certain scenarios in which bugging out is the only option, and it's important to be prepared for these too. In essence, bugging out means leaving your home to ensure your survival, whereas bugging in means staying put to reach the same goal. The common mistake many people make is to think that you can choose which option you will take before an emergency happens ... and this simply isn't the case. There's a time for bugging in, and there's a time for bugging out, and by the end of this book, you'll be able to tell —with confidence—which one is right for the situation you're faced with. To be adequately equipped for a crisis, you must be prepared for both scenarios. I cover sheltering in place in my earlier books *When Crisis Hits Suburbia* and *Prepare Your Home for a Sudden Grid-Down Situation*. You'll find additional information about stocking your pantry for a crisis in *The Prepper's Pantry*. Throughout this book, my goal is to help you prepare for an event in which bugging out is the most sensible course of action.

My family is the most important part of my life, and everything I do to prepare myself is to ensure they're safe in an emergency. I know many of you share the same goal, so rest assured that everything you discover here will be useful for taking care of everyone in your household. By the time you finish reading, you'll know exactly what you need to pack, how to prepare your family, and how to assess any emergency situation to determine the right course of action for your family's safety and survival.

Perhaps a recent weather event near you has made you sit up and take notice. Maybe a problem with your house meant you had to relocate while renovation work was carried out, leaving you acutely aware that you're unprepared for an emergency. Whatever the reason, you can rest assured that you'll find everything you need in these pages to prepare your family for a successful bug-out situation. You'll know what to pack, when to leave, where to go, how to prepare, and how to survive in your new location.

I've been studying both wilderness and urban survival for many years, and preparing my family's homestead for an emergency is an ongoing journey. My education has been practical, and everything I discuss in this book has been tried and tested—if not by myself, then by someone whose circumstances it suits better than mine. My goals are to help you put an end to your worries about what you'll do if you must evacuate your home and to leave you safe in the knowledge that you have everything you need to create a solid plan your family can follow if you have to go at a moment's notice. I've found that most books about bugging out focus on what to pack and not much else—my goal is to make sure you have the whole plan and not just a well-stocked bag you don't know what to do with.

So let's start with the essential question: How do you know when it's time to bug out, and when are you better off sheltering in place?

1

TO BUG OUT OR TO BUG IN? HOW YOU KNOW WHEN IT'S TIME TO GO

I first encountered a common problem with the idea of bugging out a few years ago while practicing with my family. The kids were super excited and desperate to know when we could do it for real. It was then that I realized the importance of not only letting them know that we were planning for an emergency (not a family camping trip), but I also needed to teach them when bugging out would and wouldn't be useful. Now, I play a game with them: When I think it might be time for a refresher, I describe different emergency situations and ask them whether it would be better to bug out or shelter in place. They're quite good at it now, and we have some interesting discussions around the dinner table about the pros and cons of evacuating the homestead in different emergencies. I think this would be a valuable activity for many people, adults and children alike. Not many people know when it's appropriate to bug out, even if they're prepared to do it. And that's why we're starting our journey here. Before we get any further into how to prepare for bugging out, we need to be confident that we know when to do it.

WHEN IT'S BETTER TO STAY PUT

Most of the time, sheltering in place is the better choice. You have a right to be in your home, and it's where all your supplies are. No matter how prepared you are, it is impossible to take as much with you as you can keep stored on your property. You also know your home intimately—where you can hide your valuables, what resources you have on hand, and ways to navigate the area confidently. Essentially, there are fewer unknowns in the location itself, so you're already on the starting blocks from the beginning. You know the escape routes (or you should!), and you know the local resources you can utilize; plus, you're around a familiar community you probably know and trust, at least to some extent. A word of warning, though: Sheltering in place requires you to be prepared. You need to make sure you have enough food and water stockpiled to see your family through an emergency, a well-stocked first aid kit and some basic first aid knowledge, and backup sources of heat and light. In my book, When Crisis Hits Suburbia, I cover these areas in much more detail. So, if you're not yet prepared for a bug-in situation, I'd recommend checking that out sooner rather than later.

I would say that for most emergencies we're likely to encounter, the most appropriate response will be to shelter in place. In each of the following scenarios, the specific details will make a difference, and there may be cases where bugging out would still be the better option, but on the whole, staying put is likely to be more appropriate. We'll take a closer look at how to assess each unique situation as it arises later in the chapter.

Viral Outbreak: In the case of a severe epidemic, it could be too dangerous to leave your home due to the risk of infection, particularly if the virus is airborne.

Economic Collapse: Large-scale economic disruption can lead to riots and other issues. If you're well-prepared, you'll be best off staying at home—especially in rural areas. However, you will need to be able to run your home without the use of the grid, produce your own food, and defend your property from looters.

ECONOMIC COLLAPSE

Civil Unrest: If looting or rioting occurs on a large scale, it could be dangerous to be outside. If there's a high level of violent activity outside your home, staying inside is your best course of action. You can always reassess when the initial chaos calms down.

CIVIL UNREST

Chemical/Biological Attack: The air outside could be extremely dangerous in the event of an attack, so this is probably a situation in which sheltering in place is a better option.

Nuclear Disaster: Although it's best to move as far away from nuclear fallout as quickly as possible, if the situation develops quickly and the affected area is large, it may not be possible to escape radiation without putting yourself in severe danger. In this case, staying indoors and riding it out is the best option.

DANGER

NUCLEAR ATTACK

Natural Disaster: Although it's possible to predict many natural disasters, you could encounter a situation where you can't get out quickly enough. If a catastrophe prevents you from using your escape route (and your home is otherwise safe), sheltering in place could be the best option.

NATURAL DISASTER

WHEN BUGGING OUT IS BEST

Although bugging in is a better option in most situations, there are times when it's safer to bug out. You will notice some overlap here with the scenarios in which sheltering in place is better. This just shows that every situation must be assessed on its own merit.

Approaching Natural Disaster: When you know something acute is coming (e.g., a hurricane is two days away from your home), evacuating the area is the best call.

An Unsafe Home: This could be the case after a natural disaster—for example, if your home is flooded or burnt. If you're at risk of domestic violence or are concerned about an intruder, leaving your home could be safer than staying put.

You Are Cut Off: If you're due to leave work or come back from vacation and a natural disaster has cut off your route, it may be safer to stay away from home for a while and avoid the danger zone.

Notification of a FEMA Camp: If government broadcasts tell you that no help will be sent to your area and specifically advise you to leave, it's time to listen. An emergency camp will likely be set up to receive you in this situation.

Civil Unrest: If looting or rioting is happening a little further away from your home and you can evacuate safely, bugging out will keep you safe if the violence moves closer to where you are.

Civil War: If the whole country is affected by civil war, the safest place may not be within the country. I'd recommend ensuring everyone in your family has a current passport and that you have funds secured to finance an overseas trip if necessary. Bear in mind, however, that you need a plan for this situation. It's crucial to know where you're going and that you'll have safe accommodation when you get there.

Nuclear War: Unless it's unsafe to evacuate the area without the risk of radiation poisoning, leaving your home for a fallout shelter will be your best course of action in a nuclear war. Timing is crucial, however, and you'll need to make sure you arrive at your destination before there's a risk that you could be exposed to radioactive fallout. If this is a risk, sheltering in place may be the better option.

BUG IN OR BUG OUT—HOW TO DECIDE

To determine the right time to bug out, you can use the REDOUT rule. Consider these six factors:

- **Resources**
- **Environment**
- **Destination**
- **Overwhelming force**
- **Unprepared**
- **Threat has increased**

Let's unpack that a bit…

Resources: If your stocks have been compromised or are low for any reason, moving somewhere with more readily available resources would be prudent. We'll look at how to prepare your evacuation route to make the most of this later in the book.

Environment: Keep an eye on your environment. Natural disasters, gas leaks, and radiation can all make a location unsafe, as can riots or outbreaks of violence. If danger escalates near your home and you can still get out safely, it's probably time to bug out.

Destination: Knowing where you're going and whether you can get there safely is crucial. If you have a secure location with more resources than you have at home and can get to it safely, it may be better to evacuate.

Overwhelming Force: Whether due to a military or civilian threat, it's best to bug out in a situation where you're outnumbered or running out of other options. Stay on top of the news and local updates to monitor the situation to escape any overwhelming force before it arrives on your doorstep.

Unprepared: Even the most thorough preppers could find themselves in a specific situation for which they are unprepared. Obviously, the goal is to be prepared for anything. Still, it's impossible to plan for every possible scenario, and if you find yourself in a situation you know you're not equipped for, bugging out may be the better option.

Increasing Threat: A new issue can arise even after the initial disaster has calmed. In the event of extreme rain, for example, flood waters could rise the day after everything had seemed safe. Keep an eye on the changes in the situation, and be prepared to leave if things get worse.

Is Bugging Out the Right Call?

Of course, bugging out is only viable if your family is prepared and their health and fitness match your evacuation needs. If you're a single person with no dependents and in good health, you'll have far more flexibility than someone with a health condition, three children, and an elderly relative to consider. We'll look more closely at bugging out with vulnerable people in Chapter Seven, so don't worry if you have special needs to consider. However, it's important to be aware of what everyone in your household can do.

First, you need to be aware of the fitness level of both yourself and your family members. Consider any long-term illnesses or disabilities among you, as well as short-term injuries that can affect your flexibility. If a slower evacuation is necessary, you'll need to weigh the benefits of getting out early to avoid being stuck against the potential benefits of sheltering in place.

The second thing to consider is the severity of the threat. The more intense or long-lasting it is, the more likely it is that bugging out is a sensible decision, and this will vary depending on your circumstances. For example, if you live in a hurricane-prone area, you're less likely to bug out in the event of a hurricane than someone living in an area less affected by such weather. Both you and your local area are likely to have measures in place to protect against the damage. Regardless of your hurricane experience, however, if you live in its direct path, you're going to want to bug out —the aftermath of a hurricane is usually relatively easy to deal with, but being in the eye of the storm is dangerous.

Last, you must consider how safe getting to your bug-out location is. Disappointing as it is to my children, bugging out is not a camping trip. Deciding to leave puts your family's life in a certain amount of danger. You could be overtaken by the same event you're trying to escape; you could find yourself lost or stranded; or you could run into trouble along the way. Bugging out is only sensible when it is safer than staying at home.

Assessing the Situation

Deciding to bug out requires you to get accurate information about the situation, which means you need to think about the communications grid. Is it still running reliably? Do you have power and cell phone service? Are any TV or radio stations operating and broadcasting safety advice? If you have an emergency radio, can you get alerts from official sources? If communications are down, this is a definite signal that the disaster has had a significant and far-reaching effect. If you cannot get the information you need from where you are, you'll need to find a way to connect with other people—ideally, a government official or law enforcement agent. It could be, however, that the emergency services aren't functioning. Look for signs in your neighborhood that tell you something's amiss. Have you had callers asking for food and water? Is there evidence of looting? Are stores and gas stations open, and are deliveries still being made? Your job is to answer as many of these questions as you can. Doing so will give you an indication of the severity and scale of the situation. If it's clear that things are bad, then it's time to consider whether it's safe to stay, especially if the grid has gone down and you don't have backup power sources at home. Look for the following clues to help you assess the severity of the situation:

- lines at gas stations, banks, and ATMs
- panic-buying in grocery, hardware, and building supply stores
- news reports detailing a potential threat
- increased military or police presence in the area

★ TAKE ACTION!

Disaster Scenario Game

Remember the game I like to play with my kids? You can do that with your family too, and I think it will help you just as much as it will help them. Every time I quiz my family on potential bug-out situations, I find myself doing a bit of extra problem-solving on the sly, which only supports my preparedness. Here are a few fictional scenarios you can try as thought experiments with your family. Feel free to make up your own too. The more practice you get brainstorming potential emergencies, the better.

Bug Out or Bug In?

⇨ There's a hurricane three towns away. Your home is secure, you have adequate provisions, and you're not in the eye of the storm.
⇨ Riots are happening in town, and it's becoming increasingly violent. Nothing has reached your immediate neighborhood yet, but you're worried it might.
⇨ Riots are happening at the end of your street.
⇨ A wildfire two miles away is rapidly spreading, and firefighters have been unable to control it. Your planned escape route is in the opposite direction to the fire.

The decision to bug out is never black-and-white, and there's no strict blueprint to follow. However, knowing how to assess the situation and understanding what your family is capable of will help you make the right decision in the moment. But knowing when to leave is no use unless you know *where* you're going, and we'll look at that in the next chapter.

2

WHERE ARE YOU GOING WITH THAT BUG-OUT BAG?

There's a good reason we're not starting this journey with the contents of your bug-out bag. You need a strong foundation before you even start thinking about your kit. You don't only need to be able to assess *when* it's time to bug out—you need to have a clear idea of your bug-out location and how you're going to get there long before an emergency ever arises. There are a couple of common mistakes preppers make regarding location, and you definitely want to avoid doing the same. The first is heading aimlessly into the hills, hoping to live off the land. I mean, it sounds sensible, but unless you really know the area and have plenty of supplies in place in case the land doesn't live up to your dreams, then it's a terrible idea and can leave you in a worse position than you started in. The second mistake many people make is to shelter in place when the better option would be to bug out—and thanks to the assessment strategies you acquired in Chapter One, that won't be you.

The secret to avoiding errors of judgment like these is to be properly prepared from the outset. That means planning your location thoughtfully and ensuring it's as well-equipped as you are.

WHAT MAKES A GOOD BUG-OUT LOCATION?

There are several factors to consider when considering your bug-out location. Don't neglect any area; remember that you're looking for an emergency retreat to keep your family as safe as possible, and every factor is crucial.

Proximity

Your bug-out location should be far away enough from the edge of the city that you're away from the traffic and chaos caused by many people fleeing the area at once. That said, it should be close enough that you can get to it within a few hours. You don't want to be driving for several days before you get to safety. It's also important to consider gas shortages and look for a place you can reach with no more than one tank of gas. We'll look at route planning in more detail later, but it's essential to have your driving routes planned, and these should be taken into account when you're choosing your location. There may be a situation where you can't drive, which means your destination should also be reachable via walking, bicycle, or motorbike. I'd recommend somewhere that won't take you more than a day if you have a family. (Although, how far away this is will depend on the physical capabilities of the group.) This also means planning for harsh weather, which may well be why you're evacuating in the first place. For example: If there's a river en route, will you still be able to cross if it's flooded? If there's a hill, will your family be able to climb it in icy conditions?

Isolation

Isolation helps minimize your chance of hostile encounters. You don't want your location to be too close to a densely populated area; ideally, you want to be away from roads and railway tracks. Aim for a place with good tree cover so that your lights are less visible, and keep any entrance gates innocuous and fully locked. The isolation factor is a bit of a balancing act. You want your bug-out location to be somewhere remote enough that outsiders won't be able to get there conveniently, yet you also want it to be accessible to your family the whole year round. The level of isolation you want also depends on your group's size. The fewer people you have with you, the more help you may need from others, and being too isolated could become a problem.

Water Sources

No matter the emergency, water is crucial to your survival, and you don't only need it for drinking—you'll also need it for cooking, washing, cleaning, and growing food. Ideally, your bug-out location will have a natural water source like a spring or a lake. Be careful with rivers, though, as these can flood in heavy rain, so if you're looking at locations near one, ensure your shelter is on high ground. If there isn't a natural water source nearby, you'll need to ensure you have a water storage facility, and it would be a good idea to install a rainwater harvesting system. A word of caution, however: Make sure you have ways to purify your water on hand. That may involve water purification tablets, a cast iron pot, a strainer, and a firepit to boil water to make it safe to drink.

Self-Sufficiency

There's always the possibility that you'll need to stay in your bug-out location for an extended period, and this means you'll need to be as self-sufficient as possible. Ideally, you'll have an independent power supply so that you don't need to rely on the grid; you'll find much more on this in my book, *Prepare Your Home for a Sudden Grid-Down Situation*. You'll also want to plant a food garden (this means keeping ample space, fertile soil, and good irrigation on your priority list). You're at an advantage if there's a supply of wild fish and game in the area and edible and medicinal plants for foraging. If you're considering raising livestock, you'll need to make sure you have suitable space and the resources to do so. You'll also need access to firewood, and if you don't have trees on the property, it may be a good idea to consider growing some fast-growing species, like Sycamore and American Elm.

Security

Security is a concern simply because if you're escaping an emergency, other people will be too, and your location should be somewhere you can defend easily. This makes consideration of your perimeter important. Ideally, your site will be on elevated ground (giving you a good vantage point) protected by natural barriers like cliffs or streams. You'll need to secure your perimeter and camouflage your property —including any vehicles you have with you. Emergency exits are also important. You'll need an escape route if your property is attacked for any reason.

Waste Management

This is important because poorly managed waste can lead to health risks. Biodegradable waste can be used as compost, but you'll also need to dispose of non-biodegradable trash like glass and plastic. This means having shovels and space (not too close to your property) where you can bury them. Human waste is the other concern. If you must dig a latrine, make sure it's downhill from your shelter and at least 50 yards from your water source. You may, however, choose something a little more permanent, in which case a compost toilet could be a good option.

Protection From the Elements

A good bug-out location must be safe from all the elements, which will be particularly important if you're escaping a natural disaster. You'll need to be aware of the potential for floods, earthquakes, tornadoes, and forest fires when choosing your location. Avoid floodplains and areas near mountain slopes, and make sure your structure is resistant to high winds and earthquakes. Of course, much of this will depend on your area. Consider the likelihood of each type of disaster, and prioritize protecting yourself against the most likely first.

Longevity

During the planning stage, you'll have no idea how long you'll need your bug-out location. And chances are, if you have to evacuate your home, you won't know in that moment either. It's best, therefore, to be prepared for an extended stay, stocking as much food, water, and fuel as possible within your budget and space restrictions. The beauty of any kind of prepping is that you can always build as you go—that's what I do. In my mind, being adequately prepared means never thinking you're done. There's always more you can do, and this is the same with your bug-out shelter. Start with what you can afford; as time goes on, you can extend it by looking for more sustainable options.

Affordability

It perhaps goes without saying that you need to consider your budget. It's even more important to remember that patience is key here: Survival properties can be expensive, and it's worth looking around, despite the urgency you may feel to get it sorted. Remember that upfront costs aren't all you're dealing with. If you're buying a piece of land, you'll have construction and development costs to factor in and any other features you want to install. Come up with a realistic budget before you start, and look for creative ways to develop it. Be cautious of buying very cheap land or property: It could cost you more in the long run if you have to do a lot of work to make it suitable for survival. You'll also need to factor in stockpiling and sourcing provisions when designing your budget.

Legalities

It's important to know about government regulations and any required permits in your bug-out location. Although these things may not be the most important in an emergency situation, they're crucial to developing the property as you wish. You'll want to check out the zoning laws, particularly if you want to raise livestock or grow crops. The chances are, you won't need any permits for a basic bug-out cabin, but it's worth knowing exactly what the rules are before you start.

Space

This may seem obvious, but you'd be surprised by how many people overlook the space their family needs to be comfortable. Ideally, you want to provide sufficient personal space for everyone; this will be particularly important if you have to stay for an extended period. You'll also need plenty of storage for your supplies and space for growing or raising food.

Structure

Obviously, a significant part of your bug-out location is shelter. You can choose an existing structure or build your own, but it must offer reliable protection from the elements. It should be able to keep your family warm and comfortable and have ample space for storing your water and food supplies. If you're looking for a safe location in an area prone to hurricanes or tornadoes, you may wish to consider underground shelters, and if you're in an earthquake zone, reinforcements will be necessary. There are many different options for shelters, and we'll look at them more closely in the next section, but for most people, a remote cabin is a good option. It's also a good idea to have another shelter you can rely on in the event of an emergency escalation—a tent or an RV, for example.

CHOOSING YOUR STRUCTURE

The best structure for you depends on the area in which you'll be bugging out, the needs of your family, and your budget. There are several options you can choose from, and we'll look at the most common and effective ones now.

Bug-Out Cabin

A bug-out cabin must be safe, strong, and able to sustain you through a crisis. For many people, a hunting cabin is a natural place to start. If you're a hunter anyway, kitting out a place you already own (providing it's accessible and in a secure location) is an easy way to begin, particularly if you're on a tight budget. If, however, you're starting from scratch, before you even consider the shelter itself, you'll need land to put it on. Land can be costly, but if you manage to find some without utilities, you'll reduce costs; I've seen places go for less than $200 an acre. This does mean you'll have to think about utilities on your own, but the chances are, in a bug-out situation, they won't be running anyway. And the bonus is, it'll be exactly the kind of land you're looking for—not too near a major highway and somewhere few people are likely to stumble upon by accident. Before you rush into anything, come up with a water collection plan—whether that's going to be digging a well or harvesting rainwater. If you decide to go ahead and buy a vacant lot, you'll need to prepare the land before you can build or add a cabin. That means thinking about power, water, and waste management.

Once the land is ready, you can opt for a pre-built structure like a hunting cabin, or if you have the skills and access to resources, you could build one yourself. One option I like is a trailer, which you can actually pick up for reasonably cheap if you're willing to put in a bit of work.

I don't claim to be an expert builder, so I won't give you complete guidance on how to build your own cabin. However, I know many of you will have the skills and determination to embark on such a project. There are a few tips I think it's important to consider if you decide to go down this route.

- Protect your cabin from wildlife by sealing or blocking gable ends with mesh screens or sheet metal.
- If you use T-11 siding, utilize construction adhesive to keep your nails spaced tightly to reduce the risk of birds pecking the siding and forming gaps bugs can access.
- Minimize your use of vents, and if you do have them, make sure they're well screened. Be sure to seal the crawl space too.
- If you have a metal roof, be sure to use waterproof caulking so that water doesn't freeze in the gutter and rip the roof off. To avoid ice and snow building up, locate any chimneys you want to add near a ridge.
- For protection against both water and wildlife, use pressure-treated wood.
- For maximum support, particularly on the roofing, use metal fastenings and screws rather than regular nails.
- To protect against intruders, secure the entrance points to your cabin by framing doors and shutters in angle iron and using carriage bolts. Add an extra layer of security to doors by equipping them with padlocks. Inside, consider adding hiding places to keep your supplies safe.
- Think about the possibility of a longer stay when you design your cabin. If you have the budget, try to include a wood-burning stove and solar panels.

LOG CABIN

RV/Campervan

The advantage of an RV or a camper van is that it can also serve as your transport, and you can move it as needed (as long as you have access to gas and can keep it running). Motorhomes are the most common type of RV, replacing the back part of a van body with a living area. They usually have a compartment over the cab with a bed in it. Campervans are smaller and don't usually have a section over the cab. There's also a third type of RV—an integrated motorhome with a driving section within the living room. These are usually larger and are more comparable to a bus than a car. While the space is appealing, they're quite noticeable and may not be the most appropriate choice for a survival situation. I would say that if you go for an RV as your bug-out home, a low profile is the most important thing.

We touched briefly on using a trailer as a bug-out cabin, but you could also use a travel trailer as a more moveable bug-out shelter. Something smaller that you can tow gives you more freedom, but only for as long as you have gas. These range from expandable trailers to teardrops to toy haulers, all of which can be towed by a regular car. The advantage of these over other types of RV is that you can disconnect them from your vehicle and set up camp elsewhere, thereby keeping a lower profile.

RV

Campsite

If you're using an RV as your shelter, a campsite could be an excellent short-term bug-out location, but I don't think I'd advise it for an emergency lasting longer than a couple of weeks. It has the advantage of being, essentially, a gated community. Furthermore, the other people using it are not only likely to have camping skills that may be useful to you, but they'll have their own shelter, so they're unlikely to be a threat to yours. Often, campsites are set up near a stream or lake, so there's a good chance of a water source. If you are considering this for a short-term emergency, I'd suggest researching campgrounds first. Your best bet is to look for family-friendly sites rather than party ones—you're more likely to find a safe and supportive community this way. Look for somewhere with lake access and a gate and consider the facilities (which may or may not be running in an emergency). Lakehouses are also an option to consider, although it's important to note that unless you own one, you can't rely on getting in during an emergency. With both of these options, although you will be sharing the space with other people, it will be relatively easy to defend that space from intruders, and the chances are you all have a common goal and enough resources of your own not to be a threat to each other.

CAMPSITE

National Park

There are pros and cons to bugging out in a national park. A big plus point is that they've been mapped out in detail, and if you have a map, you can navigate the terrain easily. You can also scout it out well in advance of an emergency, so you can plan exactly where you'd set up camp if disaster strikes. Most parks are protected by conservationists, meaning they still have all the resources you might need (unlike most unprotected land), including water sources. Again, you couldn't set up a permanent shelter like a cabin, but if you're using something like an RV, a national park would give you good options with easy access. This can also be a disadvantage, however, as the more access there is, the less security you have. Aim to find a spot well away from the main roads and trails to protect against this risk.

On the downside, although most people probably won't seek out a national park during an emergency (so your competition won't be too great), most people know where they are, and they could become a target for looters. The terrain can also be rough, so you'll need to make sure you have a safe and accessible spot picked out in advance.

NATIONAL PARK

Out-of-Town Apartment

If you have an apartment somewhere other than where you live, this is a possible option for you, as long as you can get to it relatively quickly. This is assuming the apartment is in an area unaffected by the disaster, though. So, although you need to be able to get to it, it shouldn't be too close to where you live. If you're considering this, stock up your apartment just as you would if it were a designated cabin, and be prepared to leave if the disaster comes closer to your new location. Staying with friends and family out of town is another possibility. Still, the same caveats apply, and it's worth considering how comfortable you would be if you had to continue living together for an extended period.

OUT-OF-TOWN APARTMENT

Abandoned Building

Taking shelter in an abandoned building is a risky option, but it is possible. The main problem is that they're likely to be targeted by looters and other people trying to flee the disaster. What's more, the conditions are likely to be less than ideal. There can be air quality problems, which could affect your health. They may also be in poor repair, potentially making them unsafe. On the other hand, an abandoned building will at least give you walls and shelter and may be a good stop-off point if you need to find shelter en route to your final location.

If you're considering using an abandoned building, look for multiple options, and scope them out carefully. Aim for a one-story building as it will be easier to defend and is likely to be more solid. Try to choose somewhere away from main roads and other buildings that may be prime targets for looters. Choose a small room that you can easily seal off, but try to be near an exit. This makes both security and escape easier. If insulation is lacking, use blankets to insulate the doors and windows, and keep all your supplies with you. Hopefully, you'll have your own water supply, at least for the short term, but in a crisis, you can check the water heaters and toilets. You'll need to purify any water you find in these places, but it will do in a pinch.

ABANDONED BUILDING

Boat

For many families, a boat won't even be a consideration. But if you live near water, it might not be as off-the-wall of an idea as it sounds. While we think of boats as being expensive, you can find them for as little as $50,000, and they come with tax advantages. If you're looking for a transatlantic adventure, a used boat is likely to be a money drain, but as a bug-out location, a boat doesn't necessarily need to be fully functional. Taking shelter in a stationary boat is no less effective than bugging out in a cabin. The only difference is that you're on water rather than land. Many boats have self-sufficiency built into their design. They often have water makers to allow you a constant supply of fresh water; they come with fuel storage, power systems, and sewer systems, which works to your advantage. The fishing potential is good, and it's theoretically possible to keep a container garden on deck. Storing supplies might be more difficult, particularly if you have a smaller vessel. You'll have to weigh up whether you can comfortably accommodate your whole family and store supplies.

BOAT

Multiple Locations

What I've tried to do here is give you an overview of some of your best options. Whatever you choose, be sure to research it well and weigh the pros and cons for your family. A word of warning though: An effective bug-out plan will include a backup location in addition to your primary one. Something could easily prevent you from being able to use your first choice, so it's a good idea to have a Plan B, with several possible routes clear in your mind. Ensure your backup location is in a different place—and on different routes—to your primary site. You don't want the same thing preventing you from getting to your first choice to be a problem for your second too. My family has a cabin somewhere remote but accessible, but we have a small RV too. The idea is that we can take the RV to the cabin, giving us more supplies and freedom, but if we cannot access the cabin, we can take the

RV off in the opposite direction, safe in the knowledge that we have everything we need to survive.

★ TAKE ACTION!

Bug-Out Location Assessment

Considering bug-out locations is no small task. Try using this scoring system to grade potential sites and develop the best plan for your family. The higher the number of points you have for each location, the better an option it is.

Bug-Out Location Scoring

- Easily accessible (no matter the weather)—2 points
- Not easy for others to locate or easily gain access to—2 points
- Several ways to access it—2 points
- Several escape routes—3 points
- Is on or near public, BLM, or state land—3 points
- Strong and sufficient shelter—5 points
- At least one barrier (e.g., cliff/mountain)—2 points
- At least one vantage point—2 points
- Ample storage—3 points
- You can stock it before an emergency situation—5 points
- Near to a water source (e.g., lake/well)—5 points
- Renewable sources of food (e.g., fishing/hunting/foraging/farming)—5 points
- Latrine—3 points
- Familiar area you can find and navigate easily—5 points
- Low risk of natural disasters—3 points

⇨ You know and trust somewhere near to your location—5 points

Interpreting Your Score

40-50 points: Perfect!
35-39 points: You can work with this.
Under 34 points: Major improvements must be made, or a new location should be found.

You'll need to give this section of your plan considerable thought and attention before you're ready for an emergency, but once you have this sorted, you can move on to the part of bugging out that most people think of first: that all-important bug-out bag.

3

MEET BOB: PREPARING YOUR BUG-OUT BAG

Many people fail to think beyond the bag when preparing to bug out; furthermore, a quarter of Americans don't have an emergency go bag at all. Don't worry if you're one of them. You're about to learn everything you need to know in order to remedy that.

WHAT IS A BUG-OUT BAG?

You might hear of a bug-out bag called a 72-hour bag or an emergency go bag. Essentially, it's your survival kit for when your life has been so destabilized that you must leave your home. It will be your kitchen, your pantry, and your doctor for 72 hours—which should be enough time to get you to your bug-out location, where you should have supplies stashed to cover you for a longer period of time.

The actual bag you use isn't important, but having the right kit can help with organization and making sure you have enough space for everything you need without carrying extra weight. The best bag is one you create yourself—tailored specifically to your needs. Bear in mind that everyone in your family will need a bag, as one bag for the whole party won't be enough to get you through 72 hours.

What to Consider When You're Building Your Bag

In order to build a bug-out bag that will suit your needs, you need to know your environment. Your bag is designed to get you from your home to your safe location, so that means knowing your local terrain and any possible shelter you might be using along the way, whether that's abandoned buildings, forests, or caves. You want to think about whether there are water sources on your route, and you need a good idea of the typical weather conditions in the area—particularly if extreme weather like blizzards, tornados, or hurricanes are common. Is there food you can hunt or forage along the way? Are there any likely threats? Think about dangerous plants and animals in your region and any possible human threat that may occur due to an emergency. These factors affect what equipment you may need and will guide you when planning your bug-out bag. However, knowing these things is only helpful if you know what to do with them. If you're unsure about edible plants or how to find water in a desert region, now's the time to research. Along the way, note the equipment you'll need to survive each threat you've identified.

When it comes to the bag itself, I'd recommend getting your kit together first and then deciding on the most suitable vessel. However, I realize it can be a bit of a minefield if you don't know what you're looking for. The best advice I could give you is to read product reviews and see what other customers think. Personally, I have an Eberlestock Switchblade pack, which weighs just over 3 pounds, and has a good number of inside pockets to help you keep everything organized. It has a capacity of 1,500 cubic inches, which should be enough for everything you need. I like it because it's subtle. It doesn't look like a tactical piece of gear, and that will make you less conspicuous if you have to evacuate. On the downside, although it has ample space, it won't support a lot of weight, so if you have heavier equipment, it may not be the best for you. It's also a little on the pricey side unless you can find it on a good deal, which is what I did.

GETTING YOUR GEAR

One of the most important considerations with every part of your kit is weight. I'm a big fan of spreadsheets to help with this—keeping a record of the weight of each item so that you can see how much you're building up. The whole kit (bag included) shouldn't weigh more than 25% of your own body weight (or that of whoever is carrying it). If you can carry less than this, great; it'll mean you'll have greater mobility, which will be particularly important if you're walking. Bear in mind that not everyone in your family will need everything. This means that some of the weight can be shared. For example, one person might carry the camping stove, while someone else might have the cookware. This is another reason I like a spreadsheet for this task.

The best approach to building a bug-out bag is to split it into categories, which is what we'll do here. This will help you keep your provisions organized and give you a systematic approach to ensure you don't miss anything.

Food

A healthy adult can survive without food for longer than 72 hours, but that's no reason not to consider this category carefully. You'll need to keep your energy levels up, and chances are, you'll need more energy than usual. Aim for enough food to last at least three days, and consider what you'll need for cooking; you'll need a few kitchen items as well as food provisions. Bear in mind that although you may need water for some items, it's a good idea to bring ingredients that don't require it—you don't know how scarce water might become.

Of course, what you pack will depend somewhat on your personal preferences and dietary requirements, but I'd recommend packing some dehydrated foods such as dried rice, beans, vegetables, and some jerky. You could also take dehydrated meals, meal bars, and high-energy snacks like trail mix and granola bars. Since they're light and won't take up much space, I think it's worth taking a few spices, too; it's amazing what something as simple as this can do for morale. In terms of cooking and eating, make sure you have utensils, collapsible bowls, and a can opener. Take a camp stove (with extra fuel and a way to light it), a metal cup, and a cooking pot so that you can rustle up a warm meal wherever you are. I highly recommend taking an edible plants guide with you, particularly if you're not confident with foraging.

Water

Water is absolutely essential. Everyone in your family will need a minimum of one liter a day, and you should not only carry it with you but also have a means of purifying water that you find. One consideration you may want to make when you're choosing your bag is whether it has a hydration pouch; some of these can hold three liters of water without the need for extra bottles. Make sure everyone in your family has a water bottle and that you have water purification tablets and water filters.

Heat

You'll need to be able to start a fire to stay warm and cook meals, and I'd recommend taking at least three different ways of doing so in case something fails. Consider lighters, spark rods, stormproof matches, tinder, kindling, and cotton balls that you've already soaked in Vaseline. Remember that all of these things should be kept in a waterproof container.

Fire isn't the only thing you need to consider in terms of heat, however. Take mylar blankets for every family member, as well as reusable hand warmers and waterproofs. (Rain ponchos are a good idea as they're lightweight and will fold down to a small size.)

Light

Light might not sound as important as other categories, but it's crucial. Whether you're preparing food, setting up shelter, or assessing the environment, if it's dark, you're going to need light. Again, I'd make sure you have multiple options in case one fails. Remember to bring spare batteries too! Choose from flashlights, headlamps, candles, tea lights, LED keychains, glowsticks, and solar lanterns.

Tools

It would be easy to go overboard on tools, so think carefully about what's essential and what fits within your skill set. Prioritize blades and fasteners; these will allow you to fix, break, or create something you might need. A survival knife or a multi-tool is a must. Leatherman is a good brand, but there are plenty to choose from. An ax is a good idea if you can justify the weight, as it will allow you to chop firewood, and a wire saw could be useful for accessing difficult spaces. A trowel could come in handy for burying waste, and a small sewing kit is a must for emergency repairs. Duct tape and carabiners help fix and attach things, and superglue can come in surprisingly handy too.

Navigation

No matter how well you memorize your route, it's always best to be prepared for the worst. If a road is closed or there's a riot in your path, you may need to think quickly. Make sure you have a compass and a topographic map. I also always carry binoculars so that I can see what may lie ahead.

Shelter

In an ideal world, you'll get to your bug-out location without needing extra shelter, but you don't know what may happen along the way to delay you. Taking something lightweight that you can use in an emergency is well worth the extra baggage. Remember to take the terrain, weather, and any other environmental factors specific to your area into account when you're deciding what to pack. I would suggest a lightweight and compact tent, a tarp or ground sheet, and a sleeping bag and ground pad (for everyone in the family). Depending on your environment, you may also want to consider a woolen blanket or a bug net.

Clothing

The clothing you take is obviously very dependent on your body type, fitness level, and climate. The main advice I can give you is to go for layers and re-evaluate your kit when the season changes. Make sure everyone in your family has at least two sets of clothing so that you always have something dry and comfortable. I'd recommend merino wool; it's comfortable and lightweight while still insulating, and it dries quickly. You'll need underwear and walking socks, and I'd suggest convertible pants and a light, long-sleeved shirt with a fleece sweater or jacket. Make sure you have a waterproof jacket or rain poncho and, if necessary for your climate, a warm hat and gloves. In hot climates, have a sunhat to protect yourself from UV rays.

Hygiene

This is a category that's often overlooked, but it's vital to your health, particularly since you don't know what hazards you'll run into along the way. You're likely to encounter biological elements that your body is less accustomed to, which means your immunity against these threats will be lower. This makes hygiene even more important than usual. Be sure to have wet wipes, hand sanitizer, camping soap, a compact towel and washcloth, and a toothbrush and toothpaste. You'll also need toilet rolls (I'd advise taking two rolls), feminine hygiene products if applicable, and any other personal hygiene items that are essential to you.

Medical

If you've had first aid training, you may feel the temptation to pack more equipment, but it's better to think minimally. Obviously, you want to be able to take care of your family if they become sick or injured. Still, bulky equipment like oxygen tanks will hamper your mobility and is less likely to be necessary for the few days you're in transit. I suggest building your own first aid kit in a light and easily transportable bag. Include the following items:

- acetaminophen
- alcohol pads
- anti-allergy medication
- antibiotic cream
- antidiarrheal medication
- antiseptic wipes
- aspirin
- burn cream
- eye wash
- foot powder
- gauze pads and rolls
- ibuprofen
- ice pack (break to activate)
- insect repellent
- lip balm
- moleskin
- mylar emergency blanket
- needles
- prescription medications to last a week
- safety pins
- self-adhesive plasters
- sunscreen
- suture kit
- temporary dental filling
- thermometer
- tourniquet
- trauma shears
- triangular bandage
- tweezers
- vinyl gloves
- vitamins

Communication

This area can be overlooked if you're not used to prepping. Communication equipment is vital because it allows you to keep in touch with your group, send emergency messages if necessary, and gain vital information about the emergency you're escaping from. In Chapter Five, we will look at "PACE" in the context of transport to your bug-out location, but it's also a good policy to apply to the communication you carry in your bag. PACE stands for **p**rimary, **a**lternate, **c**ontingency, and **e**mergency; in this case, your cell phone covers your primary means of communication. For an alternate means, take a tablet; for your contingency plan, take ham radio equipment (providing you have a license). For your emergency backup, take a crank radio. We'll look more at communication in Chapter Ten, and you may wish to use different pieces of equipment than this, but whatever you decide on, PACE planning is an excellent way to ensure you have ample backup. Don't forget to take solar chargers—your equipment is useless if you can't power it. I'd also recommend a whistle, flares, and a signal mirror for emergency signaling and communication.

Security

As you'll know if you've read my previous books, I'm not a firearms man, and I prefer to steer clear of this topic in my writing. However, if you do have a gun or a rifle, this may be something you'd want to include in your bug-out bag. I do carry pepper spray, and this is all I'd really recommend in this category, besides making sure you're trained in self-defense of some kind (we'll look at this in more detail later). Other things that are useful in the security category fall into other categories anyway—binoculars and a tactical flashlight, for example.

Documents

We may live in the digital age, but it's wise to keep physical copies of some documents, and you'll need to take these with you when you bug out. I'd recommend laminating paper documents to protect them from extreme weather and general wear and tear caused by your journey or storing them in a waterproof pouch. I'd recommend taking the following documents, as well as a USB drive with electronic copies of everything, along with records and memorabilia that are important to you:

- banking information for all of your accounts
- emergency contact information for family, friends, medical and insurance providers, etc.
- financial documents
- ID (include multiple forms)
- international travel documents (e.g., passports)
- legal documents
- licenses, certifications, and permits
- medical records (including prescriptions)

Morale

You can't pack morale, but you can pack things to help you keep it up, and this is important. A positive mental attitude is very important to survival, and there are a few seemingly trivial items worth packing in your bug-out bag to help you keep your spirits up and ensure that a positive attitude stays in place. What that looks like for you will depend on you and your family. For us, tea and coffee bags are a must, as well as chocolate and candy. We always have a pack of cards and a small, light book each.

Miscellaneous

Whenever you try to organize anything by category, some things just don't fit. You may have one or two of your own personal items that you'll want to take that don't fit neatly anywhere, but there are also a few important things you'll want in addition to the categories we've already covered. Consider packing the following items:

- aluminum foil
- cash
- contraception
- eye protection
- face mask
- fishing gear
- magnifying glass
- resealable bags
- salt
- spare batteries
- sunglasses
- trash bags

PACKING ON A LIMITED BUDGET

If you're looking over the list above and having heart palpitations about how much it will cost you to kit out the whole family, don't panic. You can still build a bug-out bag that will serve you well, even if you can't get everything you want straight away. Start with what's already in your house, collecting items to help you cover the key areas. It's better to start with a limited bug-out bag than no bag at all, and you can always add items later as your budget allows. Here are the critical things I think you should include in your starter preparedness kit:

- blanket
- bandages and gauze
- duct tape
- emergency contacts
- flashlight (with spare batteries)
- pre-packaged food
- lighter
- pocket knife
- raincoat
- toilet paper
- water
- wet wipes

HOW TO PACK YOUR BAG

A fully functional bug-out bag requires careful packing, and it's important that you know exactly where everything is and how to access it quickly. How you pack your bag will also affect how well you can use the space within it and how resistant it is to the weather.

The first thing to think about is weight distribution. You'll be carrying a combination of light and heavy equipment, and the best way to manage that is to pack it strategically. I would recommend the following approach:

At the bottom of your bag, pack your softer, lighter items that you won't need to access hurriedly (e.g., extra clothes, a tent, or a sleeping bag). This will be more comfortable to carry and easier to access the things you're more likely to need in an emergency. In the middle of your bag and close to your body, pack your heaviest items. This might include your camping stove or your water reserves. The closer these things are to your body, the less likely they are to impact your center of gravity, making your bag seem lighter. Also in the middle of your bag but further from your body, pack mid-weight items like food and spare batteries. At the top of your bag, add your essential but light gear—rain poncho, fire starters, and first aid kit. In the small pockets on the outside of your bag, keep items you want to access quickly without having to take your pack off. These might include your cell phone, water bottle, and snacks.

It's best to avoid attaching too much to the outside of your bag because it will be harder to keep a low profile, and you're more likely to get caught on branches or rocks. However, if you're taking trekking poles that you'll use immediately, it may be handy to store these outside your bag.

The next thing to think about is how to make the most efficient use of space, and that means looking for hacks you can use to make packing easy. One of the best examples is the military technique of making a skivvy roll, where a t-shirt, underwear, and socks are packed in a bundle. Start by lying the t-shirt out flat. Then fold the underwear in half and put it in the middle of the shirt before folding the sides into the center. Cross the foot ends of the socks over the center of the t-shirt, with the ankles sticking out the sides. Then, starting at the neck, roll the shirt tightly around the socks. You should end up with something that looks a bit like a Christmas cracker. Now, pull the ankles of the socks back inwards, stretching them over the t-shirt roll, making a burrito-like structure. This is your skivvy roll and is an effective way to pack essential clothing items compactly. Another useful tip is to collect smaller items like batteries and matches into a compact container so they're easy to find.

The final thing to consider when packing is the weather. You can buy a waterproof cover for your bag, but it's still worth protecting any moisture-sensitive equipment. Dry bags are useful for this, and they come in a huge range of sizes to cover different items.

EVALUATING YOUR BAG

No bug-out bag is complete until it's been tested, and to do this, you'll need to take it out on the road. I'd recommend four test runs. On Test 1, take a short hike with your bag and assess it for comfort. If you need to make it more comfortable, stop and rearrange your packing, and if you end the trip in pain, you know you'll need to find a bag that fits you better. On Test 2, go for a longer hike, again assessing its comfort and rearranging as necessary. On Test 3, take a backpacking trip lasting between 12 and 24 hours. This time, pay attention to what items you use and how. You may find essentials are missing. Make a note of these items, and review the contents of your bag when you get home. On Test 4, take a backpacking trip to another location. Compare your notes from both trips and look for similarities. Remove anything non-essential on both lists, and add anything you found lacking. Once you've refined your bag after all four tests, you can be confident it will serve you well.

★ TAKE ACTION!

Bug-Out Bag Checklist

It's time to build your bug-out bag. Use the checklist below to guide you, ticking each item off as you find it. Bear in mind that not every item will apply to you, and refer back to the list in the medical category above to get the contents of your first aid kit.

CATEGORY	ESSENTIAL ITEMS	SOURCED
Clothing	Convertible pants	
	Fleece	
	Gloves	
	Light, long-sleeved shirt	
	Sunhat	
	Underwear	
	Warm hat	
	Walking socks	
Communication	Cell phone	
	Crank radio	
	Flares	
	Ham radio equipment (if licensed)	
	Signal mirror	
	Solar chargers	
	Tablet	
	Whistle	

CATEGORY	ESSENTIAL ITEMS	SOURCED
Documents	Banking information	
	Emergency contact information	
	Financial documents	
	ID	
	International travel documents	
	Legal documents	
	Licenses, certifications, and permits	
	Medical documents	
	USB drive	
Food	Camp stove (and fuel)	
	Can opener	
	Collapsible bowls	
	Cooking utensils	
	Dehydrated ingredients/meals; meal bars	
	Eating utensils	
	Metal cup	
	Metal cooking pot	

Category	Essential Items	Sourced
Food	Snacks	
	Spices	
Heat	Kindling	
	Lighters	
	Mylar blankets	
	Reusable hand warmers	
	Spark rods	
	Stormproof matches	
	Tinder	
	Vaseline-soaked cotton balls	
	Waterproofs	
Hygiene	Camping soap	
	Compact towel	
	Feminine hygiene products	
	Hand sanitizer	
	Other personal hygiene items	
	Toilet roll	

Category	Essential Items	Sourced
Hygiene	Toothbrush	
	Toothpaste	
	Wash cloth	
	Wet wipes	
Light	Candles	
	Flashlight	
	Glowsticks	
	Headlamp	
	LED keychains	
	Solar lanterns	
	Tealights	
Medical	First aid kit	
	Personal medical needs e.g., asthma puffer	
	Perscription/OTC meds	
Miscellaneous	Aluminum foil	
	Cash	
	Eye/face protection	

CATEGORY	ESSENTIAL ITEMS	SOURCED
Miscellaneous	Fishing gear	
	Magnifying glass	
	Resealable bags	
	Salt	
	Spare batteries	
	Sunglasses	
	Trash bags	
Morale	Book	
	Chocolate/candy	
	Other personal items	
	Playing cards	
	Tea/coffee bags	
Navigation	Binoculars	
	Compass	
	Topographical map	
Security	Fire arms & ammunition	
	Self defense weapons e.g., taser, pepper spray	

CATEGORY	ESSENTIAL ITEMS	SOURCED
Security	Survival knife	
Shelter	Bug net	
	Ground pad	
	Groundsheet	
	Paracord	
	Sleeping bag	
	Tarp	
	Tent	
	Woolen blanket	
Tools	Axe	
	Carabiners	
	Duct tape	
	Knife	
	Multitool	
	Sewing kit	
	Superglue	
	Trowel	

CATEGORY	ESSENTIAL ITEMS	SOURCED
Tools	Wire saw	
Water	Hydration pouch	
	Water bottle	
	Water filters	
	Water purification tablets	

When you evaluate your bag, you may find that you have to make adaptations to make it comfortable and easy to carry. But in an emergency, you have only yourself and your gear. As much as adapting that gear is useful, it's also necessary to train yourself to handle an emergency situation. Luckily for you, this is what we're going to look at in the next chapter!

4

BUG-OUT BOOT CAMP: TRAINING UP FOR AN EMERGENCY

If you read the chapter title and started panicking about training your kids to handle an emergency, relax. You can actually do a lot of this by stealth. My family really enjoys camping, and I use this as an opportunity to teach the kids survival skills as we go. They love it, and they don't even notice they're learning. Outdoor activities are good for developing health and fitness too. We cycle a lot, and we love days out hiking—the perfect training program for bugging out. The point is, emergency preparedness training can be built into everyday life; the trick is to think strategically about what activities you incorporate.

Throughout this chapter, we'll look at some areas to focus on in emergency preparedness training. As you read, keep each member of your family in mind, and think about what you might be able to do to prepare them or include them in your own training activities.

THE IMPORTANCE OF PHYSICAL FITNESS

It's never a bad idea to improve your health, emergency or not, but if you're going to be able to thrive in the face of disaster, your fitness is important. You'll be less susceptible to diseases like heart attacks and strokes, and you're less likely to sprain or break something if you fall. Simply put, the fitter you are, the higher your chances of survival.

An emergency situation could require you to walk long distances. There may be rubble to dig through, an injured family member to carry, or equipment to move. All of this might be necessary on less food and sleep than you're used to, and the weather conditions might be testing. Stress alone takes a massive toll on your body, and there's no doubt that you'll be feeling more of it than usual. This can trigger health issues you may not be aware of, which you definitely want to avoid. The simple answer to training yourself for this is to exercise regularly. It might not feel like stress in the way you usually imagine it, but exercise places stress on the body, and if you're used to this, your body will handle it more effectively in an emergency. What's more, your body's natural chemical defenses are most effective when you're fit, and your ability to process stored fat for energy or access adrenaline to help you move quickly will be better.

Survival Fitness Goals

When we think of fitness goals, we tend to think about things like the number of push-ups we can do in one sitting or the distance we'd like to be able to run. Survival fitness goals are a little different. There are four overall goals you want to be working toward to prepare yourself for an emergency:

- to reduce the risk of common health conditions like heart disease, hypertension, and diabetes, the presence of which would make emergency survival more difficult
- to improve your stamina in order to facilitate walking longer distances in potentially challenging conditions
- to improve your strength for the purpose of carrying your survival kit and doing manual tasks like shelter-building and wood-chopping
- to improve your mobility to help you move through challenging environments

The question is, how do you know if you're strong and fit enough? Use this checklist to help you. The more items on the list you can do, the more prepared you are for survival.

- Carry an adult a short distance.
- Carry your bug-out bag for 10 hours (walking).
- Complete a day's gardening without hurting your back or joints.
- Escape from an opponent.
- Feel comfortable on just 1,500 calories a day with a high level of physical activity.
- Hike for 5 miles, hunt for food, and carry back your catch.
- Lift and walk a short distance with a 7-gallon container of water.
- Run for a mile on wild ground.
- Swim across a river.

Not all of these goals are easy to achieve in everyday life, but you'll get a good idea of what you can do from comparable activities. Escaping from an opponent, for example, can be tested in a martial arts class. Carrying the equivalent of a hunting haul can be emulated by carrying heavy groceries back from the store on foot rather than using the car. Think creatively, and find fun ways to challenge yourself—training for anything becomes easier when you make it fun.

Fitness Principles and Functional Training

Unfortunately, there's no cut-and-dry formula for fitness training, but the good news is that all you need to do is find out what works for you. At the basic level, simply getting yourself up and moving is a great start. You're not trying to win bodybuilding competitions or compete in ultra marathons. Think about people who are naturally fit and strong as a result of their lifestyle—the stereotypical farm boy, for example, who may not have the body of a runner or a bodybuilder but is perfectly prepped for survival. His body has been prepared by functional work, and his fitness aligns with his needs. Building your general health and wellness is a great thing to do, but it's also essential to think about functional fitness, and to be primed for survival, the best things to do are the things you would do in an emergency situation. This might include going hiking with your bug-out bag, filling and carrying water, carrying your partner if they're injured, or chopping wood.

If you'd like to work on your health and fitness in more conventional ways, this will only be a bonus. I wouldn't recommend making a ton of changes all in one go, though. If you're trying to improve your diet, for example, it isn't a good idea to eat less and better all at the same time as you're unlikely to stick with it. Start by eating a little less for a few weeks, and then start introducing healthy changes one at a time. If you're trying to lose weight, aim to eat fewer calories than you burn and put nutrition front and center. If you're trying to improve your fitness starting from a sedentary lifestyle, begin by walking before introducing more demanding cardio activities. You're more likely to stick to your new plans if you can incorporate them into your daily routine. Small changes like taking the stairs instead of the elevator or parking further away from your office can make a big difference.

If your goal is to work more exercise into your life, choose something you enjoy. You don't necessarily have to join a gym or spend a lot of money on equipment. Plenty of free activities like running, walking, and cycling can make a huge difference to your fitness levels, and these are the skills you're more likely to need in a survival situation. If you have trouble with motivation, try joining a group. My wife did this when she started running, and she found it really helped her.

Last, remember that diet and exercise aren't the only facets of health and fitness. Sleep is crucial if you're to function at your best, and stress will take its toll on both your mind and body. If you're suffering from stress in your daily life, take a look at what you can do to reduce this, and make sure you get 7-9 hours of sleep every night.

Focus on the Big Four

To be at your best for emergency survival, there are four key areas to address. They are fitness, strength, sleep, and nutrition. We've already covered the surface of each area, but let's take a closer look.

Fitness

The easiest way to improve your fitness incrementally is to do more than you're currently doing. If you're relatively inactive right now, just going for a 20-minute walk every day will make a huge difference. If you already walk daily, perhaps you'll want to walk for longer distances or change a few of your walks into jogs. The key is to build a habit. Aim to work hard enough that you get your heart rate up each time. As a bonus, running or walking in your local area will help you learn to navigate the neighborhood, which could be extremely useful in an emergency.

One part of fitness that is often overlooked is flexibility, which makes movements like climbing and slipping into small spaces much easier and reduces the likelihood of injuries like breakages while improving your coordination and balance. This is all extremely beneficial in a survival situation, and it's surprisingly easy to work training into your daily life. Simply by making a 3-minute stretch part of your morning routine, you can make considerable improvements to your mobility and flexibility. Aim for dynamic stretches, which keep you moving at the same time—for example, walking lunges, leg swings, or trunk twists.

If you're like my wife and recognize that a social element helps you stick to your exercise plan, consider joining a club or a class. Good sports for building survival fitness are soccer and basketball, which allow you to work on your agility while raising your heart rate. CrossFit is an excellent way to work on strength and fitness at the same time, while yoga and tai chi allow you to work on your flexibility and balance at the right pace and level for you.

Strength

A common misconception is that strength training requires you to go to the gym, but you can do a surprising amount at home with your own body weight, adding free weights as you wish. The great thing about this is that you can use it to prepare your body for a survival situation, and it's something you can do when you're bugging out, keeping yourself strong and supple throughout the crisis. I'd recommend crunches, planks, prone back extensions, pushups, and burpees. (These are killer and will help you with your fitness too.)

Despite all you can do at home, you may wish to go to the gym a few times a week too. If you plan to do this, aim for exercises that will work on your strength or stamina—think power lifts like deadlifts, back squats, bench presses, and kettlebell swings.

Sleep

Sleep is when your body is able to grow and repair. Hormone regulation and protein synthesis happen during this time, and your metabolism is regulated. Despite its importance, most of us get less sleep than we should. If you struggle with this, try to keep a consistent sleep schedule, waking up and going to bed at the same time every day. Avoid using screens for half an hour before you plan to sleep, and if you must use your phone, soften the blue light from your screen. Finally, avoid eating too close to bedtime. Aim for around three hours between your last meal and sleep so that your body has time to digest.

Nutrition

For some of us, losing weight will help us get our bodies into the best shape for survival; for others, it's simply a case of eating more healthily. If your goal is to lose weight, calorie intake is where you need to look. If you consume more calories than you burn, this will be stored in your body as fat. To manage this, try taking smaller portions or leaving some food on your plate every time you eat. If your goal is to eat more healthily, avoid heavily processed foods or foods laden with sugar. This has the added benefit of preparing you for a survival situation, where the only foods you can access may be foods you can catch or grow yourself. Try to up your fruit and vegetable intake, as well as complex carbohydrates, which you'll find in legumes and grains, and healthy fats, like those found in nuts and avocados. If you're eating a healthy, balanced diet, you shouldn't have any need for vitamins or supplements (unless expressly advised by your doctor), with the exception of Vitamin D. This helps your bones stay strong and is good for your immune system, but it's obtained chiefly through sunlight—which modern life doesn't always allow us much access to. No matter what dietary changes you make, be sure to drink plenty of water throughout the day.

Training to Help With Bugging Out

Whatever you do to improve your health and fitness will be beneficial. Still, if you want to thoroughly prepare yourself for the possibility of bugging out, there are a few specific activities you might want to try.

Rucking

Rucking is essentially hiking a specific distance with weight on your back. In case you were wondering, it has its roots in the military, and the name is derived from the word *rucksack*. You don't need any special equipment—simply a full backpack (perfect for testing your bug-out bag!) and somewhere to walk. Rucking regularly will help you improve your overall fitness, as well as your strength and endurance. Your bug-out bag is a perfect place to get started, but you can buy *ruck plates*, which are weights designed explicitly for rucking, if you'd rather train without your gear. Start with 10-20 pounds, and increase the weight, speed, and distance you walk over time.

Cycling

Cycling can get you a lot further more quickly than walking. The average adult walks at a speed of 3-4 miles an hour, and with your bug-out bag to carry, the chances are, your pace will be slower. The average adult cyclist, meanwhile, can move at around 12-13 miles an hour, and that extra weight will feel like far less of a burden. Cycling as a workout is a great way to improve your fitness, endurance, balance, and leg strength, and if you choose to do this to keep fit, you're preparing your body well for a crisis situation.

Self-Defense

A clever way to prepare for the worst is to combine fitness training with self-defense skills, and this is something you can even sign the kids up for. Martial arts training is excellent for helping them make decisions, learn to focus, and improve their social skills, balance, coordination, and fitness. There are so many options when it comes to martial arts, and there's really no bad choice. And if you're like me and prefer to avoid firearms in your self-defense strategy, training in other means of defense is a good idea. However, if you really want to gear your training towards survival, I'd recommend looking into muay Thai, boxing, or jiu-jitsu.

Muay Thai and jiu-jitsu will teach you valuable skills for controlling a potential attacker, while boxing will help you take an assertive stance in the face of danger. All three are great for fitness and endurance training too. Whatever you choose, aim to practice at least three times a week, and if you can, include the whole family in your training. Keep it simple, and make sure you have a full grasp of the basics before you try to do anything complicated. Eventually, the skills you learn will become second nature, and this is exactly what you want if you get taken by surprise in an emergency situation.

Survival Skills

Before we get any further into this section, I'd like to draw attention to the fact that whole books could be written on each skill we will look at. My goal here is simply to make you aware of useful skills to acquire; I'd recommend taking courses to perfect any of these skills.

Fishing

Fishing is an easier skill to acquire than hunting, and it's possible nearly everywhere. Once you're familiar with the basics, it should be possible to catch a minimum of 1,500 calories a day without more than a few hours of work. Fish have high nutritional value, and if you can catch them when you're bugging out, you're onto a winner. You can consider active fishing (e.g., casting a rod) and passive fishing (e.g., setting up a net). Although, bear in mind that passive fishing is illegal in some places, so check the laws and make sure you have the proper licenses. Active fishing takes more time than passive fishing, which many survivalists feel is a better way to optimize time and energy and can result in a better harvest if it's successful (this is the reason it's illegal in so many areas). The best times of day to fish are in the morning and the evening because this is when the fish come to the surface for food. Look for spots that fish might come to for cover (docks and rock formations are good locations), and look for areas where the water movement is different.

No matter what type of fishing you do or how experienced you are, you'll need a fishing license, which is easy to get and inexpensive. There are different licenses available depending on the state you're fishing in, the amount of time you spend fishing, the type of fish you're targeting, the method you use, and what you plan to do with your catch. Check the requirements carefully, and make sure you have the right license for your needs.

Hunting

Hunting will require a lot more training than fishing. Again, you'll need a license, and you'll need much more gear to get started. I'd highly recommend taking a course if you're a beginner and learning about the safety rules before you start. I thought carefully about what to include in this section and, in the end, decided that the most responsible thing to do would be to cover as little as possible. If you're new to hunting, you need to learn properly, and there isn't space in this book to cover what you need to know. What I will say, however, is that obtaining a hunting license is important, and as with fishing, it will need to be specific to the kind of hunting you're planning on doing. You can get a hunting license from the wildlife department in your state, along with all the information you need to know about getting one.

Foraging

Foraging is a handy skill to have in an emergency situation. You can't guarantee that you won't find yourself lost in the wild or at the end of your emergency food supplies. It's a fun skill to learn, and while you're building up your knowledge, you get to benefit from bringing new flavors to your cooking and trying out new recipes with your bounty.

While there's plenty to be written about foraging, and it wouldn't hurt to take a course, with a good edible plants book by your side, you can do a lot to develop your skills independently. Just make sure you follow a few safety rules when you're out and about:

- Don't eat anything if you're not certain what it is.
- Make sure you're familiar with the environment you're foraging in and be aware of dangers like rivers and cliffs.
- Focus on looking for plants you're familiar with rather than looking for new species that could be dangerous.
- Memorize some of the edible plants that are common where you live.
- Use a field guide to help with safe preparation and cooking.
- Be alert to wild animals when you're foraging.
- Make sure someone knows where you are when you go out.

If you're unsure where to start, your backyard could surprise you. Many edible plants are viewed as weeds, and you may find some in your lawn or local park. If you live in a humid area, you will likely find edible plants in clearings or sunnier spots. If you live in a drier area, you're more likely to find edible plants near water. If you venture out into the woods, avoid plants that are sparse. Plants that grow in abundance are less likely to be toxic and more likely to be edible. Be advised that edible plants often have similar traits to poisonous ones, and sometimes a partly edible plant may have components that are harmful to the human body. A field guide is, therefore, essential, no matter how much you think you already know.

Bushcraft

Bushcraft skills allow you to use the resources available in the natural environment to ensure your survival. They cover a range of competencies, but there are some particularly important ones I think are well worth taking the time to learn.

Lighting a fire

This is an extremely important skill that will not only provide you with heat and light but also with the means to boil water or cook a meal. As with anything, practice makes perfect, and the more you can get out there and practice your skills, the better. As your confidence grows, try to extend your skills, practicing in all seasons and weather conditions and forcing yourself to use only natural materials rather than relying on man-made materials like fire starters and Vaseline. Source dry kindling and wood, bearing in mind that this will be more difficult during the winter.

Tracking

Unlike lighting a fire, tracking is a skill that's easier to practice in the winter when icy conditions make it easier to see footprints, which means that practicing during the summer is also crucial. However, if you're new to tracking, starting in the winter is a good call because you'll find it easier to learn the traits and behaviors of specific animals that you'll then be able to use to help you in the summer.

Navigation skills

There are more horror stories than I'm comfortable with about people getting lost and meeting fatal results because their GPS went down or malfunctioned. If the grid goes down or you run out of batteries, it's crucial that you can find your way to safety using a map and compass. Odd as it may seem, a great time to practice your navigation skills is at night because the limited visibility forces you to take more notice of tiny details and work harder to keep track of your exact location. This attention to detail will be useful if you find yourself in dense woodland or difficult weather conditions during an emergency.

Making a lantern

If you're well prepared, you will have flashlights and batteries with you in an emergency situation. Nonetheless, if you have to bug out during the winter when the days are shorter, you may find a greater need for light and battery preservation. Making a lantern is, therefore, a valuable skill and gives you a backup plan in case your flashlights or batteries fail. There are a few different approaches to this. You could make a candle holder using sticks and bark, or you could use the ends of used candles to make a bigger candle by melting them into a tin and adding a fresh wick. To really go full bushcraft, you could craft a lantern out of only natural materials like birch bark or pine resin. These may not burn for as long as other materials, but you can experiment to find the best options to use in an emergency.

Melting snow to drink

Bugging out in icy conditions is, in many ways, far from ideal. However, snow can be a valuable asset when it comes to your water supply if you know how to access it. One option is to fill a pan with snow and heat it until it melts. The problem with this method is that the snow takes up more space than the water due to the quantity of air it contains, causing a space between the melted and unmelted snow, and in an aluminum pan, this can result in a hole being burned in the bottom. A better option is to add some water (if you have access to it) to the pan first, gradually adding snow and allowing it to melt. This also helps with the problem that it can take quite a long time to produce not very much water when you start with snow; starting with water will allow the snow to melt more quickly and efficiently. It's a good idea to practice this skill if possible, as you'll very quickly see that snow is variable, and each harvest will melt differently. An alternative solution would be to fill a piece of clothing with snow, hang it beside a fire, and allow it to melt into a container through the fabric.

Ax skills

Ax skills aren't of much use to many people in regular life, but they'll be crucial in a survival situation when firewood is critical to your survival. You need to be able to process dead, dry wood into firewood, covering a range of sizes from kindling to medium logs.

MAKING A TRIAL RUN

One of the most important things to practice is bugging out itself. At a bare minimum, you should do a full trial run of navigating your planned route with your bug-out bag once. This is the only way that you'll spot potential problems and fix them before they become a hazard. I'd personally recommend doing your dummy run several times. Try it in all weather conditions and adapt your supplies accordingly. Remember to assess your bug-out bag and make necessary adjustments according to your experiences on trial runs. And a final word to the wise: Be sure to test out all your equipment too. A trial run doesn't just pertain to the route but to making sure all your equipment is fully functional too.

★ TAKE ACTION!

Devise a Training Plan

When there's so much to cover, training for bugging out can seem daunting, and the danger is that you might want to avoid doing it. I'd recommend coming up with a training plan before you start. This will give you something you can follow logically, breaking it down piece by piece. Only you know your fitness level and lifestyle, so this is best done by you, and any template I could give you would fail to take into account your unique needs. Identify what areas you need to work on, and develop milestones you'd like to hit at particular times. Ultimately, it doesn't matter if you hit them on time; all that matters is that you keep moving forward.

Improving your fitness and training for an emergency is sensible, but it won't necessarily be the case that you'll be entirely on foot if you have to bug out. In the next chapter, we'll look at how you'll get to your bug-out location. However that is, this is something you should cover in your trial run. Before we get to that, though, let's take a moment to appreciate what we've achieved so far.

A QUICK BREATHER TO FOCUS ON WHAT YOU'VE ACHIEVED

"Tell me and I forget, teach me and I may remember, involve me and I learn."

— BENJAMIN FRANKLIN

Although there are plenty of specific areas to train in, many of them physical, it's important to recognize the advances you're already making. Every new piece of information you gather, every additional thought you give to your bug-out plan, is in itself training.

If you think about any course you've been on that ends with a practical exam, you'll notice that every part of that course was important. You may not have used every detail in the exam itself, but it was that understanding of the broad picture that got you to where you needed to be in order to pass.

So if ever you feel downhearted when you look at the amount of training and preparation still ahead of you, take a moment to appreciate everything you've achieved so far. Even if all you've done at this point is reading, that's an essential step that will allow you to execute every part of your planning process more successfully.

I know how daunting it can feel, and trust me, I've felt it myself, so I try to slow down here and there to share a word of encouragement. My goal is to help as many people as I can to prepare fully for an emergency situation, and that includes every part of the picture.

This is your opportunity to help me…

By leaving a review of this book on Amazon, you'll show new readers where they can find all the information they need to start preparing and training themselves up for a potential emergency.

Simply by letting other people know how this book has helped you and what they'll find inside, you'll be helping them with their own training program—and working on yours at the same time. When we share the information we've learned and think about it from the point of view of how it will help others, we consolidate and deepen our understanding—and that will only serve your preparation efforts.

Thank you for your helping me to make sure this guidance reaches as many people as it can. If you've read my other books, you'll already know my motto: Stay healthy; stay strong; stay prepared… and for that, every one of us needs all the training we can get.

5

WHICH WAY... AND HOW?
PLANNING YOUR TRANSIT

We looked at choosing the best bug-out location for your family in Chapter Two, but each option depends on you being able to get to them in an emergency. You should have several alternative ways of getting to each of your potential locations to account for any disaster that may get in your way. You might remember I told you about my family's two locations—a remote cabin and an RV. The RV is both a potential bug-out location and a means of travel, but we have several options when it comes to getting to the cabin. Were we unable to use the RV for any reason, or should the roads all be blocked, we also have two different walking routes that we could use. Additionally, we have bikes kitted out to carry all our gear, so if we needed to get away quickly but were unable to use the RV, we could cycle.

WHY IT'S IMPORTANT TO HAVE DIFFERENT OPTIONS

Someone once told me I was going overboard having this many alternatives planned, but the truth is that being properly prepared means being overprepared. You need to be ready for as much as you can—including things going wrong with Plan A. By its nature, an emergency situation is unpredictable, and you have no guarantee that your original plan will be possible. Some routes may be blocked, either by the disaster itself or by the police or the military. This means it's important to know secondary roads, rail tracks, or lesser-known trails too, and it's crucial that your location be accessible in several different ways. It's also a reason that distance is important. If the only way you can access it is by car, you're immediately cut off if there's something to prevent you from driving. Ideally, you want to plan a route for every type of transit available to you—just as I have with driving, walking, and cycling.

PACE planning, which you may remember from Chapter Three, is a good way to approach this. That means having a primary, alternative, contingency, and emergency plan for both your location and routes. Alternative routes probably involve roads less traveled, and your contingency and emergency routes may seem less than ideal in ordinary life. The most viable route will be your primary route. I'd suggest color-coding your plans on a map so that you can clearly see the exact route for each part of the PACE acronym.

WHAT ARE YOUR OPTIONS?

Before you can effectively begin your PACE planning, you need to know what your options are. For most people, this comes down to five different modes of transportation: walking, cycling, motorcycling, driving, or sailing.

Bugging Out on Foot

Whether it will be possible for you to bug out on foot depends on a few factors, the most pressing of which is the situation at the time. If you need to bug out, it means you have no option but to leave your home, and that means there's a situation in front of you that you must assess carefully. Will it be safe for your family to escape on foot? Is everyone capable of making the journey? You'll need to consider your physical strength and that of your family (and this is why training up is essential). This is something you can plan for to an extent, but if someone sustains an injury in the disaster, you may need to rethink your plans. You will, of course, need to consider your bug-out location too; it needs to be within three days' walking distance, and you need to be able to reach it in potentially severe weather conditions.

If you're confident that bugging out on foot is the right option, you'll need to make sure you're adequately prepared. Footwear is crucial: Everyone in your party needs a good pair of walking shoes, which should be broken in and supported with good, thick socks. Your clothing should be weather appropriate—light enough that you don't overheat in the summer (while still protecting you from the sun) or warm enough to help you survive in a cold climate. You can plan for this by knowing your climate and the changes you can expect throughout the seasons, although extreme weather may force you to reevaluate your plans.

You should know your route and your paths inside out, but it's wise to have some backup routes planned in case there's some reason you can't go with your original.

Once you're on the road, you might find it tempting to press on and get to your destination as quickly as possible, but remember that rest is important. Taking breaks frequently will help you conserve energy, give you a chance to fuel and relieve yourself, and help younger or more vulnerable members of your family gather their strength. If you do need to stop, it's wise to keep someone on guard duty at all times, particularly if you're concerned about civil unrest.

Bugging Out by Bike

Getting to your bug-out location by bike offers you significant advantages. The most obvious of these is the speed compared to walking. It would take most people around three hours to walk 10 miles, but that distance could be cycled in an hour—without having to carry the weight of your bug-out bag on your back. Bikes can easily be carried when the ground becomes too tricky for cycling, and they're quiet, allowing you to keep a low profile when you're on the move. They also offer an advantage in heavy traffic, as you can weave through or veer off down sidewalks or smaller paths. Again, fitness is a must, and if you are cycling with your family, you'll need to be sure that everyone has the confidence and experience to cycle to your location safely.

The disadvantages of cycling are few, but they're worth considering. The biggest risk is something going wrong mechanically, but if you choose the right bike and make sure you have a comprehensive repair kit, you can mitigate most of the risk. Another issue is that if you become compromised, it might be difficult for you to remove your supplies from the bike, putting them in jeopardy of being looted. Lastly, there's the risk of injury. This could, of course, happen on foot too, but with a bike, there's a chance that you could fall off and sustain a much more difficult injury. That said, I don't think any of this is enough to make a bike a bad option; just make sure that yours is up to the task, or buy one with bugging out in mind.

If you're buying a bike specifically for the purpose, the main things to consider are strength and weight. A mountain bike is probably your best bet for survival conditions: It's a comfortable and durable type of bike, and it can handle unpredictable terrain. Be aware, however, that a mountain bike is simply a type of bike, and there's still a lot of variation within the category. The frames can vary widely, and you'll need to choose wisely. The winning formula is lightweight yet durable, and for this, your best bets are aluminum or titanium (although this is a pricey option).

You'll also need to make sure your bike can carry everything you need. There's a vast range of accessories on the market, and you'll be able to find a combination that allows you to bring all your survival gear with you—everything from water to a sleeping bag and food supplies. Saddlebags and panniers should be more than adequate, but if you want to carry a little more, you could also opt for a trailer. Some can generate electricity, enabling you to charge smaller electrical devices on the go. You will also need lights, and to avoid any issues with batteries, I'd advise choosing ones powered by the bike as you pedal.

Make sure you have a good bicycle repair kit but remember that this will be useless unless you know how to use it. Teach yourself how to fix a flat tire, replace worn breaks or a broken chain, and patch an inner tube well in advance of any emergency.

Bugging Out With a Motorbike

With a motorbike, you have most of the same advantages as a bicycle, with the added efficiency of a car. This probably isn't an option if you'll be traveling with your family, but if you're a group of adults and all have the skills and experience to ride legally and safely, it's a good option to consider. The downside when you compare them with bicycles is that they're not as quiet, and if you come across difficult terrain, you'll have to push them.

If you're thinking of buying a motorcycle specifically for the purpose, avoid lightweight engines and small frames: It needs to be powerful enough to carry both you and your gear. Consider the terrain you'll likely need to cross. If your getaway mostly involves roads, a commuter bike may be all you need, but if you need to navigate rougher conditions, you'll need a sturdier model. Check that the parts are easy to come by. If something goes wrong, you'll need to be able to get hold of the parts you need to repair it, and you'll need to know how to do this.

Again, you'll need to accessorize to make sure you can carry all your gear. Choose a bike with saddle bags or to which you can add your own, and make sure you have enough space to carry everything you need.

Bugging Out by Car

We touched on using an RV or a motorhome as both a means of transportation and a bug-out location in Chapter Two, but you may wish to use your car to get to a designated location. If this is something you're considering, I'd advise you to choose your next car with this in mind, as not every vehicle is up to the task. You'll need to make sure it's big enough to carry your whole family and all your gear, and you'll need to know what kind of fuel you'll need and assess whether this is something you'll have access to in an emergency. You'll need to consider its speed capabilities, whether it can get you to safety quickly, and whether it can handle difficult terrain and potentially severe weather conditions. For any vehicle you take, it's wise to be aware of potential maintenance issues that may arise and be confident that you can do basic repairs if necessary. It's also worth thinking about its resistance to damage and how well it will be able to protect you from potential threats. Beyond the vehicle itself, you'll need to consider your location and whether you'll be able to keep your car nearby—preferably out of sight, to avoid drawing attention to yourself.

When it comes to choosing the vehicle itself, a car may be right for your family, but bear in mind that there are a few other options to consider. Trucks such as Fords, Jeep Wranglers, and GMC trucks may well suit a family better, allowing plenty of space for storing supplies as well as carrying everyone. They're also well equipped for rougher terrain, and this may bring peace of mind in an emergency situation. For larger families, an SUV is a good option, again allowing you to navigate difficult terrain and carry plenty of supplies. Campers and RVs, as we've already discussed, allow you to combine your transit with your shelter and keep moving all the time. I certainly like this option for my family, and it's a good choice if any member of your party is less mobile.

Bugging Out by Boat

If you live near a river or a large lake, a boat could be perfect for your escape. Waterways are far less likely to be blocked by traffic than roads, and as long as you know exactly how to get to your destination on the other side, they could be your quickest way out. This option won't work for everyone, however, and it's only worth considering if you live near water and have a safe location on the other side. It goes without saying that you will need a boat, as well as the skills and experience to take your family safely across the water. Unless you're confident in your ability to handle a boat, even if you live near water, it may not be your best option.

PLANNING YOUR ROUTE

Your ultimate goal is to escape whatever disaster is threatening you as quickly as possible, and that means knowing where you're going. This isn't as simple as knowing your daily drive to work. You'll need to know potential detours to take if the roads are cut off or if something prevents you from taking your planned route. That's all a lot to recall under pressure, so I'd highly recommend writing it down or drawing it onto a map. If you live in a city, a detailed map of the roads into the suburbs will be the best choice, but if you live somewhere more remote, a highway map will probably suit you better. If your bug-out location isn't included on the map, you'll need a second one to make sure you can navigate the whole route easily.

What to Consider When You're Planning Your Route

It would be easy to plan a route from home without considering other options, but the reality is that you don't know where you'll be when disaster strikes. You may not be able to account for every possible scenario, but if you know that you're often at work, with your in-laws, or at a particular friend's house, it would be wise to plot a route from those locations too. This may become more complicated if you're also trying to get home to collect your family, so make sure you plan a route that will allow you to do this, circumstances willing. You also need to know your endpoint, and that's exactly why we looked at deciding on a bug-out location before we went any further. Your route will need to take into account the people you'll be traveling with and what they're able to handle, and it will need to account for the mode of transport you're planning to use. Bear in mind, however, that it would be wise to know the walking routes, even if you plan to drive. You need to be able to solve the problem if you break down and find yourself stranded. Make sure your bug-out bag accounts for all possible options—and if, once you get to route planning, you notice that there are things you haven't accounted for, view this as an opportunity to go back to your bug-out bag and make it even better.

Conducting a Route Assessment

To be confident in your route, you'll need to conduct an assessment, for which you'll need a compass, your bug-out bag, sufficient water, and a notebook and pen to keep track of things that come up.

A good route assessment can be split into five key steps.

Step 1: Area Familiarization

Before you do anything else, you need to make sure you're familiar with the area. Identify any areas that may be useful to you on your journey, and make a note of each of them. It's important to do this even if your route won't pass them all; you may need to adjust further down the line. The points you'll need to take account of are your start and end points, any meeting points you plan to include, friendly spaces like hospitals or safe houses, unfriendly places like difficult neighborhoods or places devoid of resources, potential choke points, water crossings, towns, places where you can stock up on food, water, and fuel, and visual markers that you can use to get your bearings.

Familiarizing yourself with the area also means anticipating problems. I mentioned identifying choke points. These are areas where you may need to travel through a narrow space (a bridge, for example). Your route must account for these and include alternatives in case they're blocked. You'll also need to be aware of the potential for the landscape to change in different weather conditions; make sure you plan for all scenarios. If you plan to use side roads or dirt tracks (a wise choice to avoid congestion), drive them regularly to ensure they're not closed off.

Step 2: Identifying and Prioritizing Routes

The next step is to identify different routes between your starting point and endpoint, taking into account areas of interest you've already made a note of and the type of transportation you'll be using. Use your PACE planning to come up with several possible alternatives. Now that you've noted the areas you want to avoid, your routes can take these into account and sidestep them.

Step 3: Documenting the Routes

Once you have your routes figured out, you'll need to document them so that you don't need to rely on memory, and you can make adjustments easily if you need to. I would suggest using both a written plan and visual representations of your routes on a map. Be careful with your written route—make sure you include each leg and make a note of every area of interest. You can also add any notes that you feel are pertinent.

Step 4: Running the Routes

A route assessment isn't complete until you've tried out each route using whatever mode of transport you plan to use in an emergency. Follow your own notes, and make changes where you notice that you haven't been clear or precise enough. To level it up, you could even take pictures of the different points of interest so that you have visuals you can refer to later. A good rule of thumb is that someone else should be able to follow your notes with no previous experience in the area.

Step 5: Completing the Document

Once you've tested your routes, it's time to finish your document, taking into account any new notes you made on the run-through. You should have a map and a set of clear instructions, ideally with photos. Make use of color coding on your map, using this to show different routes and areas you want to avoid. To have complete faith in your finished document, give it to someone else to try out and incorporate their feedback. When I did this, I asked my wife to test out my instructions, and she found a few points where I'd failed to be clear enough. Her input was vital to us having a final document we could really rely on.

CREATING A FAMILY EVACUATION PLAN

Part of planning your escape means planning for how you'll get your family together quickly so you can leave as safely as possible. Creating a family evacuation plan is a must (and you'll have an opportunity to get the ball rolling in the last part of the chapter). Your plan should identify your starting point, potential triggers for evacuation, your destination, the route you'll take and how you'll get there, and the supplies you'll be taking with you.

When it comes to the starting point, it may be that different family members will be in different places. Therefore, you need to account for how everyone will communicate and how you'll gather everyone together. Discuss the potential triggers as a family, and make sure everyone is aware of what scenarios will trigger an evacuation. If your kids are anything like mine, you'll be thrown a few wild cards you'll have to weed out (a tiger attack was posed by my youngest son once!), but everyone's ideas are valuable, and discussing this will mean you're more likely to catch all potential threats.

★ TAKE ACTION!

Create a Family Evacuation Plan

If you don't have a family emergency plan already, it's time to make one. I've designed a template you can use to get you started, although you may want to make adjustments if you think there are things your family needs to know that I haven't covered. Before you get started, conduct a risk assessment, considering each member of the family's individual needs. Your goal is that everyone stays safe, you sustain minimal losses, and you can be reunited quickly if you're separated.

Family Information (repeat for each family member)

✎ Name:

✎ Mobile number:

✎ Social media handles:

✎ Email:

✎ Important medical information:

✎ Other information:

Emergency Plans (repeat for each family member):

✎ Workplace/school/childcare contact details:

✎ Name:

✎ Address:

✎ Contact number:

✎ Email:

✎ Emergency plan:

Emergency contacts (repeat for each contact):

- Name:
- Address:
- Contact number:
- Email:

Emergency meeting place:

- Location:
- Instructions:

Medical information:

- Doctor name:
- Medical practice address:
- Medical practice number:
- Medical insurance provider:
- Medical insurance policy:
- Medical insurance contact number:
- Vet name:
- Vet address:
- Vet contact number:

Other important contacts:

✎ Police:

✎ Fire department:

You have your location identified, and you know how you will get there, but that isn't the end of the story. It's vital that the location itself is well prepared and can support you in an emergency, and this is what we'll look at in the next chapter.

6

HOME AWAY FROM HOME: PREPARING YOUR BUG-OUT SPOT

Your bug-out bag is designed to support you for 72 hours, but chances are, you'll need to be away from your home for longer than this. You can't carry everything you need for an indefinite period of time, so it's vital that your bug-out location is set up to support your family's survival. This means you'll need to equip it in advance or, at the very least, have a solid plan for how you will access the basics. Personally, I'd recommend stocking your location fully—it's amazing how much peace of mind this brings. Both my cabin and RV are fully kitted out, and I'm confident that either could support my family in an emergency. Plus, if we had to use the RV to get to the cabin, we'd have an insurance policy in the form of backup supplies.

THE FUNDAMENTALS OF PREPARATION

It's important to remember that an emergency situation doesn't necessarily equate to the need to bug out. As we discussed in Chapter One, in the majority of cases, bugging in is going to be the better option, so it's important that your home is equipped to support you in an emergency. Prepping your bug-out location should not be done *instead of* preparing your home; rather, it is an addition to making sure you're ready for all possibilities.

Over the course of this chapter, we'll take a look at the essential elements of preparation that should be taken into consideration, but preparing a bug-out location is the same as readying your home for an emergency, and everything that you would do to your home is applicable here. For more detail on each area, I'd recommend reading my previous books, which look in much more depth at preparing your home and your larder. To avoid repeating information (and because each area requires far more detail than we have room for in this book), I have included a starting point for further reading in each section.

Food

You'll find much more detail on this in *The Prepper's Pantry*, and I'd recommend reading this or another in-depth guide to food preparation for an emergency.

Your focus should be on foods that have a long shelf life or are non-perishable and will deliver you nutrient-dense meals, no matter how long you have to be there. Bear in mind that even long-life foods have an expiration date, so you will need to keep on top of your stocks, using them up at home and replacing them with newer items regularly.

Foods worth having on your list include:

- canned food (including meat and fish)
- coffee and tea
- cooking oil
- dried beans
- dried fruit
- dried nuts and nut butters
- dried potato flakes
- freeze-dried foods
- granola bars
- herbs and spices
- honey
- jams and jellies
- multivitamins
- pasta
- pet food (if applicable)
- powdered eggs
- powdered milk
- protein bars
- salt
- seeds
- stock cubes
- sugar
- white rice
- whole grains

Water

If possible, I'd recommend implementing a rainwater harvesting system at your bug-out location. Remember that this must be filtered before you can use it for drinking or cooking. You'll find much more detail on this in *Prepare*

Your Home for a Sudden Grid-Down Situation. Unless you know that you have a reliable source of water (such as a stream) near your location, it would be wise to stock bottled water or larger vessels like water bricks, particularly if you can't rely on rainfall in your area. As a rough guide, you will need 3 gallons of water per person daily. My cabin is prepped to keep my family in water for a month, and we have a rainwater harvesting system in place as well.

Power

Again, I'd refer you to *Prepare Your Home for a Sudden Grid-Down Situation* to make sure your bug-out location is prepared to keep the lights on in an emergency. If you can, I advise you to make sure your location can keep you in power even if it is cut off from the grid. Solar panels are probably your best option, but you could also look at wind or water power if the conditions are right. If you're unable to do this, a backup generator is a good idea. Remember that solar chargers can power smaller items, and heat and light can be generated through fires, candles, and lanterns. Be sure you stock your location with enough fuel for whatever sources you intend to use, be that firewood or gas. You will need this for cooking as well as for keeping warm.

Security

Choosing the right place for your bug-out location is key to your overall security. The ideal location is secluded, has ample tree cover, and is difficult to access (although not so tricky that you can't get to it yourself!). These preliminary considerations go a long way to keeping your location secure. It's also important to know the strengths and weaknesses of your site. If you've already observed that the front door, for instance, is less secure than the one you have at home, take measures to bolster it.

If security is a concern, however, you may want to go a step further, and we'll look at this in a little more detail in Chapter Nine. You can fortify your perimeter by planting thorny bushes and increasing the density of the coverage to hide your property. If you want to go a step further, you could even consider adding booby traps, although this isn't something I've done myself. In my opinion, the safety of the family comes first, and I think there's more risk of one of the kids being hurt by a trap than there is of needing to rely on them to deter an intruder. DIY alarms placed both near the entrances and a little further away are a good way of staying alert to potential trouble. If you have the power to accommodate them, security cameras may be a consideration, as well as motion sensor lights, which not only alert you to intruders but deter them as well. If you have a dog with you, you have a natural deterrent already—I know mine will certainly raise the alarm if necessary (and also when it's not!)

Sanitation

The precautions you'll need to take at your bug-out location are much the same as the ones you'll need to take at home, although there will be some variations. You may, for example, not have a toilet that you can flush with a bucket of rainwater, in which case you may need to consider digging a latrine. There are more details on this in *Prepare Your Home for a Sudden Grid-Down Situation*. The key is to know the limitations of your location and plan accordingly. Similarly, you may have to get creative as far as trash disposal is concerned. Waste that cannot be repurposed can be burned, but be aware that the smoke could draw attention to your location. A trash pit, therefore, might be a better idea.

Clothing, Hygiene, and Medical

There isn't much to say about clothing other than to make sure you have it. The clothes in your bag won't be sufficient for a longer stay, so make sure your family has a stash of season-appropriate clothing at the bug-out location too. You know your climate; make sure everyone has everything they need to stay comfortable and dry for the duration of your stay.

We looked at building a first aid kit for your bug-out bag in Chapter Three. Your location should also be equipped with first aid supplies. You'll need the same equipment you need for your bag, but it's also a good idea to add some extras. After all, you won't need to carry them, and you could be at your location for some time. Additional items I'd recommend keeping are:

- IV kit
- magnifying glass
- scissors
- splint
- wound irrigation syringe

Ensure your location is sufficiently stocked with toilet paper, toiletries, antibacterial soap, and all the cleaning supplies you need to keep your family in good hygiene for the duration of your stay. You'll find more details about essential hygiene supplies in *When Crisis Hits Suburbia*.

Information

You're unlikely to have the internet, and you may not be connected to the grid. For this reason, it's a good idea to keep hard copies of survival books and information at your bug-out location. I'd recommend keeping books on first aid, foraging, medicinal plants, and insect identification at your retreat, as well as maps and guidebooks of the area.

★ TAKE ACTION!

Your Bug-Out Spot Checklist

Use this rudimentary checklist to make sure you've covered all your bases. If you've already prepared your home, this should be easy for you. If you haven't, I'd recommend further reading on each of the sections we've discussed before preparing both of sites. This list is designed as a guide, and you will need much more depth in your preparation.

Food

- canned food
- coffee and tea
- cooking equipment
- cooking oil
- dried food
- eating utensils
- multivitamins
- nuts and seeds
- pasta and rice
- pet food (if applicable)
- powdered milk and eggs

- protein and granola bars
- seasonings
- whole grains

Water

- access to fresh water
- water harvesting system
- water storage sufficient for 3 gallons per person per day for one month

Power

- a way to generate solar/hydro/wind power
- backup generator
- candles
- lanterns
- means to build, light, and maintain a fire
- sufficient fuel for one month
- torches

Security

- DIY alarms
- good tree coverage
- motion sensor lights
- secured doors and windows

Sanitation

- a solid plan for human waste management
- a solid plan for waste disposal

Clothing/Hygiene/Medicine

- antibacterial soap
- climate-appropriate clothing for the whole family
- first aid kit
- laundry and dishwashing necessities
- personal medications for each member of the family
- toilet roll
- toiletries

Information

- edible/medicinal plant guides
- insect guide
- maps and guides of the area
- survival books

Preparing to bug out effectively is a personal journey for every family, but it's imperative to pay attention to your needs if you have vulnerable people and/or animals with you. This is what we'll look at in the next chapter.

7

NO PERSON (OR DOG!) LEFT BEHIND: BUGGING OUT WITH VULNERABLE PEOPLE AND ANIMALS

My children are older now, and well versed in survival skills, but when they were younger, I had to make different accommodations for them. My plans still take into account their ages and capabilities even now, so I'm constantly updating them as they grow stronger and learn more skills. I also have plans for my three dogs. They're all fit and capable, so it's just a matter of making sure I have everything they need, but were they smaller or older, I'd have to make different adjustments. If you have children, elderly or sick relatives, or animals with you in an emergency, your bug-out plans will need to accommodate them. Everyone in your party must be able to get to the location and stay safe and healthy once they're there, and your plan needs to support this.

BUGGING OUT WITH CHILDREN

As you well know, the needs of your children vary depending on their age, and the adjustments you'll need to make for an infant are far different from those you'll need to make for older children and teenagers. I've split this advice into three broad categories, but you know your children. The most important thing is that you plan with wherever they are developmentally in mind. In each of the following sections, we'll cover mobility, comfort, safety, and provisions, and these are the four categories you'll need to keep in mind when you're planning for your children.

Infants, Toddlers, and Preschoolers

If you have a baby, you'll obviously be carrying them. But bear in mind that toddlers and preschoolers have a limited amount of distance in them too, and they'll struggle on rugged terrain, ultimately slowing the whole party down. You'll therefore need to be prepared to carry them at any point that you'll be on foot, and that means factoring in the extra weight when you're considering your supplies. Whatever child-carrying method you invest in, be that a sling, a back carrier, or a trailer, it will need to be both comfortable for your little one and allow you to cross any kind of terrain you encounter. Be cautious of strollers: While they do help with the weight, they mean your hands aren't free, and they may struggle on difficult ground. Before any emergency, you can prepare your children by getting them to practice standing up independently after they fall over, showing them how to walk carefully on difficult ground, and teaching them to climb stairs without your help. These mobility skills will serve them well anyway, but they will also help their mobility in an emergency situation.

An extra consideration you must make with children of all ages is the amount of strange and scary noises they may be exposed to. In an emergency situation, there's likely to be a lot of noise, be that in the form of shouting, screaming, or sirens, which will upset your little one. You can reduce the impact of this by having them wear earplugs or head coverings, playing ambient music to them, or traveling during the night when the noise is likely to be less. The more comfortable you can make your little one, the less traumatic the experience will be, and the easier it will be for you. On the flip side of the noise issue is the noise children make themselves. Infants and toddlers are too young to understand that crying and laughing could put the family at risk, and the only way they have to express their needs is vocally. You can decrease the risk by anticipating the needs of your little one and teaching toddlers and preschoolers signs to communicate. For example, you could teach them to tug your shirt to tell you they're hungry or thirsty.

If your child is not yet toilet trained, you'll need to plan for the disposal or washing of diapers. One possibility is to try diaperless training in advance to avoid this problem. Otherwise, you'll need to plan for how you'll get rid of the waste—carrying dirty diapers around with you is the last thing you want when you're on the move or surviving in cramped conditions. Taking a combination of cloth and disposable diapers could be a good call, giving you more options. So that they take up less room, you can use a vacuum sealer to pack disposable ones. Take zip-top bags to store soiled diapers until you can dispose of them properly.

As all parents know, toddlers and preschoolers can be defiant, and if they don't feel like wearing that raincoat, they'll fight for the freedom not to. That's the last thing you want in an emergency when it's pouring down rain and you need to keep moving. You can reduce the risk of this battle by teaching them the importance of protecting themselves from the weather, reminding them each day that the weather helps them decide what to wear.

As far as supplies go, while babies don't need to be factored into your water provisions, toddlers and preschoolers do. Children between the ages of one and three will need about four 2-4 ounce cups of water daily, and four-year-olds will need five. Toddlers require around 1,200 calories a day, which increases to around 1,400 calories once they reach the age of four. For infants, you'll need to factor in the health and needs of the mother. If she's nursing, it's still a good idea to take formula with you, as the likely reduction in calories combined with the stress of the situation could affect the production of breast milk.

Guideline Provisions for Infants, Toddlers, and Preschoolers

- 3 gallons of water per day for washing bottles
- baby food
- bike seat or trailer for small children (if using a bike)
- bottled water (for formula)
- diapers (mixture of cloth and disposable)
- electrolyte packets
- entertainment
- evaporated milk/powdered milk (to make emergency formula)
- extra clothes
- eyedropper/syringe
- harness
- infant carrier
- infant medication
- infant acetaminophen
- instant/ powdered formula

- pacifier
- pre-sterilized bottles
- prenatal or vitamins (for nursing mothers)
- stroller built for all terrains (if using)
- weather-proof clothing
- zip-top bags for temporarily storing dirty diapers

Elementary School-Aged Children

At this age, children are capable of walking further, but it's still a good idea to plan for a way to carry them if necessary —for example, if they get injured or tire out. If they're light enough, this can be a carrier, but for most children this age, you'll want something you can pull, such as a wagon or sled or a child seat attached to your bike. Make sure your plan includes rest stops along the way so that they can walk further distances for longer. You can get children used to walking greater distances or cycling for longer in advance by going on family walks, runs, or bike rides. Show them how to pay attention to the ground, and teach them techniques for walking on mud or slippery surfaces. You can even practice early orienteering skills at home or in a local park and teach them basic survival skills to normalize them if they become necessary. That can be as simple as letting them lead the way to school, teaching them to pay attention to signs and markings, and pointing out safe places like churches and hospitals. You can also teach them simple safety procedures through fire drills or tornado drills (if appropriate in your region) and show them how to build a fire or a shelter. Summer camps are also a good way for them to pick up these skills.

Again, noise is a concern for this age group. Children this age are old enough to know that things aren't right, which can make them uncomfortable; distressing sounds will only add to this. You can use the same distraction tactics as you would with younger children, and entertainment in the form of coloring books, games, or puzzles can also help during times when you're resting. Don't underestimate the power of comfort items like a favorite cuddly toy or blanket.

As much as noise can be a problem for them, noise is a problem they may create too. Children this age can be talkative if boredom strikes, so plan for ways to keep them calm and engaged. Explain to them what's happening as much as you can, and keep reassuring them that you're keeping them safe, and that's why you're bugging out.

When you're thinking about provisions, bear in mind that your child will be able to carry their own backpack, but they're limited in how much they can carry. They shouldn't carry anything over 10% of their body weight, so you'll have to take everything else.

Guideline Provisions for Elementary School-Aged Children

- anti-pollution child mask
- books, lightweight toys, and games
- coloring or puzzle books and pens/crayons
- family photos
- favorite cuddly toy
- flashlight/headlamp
- glow sticks
- lollipops (to keep them quiet!)
- medical ID
- natural sleep aid for children
- personal hygiene provisions

- ready-to-eat meals
- safety wrist strap
- signaling whistle and mirror
- small backpack
- snacks
- spare socks, clothing, and shoes
- strong wagon
- water bottle
- weather-proof clothing and accessories (gloves, hat, sunglasses, etc.)

Middle and High School-Aged Children

Once children get to this age, mobility is less of a concern. They're mostly able to walk longer distances, and they can carry more of their own supplies. To make sure this is effective, choose their backpack carefully so that it fits well and allows the weight to be balanced. To minimize the risk of a traumatic experience, make sure they have everything they need to feel comfortable. Older kids sometimes want to appear tougher than they are, so although they should be able to pack their own bag, keep an eye out for this and double-check their supplies to ensure their packing is appropriate. Remember that they can be sensitive at this age, and their social life is important to them—no matter how confident they appear, they may become withdrawn and struggle to adjust to a different way of life.

Make sure your child knows the plan and what they need to do to stay safe if something happens. With this age group, you have the advantage that they can be told more about the emergency. Be careful that your reassurance isn't so great that it outweighs their sense of the gravity of the situation. Ensure they have all the necessary supplies and know how to use them if separated from the group. You can prepare them in advance by showing them how to pay attention to their surroundings every day and make sure they can find their bearings using a compass, landmarks, or the sun and stars. Ensure they know how to get home and to other places they go regularly, and check that they know how to access your bug-out location from all of these places. They should also learn to contact a trusted friend or family member in an emergency in case they can't reach you. Make their responsibilities in an emergency situation clear to them, and allow them to take on adult responsibilities, which will give them a sense of purpose and distract them from the things they've been forced to leave behind.

Regarding provisions, most teenagers should be able to carry their own. Factor in their calorie requirements, which can be up to 3,000 a day if they're active (which they will be if you're bugging out).

Guideline Provisions for Elementary School-Aged Children

- alternative way to communicate (e.g., backup cell phone)
- collapsible bike and trailer
- compass
- emergency contact information
- family photos
- fire starting provisions
- first aid kit
- food
- knife (if able to use effectively)
- map
- medical ID

- N95 respirator mask
- personal hygiene provisions
- playing cards
- ready-to-eat meals
- shelter materials
- signaling mirror and whistle
- spare socks/clothing/shoes
- sudoku/crossword/logic puzzles
- water bottle and filter

BUGGING OUT WITH ELDERLY PEOPLE

The first thing to consider with older adults is their medical needs. Make sure they have a list of their medications and know their dosing schedule, and stockpile enough medication to last at least a month (paying careful attention to expiration dates). If there are natural alternatives for their condition, it would be wise to have some of these as a backup too. If any medical equipment is needed, make sure that you have spare batteries and a backup generator if necessary, and if incontinence is an issue, ensure that you have pads to accommodate this.

Mobility may also be a concern. If they use a battery-powered scooter or wheelchair, ensure it's always charged and that you have a spare battery with your supplies. It's a good idea to upgrade wheelchair wheels so that they can navigate rugged terrain too. If possible, carry a spare walker and any other mobility assistance equipment that may be necessary.

While they should be able to pack their own bug-out bag, they may need a detailed checklist to follow to ensure they don't leave anything out. You know your loved one and what level of support they'll need for this. If, however, they live in a nursing home, you will probably need to do more for them. Make sure you have a bug-out bag prepared for them and a plan for how you will carry it if they're unable to. Make sure you have copies of their medical needs and all the supplies you need to cater to them.

BUGGING OUT WITH SOMEONE WITH A HEALTH CONDITION

The main thing here is to know what you're dealing with. You need to know the health condition and what treatments it needs in order to continue those treatments for as long as possible in the case of an emergency. Of course, not every condition is treatable, and in these cases, you'll need to know how to manage the situation and what you can do to help your loved one survive a disaster until medical assistance is available. If possible, look for treatments that don't rely on electricity and that you can fall back on if the worst happens. The goal is to avoid a sharp decline in health if you find yourself suddenly without power or cut off from your usual treatment options. This can pose a problem when it comes to stockpiling medication, as there are laws and regulations that make it difficult to stock up. Some mail-order prescription services will deliver 90 days' worth of medication in one go, and this is worth considering if your loved one's medication isn't subject to regular change. It's also worth looking into alternative medications that will help some symptoms in a pinch, including vitamins and supplements to support their overall health.

Diet plays a considerable role in our health, and this is even more pronounced when a medical condition is in play. Make sure your loved one knows which foods aggravate and alleviate their symptoms, and plan for this in your supply inventory.

BUGGING OUT WITH ANIMALS

The first thing to consider is whether your pet is capable of bugging out. For some animals, it may be kinder to leave plenty of food and water out and leave them at home. Certainly, smaller pets like rodents, fish, and rabbits will make your journey much more difficult, and they will rely on you for everything. In some cases, it may be appropriate to take your cat, but you will need to carry them the whole way, and it may be difficult to keep track of them once you reach your location.

Dogs are the pets most compatible with a bug-out situation, and for many, coming with you will be appropriate. I'm confident that my three are well-prepared and could come with us, but if their health deteriorates, I know we'll have to reassess the situation. Weigh the pros and cons before you make your decision. On the plus side, they provide valuable companionship and add to the group's warmth and security. On the downside, they are an extra mouth to feed and mean you need extra supplies. They are an extra responsibility, and they may struggle to keep up with the pace. Unless you can train them not to bark when it's not necessary, they can also be as much of a danger as they are a security asset, potentially giving away your location. You know your dog: Think carefully about whether they're capable of bugging out. Take into account their age, their health, and the conditions they will need to navigate.

If you decide to take your dog with you, you'll need to train them. Gradually increase the length of their daily walk (the bonus here is that you'll be training yourself, too!) and get them used to wearing a saddlebag. Start with an empty pack, gradually upping the weight until they're used to carrying everything they'll need to. Take them on overnight camping trips to get them used to various conditions, and make sure they're well-trained both on and off the leash.

The Doggy Bug-Out Bag

Food: Your dog will need extra calories in a survival situation, particularly if you'll be walking intensely. They may need between 50% and 100% more calories. Rather than canned food, go for freeze-dried kibble, which packs a lot of calories in a smaller amount of weight. Some dog energy bars would also be a good idea for when a quick burst of energy would be useful.

Water: To determine how much water your dog will need, divide their weight by eight. The result is the number of cups of water they'll need daily.

First aid: Having been on one myself, I'd recommend taking a first aid course for dogs. Many of the things you have in your first aid kit will also work for your dog, but you will need a few extras too. You'll need their monthly flea and tick treatment, a supply of Sulfadene or another canine skin ointment, hydrogen peroxide for cleaning wounds, Metronidazole (for treating waterborne diseases), electrolyte powders (in case of dehydration), and an antibiotic ointment and gauze.

Clothing: This is breed-dependent, but you may need raincoats and sweaters if you have a less hardy dog. Dog booties are a good idea for all dogs. Rough terrain can be tough on paws, and these will help protect them and keep them injury-free. Remember that you'll need to get your dog used to wearing these first.

★ TAKE ACTION!

Doggy BOB Checklist

Use this checklist to make sure your dog is bug-out ready. Remember that you will need to train them to carry a pack before they can do this reliably. I have added a few extra items that didn't fit into the main categories. You know your dog's needs, and if you think something isn't appropriate for them, feel free to leave it off your list.

- collapsible bowl
- collar with ID and vaccination evidence
- dog booties
- dog food
- extra water
- favorite toy
- first aid kit
- muzzle (if appropriate)
- paw wax
- raincoat/jacket/sweater as appropriate
- reflective dog jacket
- secure leash
- sleeping mat
- towel
- well-fitting saddlebag (with waterproof cover)

You have your location, your route, and your transport all set. You have as much as you can carry in your bug-out bag, and you know your location is as well-prepared for all members of your group as possible. But you need one more thing in your arsenal: a survival cache located somewhere on your route. This is what we'll look at in the next chapter.

8

TREASURES ON THE ROAD: PREPARE YOUR SURVIVAL CACHE

I don't know how many times I used the expression, "Don't put all your eggs in one basket," before its meaning truly hit home. We were on vacation once, and we stopped at a diner for something to eat on the way. The parking lot was full, and we parked a little way down the road, knowing nothing of the neighborhood or how safe the car would be. Honestly, I didn't think twice about it. We returned to pick up the car, revived and ready for the next leg of the journey, only to find it missing, along with everything we needed for our trip. I had put all my eggs in one basket, and that basket had been stolen. I tell you this story because it was an important lesson in survival planning, and that eggs-in-a-basket expression is important when you're thinking about your bug-out bag. Your bag is your basket, and your supplies are your eggs—lose your bag, and you lose all your supplies too. That's why you need a backup plan, and that backup plan is your survival cache.

WHAT IS A SURVIVAL CACHE?

In simple terms, a survival cache is a secret hiding place for survival supplies. It gives you an alternative way of accessing emergency supplies if something goes wrong. That could be that you're away from home when disaster strikes and you don't have your bug-out bag or access to the supplies you have at home, or it could be that your bag is lost, stolen, or damaged while you're on the move. A survival cache can also be used as a restocking point along the way to your location, allowing you to carry a lighter load. And you can have more than one; in that case, it can be used to spread your gear out in different locations en route to your final destination.

WHAT SHOULD YOUR SURVIVAL CACHE CONTAIN?

The contents of your survival cache will be similar to those of your bug-out bag, but there are a few ways in which they will differ. For a start, I'd recommend keeping the less expensive versions of an item in the cache—keep your good knife for your bag, for example, and put the cheaper version in the cache. If the sole purpose of your cache is a backup to your bug-out bag, you don't need to think much beyond this. However, if you have several caches in place and plan to use them for different purposes, you'll have to think more carefully, and this is the approach I'd recommend.

To illustrate this, let's consider a scenario in which your bug-out location is 50 miles away, and you need to get there on foot. Your cache at the 10-mile mark may contain extra rations of water, a fresh set of clothes, and a tent—everything you need for the first night of the journey. At the halfway point, you might stash extra food, water, and your fishing kit. Consider the number of caches you want and how you plan to use them before you decide exactly what they should contain.

What we'll look at here is a broad overview of what you might need to store in your cache, but plan carefully for your own route, location, and the number of stashes. That said, some basic supplies should be included in any cache you have, no matter how many there are or what else you plan to store in them:

- batteries
- clothes
- emergency blanket
- firestarter/matches
- first aid kit
- flashlight
- food
- knife
- rope
- tarp
- tent
- water

As you know, I tend to steer clear of firearms, but if you're using them, spare ammunition is something you'll want to store in some of your caches. I'm assuming you've packed water filters in your bug-out bag, and if you have several, you may not feel the need for a backup. However, since they don't take up much room, an emergency stash is always a good idea, and I'd include an extra one in your cache. Although you already have a flashlight and batteries on your list, a few candles as an emergency fallback plan wouldn't go amiss. A multi-tool, a fishing kit, a backup communication device, and copies of your maps are also good ideas. You'll probably want to add some essential hygiene items, and if you have the space, you could even include one or two things you could use for bartering if necessary. This might be some extra first aid supplies or some alcohol—things that could become precious resources in an emergency.

THE CONTAINER

Choosing the right container for your cache is more important than you might realize. Get it wrong, and your supplies can easily deteriorate. The best container for you will depend on the environment in which you'll be stashing it, but wood is a bad choice in most cases. Wood rots easily, and this puts your supplies in jeopardy.

Your main enemy will be moisture, so in most cases, the best containers will be made of either plastic or metal. Although metal is likely to rust over a long period of time, it does have the advantage of keeping pests out, and rust isn't a problem if you're placing it in a low-moisture environment. If you'll be hiding your cache in moist soil, however, your best bet is a plastic container with a waterproof seal. Rodents are a risk in this case, as they're capable of gnawing through plastic, and that will make the watertight seal redundant. Weigh the pros of cons of each within the environment you'll be storing it in before you make your decision. Whatever you decide on, I'd recommend placing all your supplies in zip-top bags with oxygen absorbers for extra protection.

I've tried and tested a few different containers over the years, and having weeded out the least successful, these are my suggestions:

PVC Pipe

A PVC pipe container has several size options and is a nice affordable choice. They're great if you want to store your cache underground, as they're watertight and easy to bury. And the chances are, if someone comes across them, they'll just think they're pieces of pipe and won't be inspired to loot. To be on the safe side, use a strong sealant to make sure it's completely waterproof.

To secure a cap to the end of your pipe, simply use PVC cement. Word to the wise though: If you do this to both ends, you'll need something to cut the tube open, or you won't be able to access your store. Trust me: I've made this mistake on a trial run. Instead, you can insert a rubber gasket into the other end. As you tighten its wing nut, the rubber will be pushed to the inside of the tube, creating a seal. You can then add a cap to close the pipe. In the Take Action section at the end of this chapter, we'll run through exactly how to make a PVC pipe container.

PVC PIPE

Ammo Can

Ammo cans are a good option for dry climates like the desert. As they're made of metal, they're less suitable for a high-moisture environment as rust is a risk. Most come with a waterproof seal, but they're still prone to rust and corrosion, so unless you live somewhere dry, they're better as a short-term option.

AMMO CAN

Metal/Plastic Storage Container

Your local hardware store will stock a range of metal and plastic storage containers. They're well built, weather resistant, and come in many different sizes. Again, you'll need to add a strong sealant to ensure they're waterproof. You could also look into waterproof boxes, which shouldn't require any extra sealant. Remember that larger containers will be harder to bury, so keep your container as small as possible for what you intend to store.

CONTAINER

Metal/Plastic Trash Can

These are a great option, but you'll need to be more careful with sealant as trash cans aren't designed to be waterproof. Don't be tempted to go for large cans. While the storage space may be appealing, they're far less convenient. A medium-sized or small trash can will suffice.

TRASH CAN

THE ADVANTAGE OF HAVING MULTIPLE CACHES

Having more survival caches only means being better prepared. You'll be able to restock more easily if you need to, and the more of them you have, the less need for them to be large. You can't really have too many; you just have to make sure you know what's in them so you know where to go for what you need. This may not be so easy when they're spread out along your route. You need to think about what you'll need for each stage of your journey, but if you have them spread out around your bug-out location, you'll have a backup if you start to run out of supplies. Returning to the proverb we began the chapter with, the more baskets you can spread your eggs among, the less likely you are to lose everything if one disaster happens. If you do have a lot of caches, though, I'd suggest marking them all on your map so that you don't forget where you've hidden them. We'll look more closely at ways to remember where your caches are further down the chapter.

THE BEST LOCATIONS FOR A SURVIVAL CACHE

The key to choosing the best place to hide your cache lies in remembering what it's there for. It's there to fall back on if your bug-out bag is compromised or you can't get to it for some reason; it's there to allow you to restock your supplies; and it's there to provide you with what you need en route to your destination. With all these factors in mind, deciding where to place your cache should reveal itself to you naturally.

You'll want to hide it on the route to your bug-out location (and remember, that will mean having one on each of your routes), somewhere secluded but easy for you to reach. You may also want to place them around your bug-out location so you can restock easily or for peace of mind that you'll still have supplies if your hideout gets looted. I'd also recommend hiding an extra one in your home. That way, if bugging in is the more appropriate course of action but your home is looted, you'll still have some supplies on hand. Personally, I have a network of caches spread out everywhere—my home and my bug-out location, with alternative stashes on each route.

Any hiding place you use should be well away from where you live, ideally in a remote area that you can access easily but where you'll be unseen when hiding or retrieving your supplies. The best way to choose those hiding places is by process of elimination: There are certain places where hiding a cache would be a bad idea. I've heard many tales of people hiding caches in abandoned buildings, but this isn't wise. In an emergency, these places may be used as refuges, and if that happens, you won't be able to access your cache discreetly. They also often get burned down, meaning you wouldn't have a stash to fall back on at all. Commercial storage units aren't a sensible choice either, as they'd be prime targets in a crisis, and if you suspect that a location might be used for development, you'll want to avoid that too. If there's any chance your cache could be destroyed or discovered during construction work, it's not a good hiding place.

You also want to avoid flood zones, which, if your cache hadn't already been destroyed by flooding, it might be dangerous to retrieve it. You should also steer clear of a main road or escape route; you want it to be hidden from sight and possible to retrieve discreetly.

CHOOSING A HIDING PLACE

The first decision you must make is whether to hide your cache in a natural location or use an existing structure. Natural hiding spots are entirely dependent on your environment and could include fallen trees or shrubs, river banks, or caves. In these cases, your natural environment is what you trust to keep the cache hidden. Your other option is to hide it within an existing structure, although, as we've discussed, many of these (such as abandoned buildings) aren't wise choices. However, a few structures could work for you. Perhaps you have a shed on an allotment along your route, or maybe you have a mobile home you could stash it under.

There's some debate about the best way to hide a cache, but most agree that burying it is a solid option. If you take this route, you want to bury it somewhere that you can access easily, and you want to bury it deep enough that it remains hidden but not so deep that digging it up is a major project. Make sure the top of your cache is a few feet below ground level, and take note of the natural markers in the area so that you know exactly where it is. You're not a squirrel, though, and for most of us, even a natural marker won't help us remember exactly where we buried our treasure, so make sure you mark the location on your map.

Burying a cache isn't a guaranteed way to protect it, and water damage is a risk. You can guard against this to some extent by not burying it too deep and making sure your container is watertight. Remember that a natural landmark may not be there forever—logs and rocks can be moved, and even trees can be taken down, so make sure you have a few ways of identifying where you buried your cache. Ensure your map is detailed enough to find it even if all your landmarks disappear. Use GPS coordinates and count paces from a road, for example, to the exact spot where you buried your cache.

Just as you need to rotate your supplies, you'll need to check in on your cache even after it's been buried. You should dig it up at least once a year to make sure it's still there and that your supplies are still in good condition. It would also be wise to stay on top of local news to make sure there's no development being planned near your hiding place. As soon as you hear of something like this in the works, you know it's time to move your cache.

Another option is to submerge your container in shallow water, but if you do this, you'll need to be absolutely sure that it's 100% watertight. If you live near a pond, river, or stream, burying it on the bank might be an option, or you could submerge it further out. If you do this, however, you'll need a way to retrieve it—most likely a rope and a float and access to it by boat. This is a risky option, but if it's plausible for you, it does make your cache far less likely to be discovered by someone else.

PROTECTING AND FINDING YOUR CACHE

Once your cache is out in the wild, there's only so much you can do to protect it. Most of the protection comes in the hiding stage—the better hidden it is, the more protected it is. When considering your hiding place, factor in who might be traveling past and why they might be there. If you know, for example, that metal detectorists tend to visit a particular area, you know that this won't be a good place to hide your cache. Once your cache is hidden, checking it regularly and rotating your supplies will keep you informed if something has gone awry and allow you to make sure everything is in the best condition possible.

We've discussed using natural markers and maps to make sure you can find your cache again; to be sure you can track it down quickly, I'd recommend having a distinct map purely to find your cache. Ideally, that map will be drawn so that only you and your family can read it. This will protect the secrecy of your hiding place. It may sound a bit over the top, but the strategy I've taken for this is drawing my map on two pieces of tracing paper, with only half the map on each one. The only way the map is complete is when those pieces of paper are placed over top of each other. I keep both sheets in different places, and I'm confident that if someone were to find one, they wouldn't be able to understand the full picture of the map. You could also use GPS tracking, although you'll need a high-quality tracker and rechargeable batteries for this.

The last thing to note about finding your cache is that it's crucial that anyone in your family can find it. You don't want someone who's stumbled upon your map accidentally to be able to read it, but you do want to be sure that if your family became separated, any one of you would be able to access your emergency supplies if necessary.

★ TAKE ACTION!

DIY PVC Pipe Survival Cache

I'm a big fan of the PVC pipe as a survival cache, and I have several of these stashed along each alternative route to my bug-out location. We've touched on them a little already, but a quick tutorial will set you on the road if you've never made one. Have a go, and you'll soon be convinced.

What You'll Need:

- PVC pipe (any diameter you choose)
- 2x PVC caps
- 1 test plug
- PVC cement
- saw (if you need to cut the pipe to length)
- silica gel
- thin sock

Method:

1. Cut PVC to your desired length if necessary.
2. Attach a cap to one end of the pipe using PVC cement.
3. Allow the cement to cure fully.
4. Pour silica gel into a clean sock, secure it with a knot, and place this in the pipe.
5. Add your supplies to the pipe.
6. Insert the test plug into the open end of the pipe and tighten it.

Now, with your home, your bug-out location, and everything you need to get you there safely in place, it's time to start thinking about securing your bases, and that's what we'll come to in the next chapter.

9

SECURING YOUR BASES ... BOTH AT HOME AND ON THE ROAD

Did you ever play Capture the Flag as a kid? Bear with me ... It's more relevant than it sounds! The goal is for each team to capture an opposing team's flag and take it back to their territory. The thing is, it isn't just about capturing the flag—you also have to protect your own flag and avoid capture on the way back to your territory. You want to keep and protect your flag from everyone else who wants it—because it's in everyone's best interest to have that flag in their territory. This is comparable to the value of your bug-out location—you're not the only one who wants a safe and well-equipped place to shelter, and in an emergency situation, you may face some rivalry. In this chapter, we'll look at how you can protect against that rivalry, as well as skills you can learn to keep yourself safe when you're in transit.

As we discussed in Chapter Six, a large part of making sure your bug-out location is secure relates to choosing the right spot in the first place. It should be in a secluded area with plenty of tree cover, ideally with a natural barrier like a river or a mountain to make it more difficult for others to reach. You can use this natural camouflage to its best possible advantage by also making sure there are strategic places that will allow you to keep an eye out for potential threats. You should also be aware of your location's strengths and weaknesses, utilizing that knowledge as well as you can to keep a closer eye on weaker spots and spend less time on areas that are naturally more secure. Getting these fundamental components right in the early stages will go a long way toward keeping your location safe, but there are a few extra precautions you can take to increase your security.

ADDITIONAL SECURITY PRECAUTIONS

As you know by now, I see being prepared as a never-ending journey. There's always more you can do to prepare both your home and your bug-out location for an emergency, and these additional precautions are all details you can work on or add to over the years. As long as your site is in a good, secluded spot and you're confident that it won't be an immediate target for rivals, you can focus on stocking up and preparing your supplies first so that you know you'll have everything you need if disaster strikes. All these additional security elements can be added as you go along.

Cameras

The best security cameras run on batteries and are equipped with motion sensors. These will let you know if someone is on your property, allow you to see what's going on, and give you something to look back on if you require proof of an intrusion later on. The advantage of seeing what's going on if someone stumbles onto your property is that you have time to take precautions rather than being caught unawares. Those extra few minutes may seem small, but they're enough to allow you a hasty exit if necessary. I'd advise against fake cameras designed simply to scare away intruders. These may work for protecting your house against burglars under ordinary circumstances, but they're unlikely to deter someone in desperate circumstances. You could, however, use game cameras if you're using your location regularly (for example, if it's also a hunting lodge). These are easy to transport and can be set up anywhere you choose.

Motion Sensor Floodlights

Motion sensor floodlights are available in solar models, and I'd highly recommend these for your bug-out location. They'll deter unwelcome animals and people, and they can be carried with you or stored inside and set up when you need them. Not only will they deter trespassers, but they'll also alert you to their presence after daylight hours, giving you time to take precautions.

Thorny Bushes

Ideally, your bug-out location already has plenty of tree coverage, but you can add to this by planting thorny bushes like roses and cacti (depending on where you live). These will make it more difficult for intruders to make their way onto your property and keep animals at bay. Bear in mind that planting any kind of bush is a long-term plan, however, as they take time to grow. You'll want to do this as soon as you can, and it may only be possible if you own your property and the land it sits on.

Electric Shock Fences and Boobie Traps

The chances are that an electric shock fence labeled as such will be enough to send out a clear message that strangers are unwelcome without anyone needing to get hurt. That said, electric shock fences deliver minimal shocks, and no one will be seriously harmed if they touch one. You can also use boobie traps, increasing in intensity as they get closer to your property. I would advise, however, that you use these cautiously, particularly if you have children or vulnerable people with you. I personally try to avoid using boobie traps because of the risk to my own children.

In a similar vein but less harmful, however, are DIY alarms, which you can place at the entry points to your property to warn you if someone is approaching. We'll look at how to make a mousetrap-tripwire alarm in our Take Action section at the end of the chapter.

Your Relationship With the Community

It may not sound like much of a defense strategy, but your relationship with the community is important. Your location should be secluded, but that doesn't necessarily mean that there will be no one in the vicinity. Get to know anyone who lives there and make an effort to get to know the area and the crime rates in the nearest neighborhood. All of this gives you useful data points and tells you a certain amount about your potential security in times of crisis. Getting to know the neighbors, meanwhile, means there are more of you to look out for each other in an emergency situation.

Safety in Numbers

There's safety in numbers, and while a bigger group may draw more attention, it's also more likely to be able to protect itself in the event of an attack. This is something you'll want to consider in your overall bug-out plan. Will it just be you and your immediate family, or will you pair up with another family or include some friends? If you have more people on your team, you can also afford to employ extra security measures like having someone on sentry duty patrol the property and alert the rest of the group to danger. A dog can also be a good asset here, but remember that unwanted barking may draw attention.

Being Wise About Valuables

While you do want your bug-out location to be adequately stocked and ready to move into at a moment's notice, I'd advise against leaving anything valuable there. Important personal documents should be kept on your person. If you would like to store valuable things away from home, a well-hidden survival cache is a better idea than keeping them at your bug-out location.

BEYOND PHYSICAL PRECAUTIONS

While making sure your bug-out location is as secure as possible is important, a good security plan goes beyond any of the physical precautions you can take. We live in a world where our personal data is everywhere, and protecting it in an emergency is just as important as protecting our physical possessions. As with any preparations, this should be done well in advance of an emergency because, chances are, a computer virus or worm is likely to hit you before any physical disaster does. Make sure you have a copy of essential documents like your birth certificates, social security cards, recent pictures of each family member, and all your contact information. Ideally, that data should be stored in several locations, including an external hard drive that you can carry with you.

It would be wise to back up additional data too—things like world knowledge and online encyclopedias. That way, if the internet goes down, you still have access to some of the information that would have been available to you under normal circumstances. You could even keep copies of novels that are out of their copyright period. Project Gutenberg is a good place to go for this. If an emergency goes on for a long time and life as we know it completely changes, that reading material could be a real sanity saver.

SECURING YOURSELF AND YOUR FAMILY

Ultimately, any security measures you put in place are working toward the same goal: protecting you and your family. To do this effectively, you'll also need to be streetwise and know how to defend yourself if danger approaches. I've broken this down into three key areas to think about.

Situational Awareness

Situational awareness simply means being aware of the world around you, which is something to train yourself in well before any emergency. Try not to walk around with your nose in your phone. Pay attention to your environment and the people around you. Looking alert is a surprisingly effective way to protect yourself. Someone buried in their phone and not paying attention to who's nearby is far more likely to get mugged than someone looking at their environment. While you don't want to be paranoid about every little thing, it's important to pay attention to any potential danger so that you can react when you need to, and this will serve you well in a crisis situation. You can train your kids to do this by asking them questions about their environment or giving them particular things to look out for—like an on-the-go version of Eye Spy.

Blending In

In a survival situation, the last thing you want to do is stand out. For example, you don't want to be remembered for buying large amounts of food or supplies. Do what you can to minimize this risk, avoiding particularly remarkable outfits that draw attention. Wear neutral tones and avoid bright colors that will attract attention. Blending in is an extension of situational awareness; pay attention to those around you and match your behavior to theirs so that you don't stand out. This is also a great game you can play with your kids, and it's super useful as a child-taming strategy when they're being a bit wild! Get them to pay attention to the people around them and act as if they are one of them. My kids can play this game for hours, and they're getting very good at it.

Self Defense

Again, I'd like to leave firearms out of this discussion, but if you live in an area where you're allowed to carry a weapon, this may be something you want to consider. If you do this, however, be sure to get proper training and follow the appropriate licensing procedures. Whether or not you have firearms, learning how to defend yourself without one is a must. I'd recommend martial arts classes for this; again, this is something everyone in the family can get involved in. Martial arts classes prepare you well in a number of ways. Not only do you learn how to defend yourself, but you also learn how to fall well, thus avoiding injury and building your self-confidence, which can deter potential attackers on its own.

Martial arts is a very broad umbrella, and there are many you can choose from. We touched on this in Chapter Four, and you may remember that my particular recommendations were muay Thai, boxing, and jiu-jitsu. There are a few other defensive styles you may wish to look into as well, one being krav maga, which was developed by the Israeli Defense Forces. It is perfect for quickly disabling an attacker and combines well-known arts like boxing, judo, and jujitsu with real-life situations you might encounter.

Of course, any martial art you learn is determined, to some extent, by what's available in your area. Read reviews and make sure you find a reputable instructor before you commit to a class. My whole family is currently learning judo, all at age-appropriate levels. This is part of our long-term training plan, and the kids love it.

★ TAKE ACTION!

Make a Mousetrap Trip Wire

A mousetrap isn't just good for catching mice. It's also a good starting point for a tripwire alarm. I prefer this kind of DIY project to a boobie trap, but if you have children, be mindful of where you place it. Although it won't cause any harm to an intruder and simply works to alert you of a threat, it could be a hazard to a small child or elderly person. Place it wisely, and make sure everyone in your party knows about it.

What You'll Need:

- a mousetrap
- wire cutters
- ring caps
- fishing line
- zip ties

Method:

1. Remove the holding bar from the nail on the mousetrap, carefully leaving the loop intact.
2. Use wire cutters to trim the bar behind the arch so that you're left with a straight bar.
3. Remove the bait holder catch.
4. Pull the hammer back a couple of times, allowing it to spring back and mark the wood to show you the contact points.
5. Remove the arm of the spring from the hammer and turn the hammer to the side.
6. At each of the contact points, add a small nail, leaving the head slightly raised from the wood.
7. Turn the hammer back to its original position and reattach the spring.
8. Pull back the hammer, and slide the holding bar through the U-shaped nail to hold it in place.
9. Place a ring cap on each nail.
10. Tie a knot in a piece of fishing line, creating a loop that you can slide onto the holding bar.
11. Put your tripwire in place by tying the other end of the fishing wire to something strong and secure, and mount the trap using zip ties.

12. Your tripwire is alarmed and ready! If someone's foot touches the fishing line, the bar will be pulled, and the alarm will sound.

Although it's important that your bug-out location is secure, it's also important to make sure the home you're leaving behind is safe. You can learn more about this in my earlier book, *When Crisis Hits Suburbia*, but remember that all of the precautions we've discussed in this chapter can also be applied to your home.

You now know everything you need to bug out effectively in an emergency, which leaves us with one final piece of the puzzle. In the next chapter, we'll look at how to plan your exit—without cutting yourself off in the process.

10

MAKE A SWIFT EXIT WITHOUT CUTTING YOURSELF OFF: PLANNING AND COMMUNICATION

The very first time I did a test run to my bug-out location, I discovered that I'd overlooked an essential part of the plan: I hadn't covered my route out of the city thoroughly enough. As soon as I hit heavy traffic, I realized that if there was an emergency and everyone was trying to flee, this would be a problem. I instantly knew my plan needed work. The first thing I'd have to do to correct the problem would be to make a proper exit plan—with backups. We discussed this in Chapter Five, but now we need to take it a step further. Planning your exit isn't just about planning how you'll get to your location; it's planning the whole evacuation from the moment you make the call to leave to the moment you arrive at your bug-out spot.

PRE-PLANNING

It's a strange way to put it (after all, planning *is* preplanning—being prepared in advance), but I find this a helpful way to think about the planning process. When I talk about pre-planning, I'm really talking about everything we've covered so far—training yourself and your family, organizing your bug-out bag, and preparing your location. Self-awareness is a key component of ensuring all of this works for you. Knowing what you're good at already and what you need to work on will help you know where you still need to train. After all, preparing your location and supplies is useless if you don't know what to do with anything you've prepared. Making sure you have the right mindset is also important; it's amazing how much more you can accomplish when you believe in your abilities, and a positive attitude goes a long way in lifting everyone else up and motivating them too.

A certain amount of forward-thinking and hypothesizing is helpful as well. Consider what disasters are likely in the area you live in. That means learning about the area's history and knowing what natural disasters have happened there in the past. Have there been floods, for example, or is it in an earthquake zone? Factoring these details into your plan makes it much easier to develop a concrete strategy, as you can eliminate some options from the outset. The same concept can be applied to what you've already ascertained about your strengths and weaknesses. Taking these into account not only helps you direct your training in the most beneficial way, but it also means you can tailor your plan to use your strengths to their best advantage. If, for example, you know your fitness is good, you may be able to plan for a longer route or to carry more supplies. Your weaknesses, meanwhile, will tell you what you need to study and practice.

One important calculation you'll need to make has to do with your travel speed. If you're able to calculate the rate at which you travel, you can work out how long it will realistically take you to reach your bug-out location, and in turn, this will help you plan for the number of supplies you'll need to carry or cache. Remember that this isn't as simple as calculating your walking or cycling speed under ordinary circumstances. You'll need to factor in the weight of your bug-out bag and the terrain you'll have to navigate. This is why trial runs are so important. You'll need to have a good idea of what you can carry and how the landscape will affect your speed, and you'll need to adjust your plans to accommodate what you discover. Of course, you're not the only person to consider in this equation, and once you've tried out the route yourself, you'll need to do it with the whole family and make adjustments accordingly. I know I had to shift my own plans somewhat when I realized my youngest son was struggling to keep up with the weight of his bag.

FINALIZING AN EXIT PLAN

You can plan your escape routes to a certain extent, but ultimately, they'll be determined by what happens in the specific emergency. This means you'll need options, which you'll need to work out with your whole family. When I did this, I bribed them with cake and insisted we all sat around the kitchen table with a map. Your goal is to come up with meeting points that everybody is familiar with, and you'll need several points in each cardinal direction. I'd recommend having a minimum of three possibilities in each direction: one close to home, one on the city's outskirts, and one outside it. If your family isn't familiar with any of them and you can't find options they do know, make sure to visit each one so they're all clear on where you should meet.

Think of route planning as a long-term project. This isn't necessarily something that can be done effectively in one afternoon. Practice going to work by as many different routes as possible, getting to know the secrets of your city. You'll learn a lot about the different options available to you that way, and you'll pick up important details about the landscape that you probably weren't aware of. Aim for lesser-known paths for each of your routes, and factor in traffic at the busiest times of the day—these are likely to be reflective of the congestion levels in an emergency.

KEY QUESTIONS TO ASK YOURSELF

How effective your evacuation will be is determined by the timing and efficiency with which it's executed. You're unlikely to have much warning when a crisis hits, and your response will be dictated by the circumstances at the time. The best way to deal with this is to nurture a crisis mindset, which starts with remaining calm under pressure. From there, there are eight key questions you can ask yourself that will help you assess whether it's time to bug out and how you will do so effectively. If you're not convinced you'll remember these questions in an emergency, copy them and keep them with your emergency plan.

1. Is everyone OK?
2. Exactly what has happened?
3. Is it safe to remain at home?
4. If we need to evacuate, how quickly do we need to move?
5. Which direction is the wind blowing in? (Be aware of airborne dangers.)
6. What supplies do I have with me?

7. What are the weather conditions?
8. Which direction should I move in (based on the specific emergency)?

COMMUNICATION PLANNING

If the circumstances require you to bug out, it's likely that the environment is changing rapidly, and that means you'll need up-to-date information in order to stay safe. This makes communication extremely important, both for the purposes of accessing information and staying in contact with your loved ones. A successful exit strategy requires you not only to leave safely but also to avoid cutting yourself off in the process.

The first thing to ensure is that you have a physical copy of all the contact details for your friends and family, as well as emergency numbers and the contact information for official government agencies. These will help you to stay in contact and access updates about the emergency.

It's likely that mobile phone networks will go down fairly quickly in a disaster, but you may be lucky for a few hours. If that happens, you'll be able to initiate your evacuation plan with messages, but it's unwise to rely solely on this strategy. Walkie-talkies are a good backup plan for communicating within the group, but getting information from the wider world is also important, and you have a few options here. All of these options are discussed in more detail in my previous book, *Prepare Your Home for a Sudden Grid-Down Situation*, but we'll cover them briefly here. Bear in mind that there are also other signaling options for when you need to catch someone's attention or send a message silently. These include mirrors, lights, and glow sticks, and these will be essential for some of the subtle communication strategies we'll look at shortly.

Hand Crank Radio

A hand crank radio will allow you to tap into radio waves, even over some distance, particularly AM frequencies., and this will be extremely useful for getting weather updates. This is especially important when escaping a weather-related emergency like a hurricane or a wildfire. If you don't already have a hand crank radio, I'd suggest getting one with solar capabilities that comes with a flashlight, a phone charger, and NOAA weather.

Ham Radio

Ham radio is extremely effective for long-distance communication, and there are plenty of handheld devices you can use without needing to set up a huge station. You can easily keep your costs down to under $200, but this will only be worth it if you know how to use it. It can be a steep learning curve if you're a beginner, and I'd recommend going on a course if you seriously intend to use it. Bear in mind that you will also need a Federal Communications Commission (FCC) license to operate ham radio legally.

CB Radio

Because it doesn't require you to pass a licensing exam and it's nowhere near as challenging to learn as ham radio, a CB radio is a more realistic option for most people. You can't transmit over as long of distances as you can with ham radio, but in a bug-out scenario, its reach will probably be sufficient. You can get both vehicle units and handheld models, so you can pick what best suits your plan. I'd recommend Cobra as a starting point when you're researching brands.

Walkie-Talkies

Walkie-talkies are simple yet very useful in a bug-out situation. If someone in your group has to leave your location for supplies, walkie-talkies allow you to stay in touch. Also, if someone is away from the shelter and has an accident or encounters danger, they can call for help. Again, you can get vehicle units or handheld models, and they're great to have as a backup, even if you also have a radio for accessing information about the local environment.

Satellite Phone

Satellite phones are expensive, and there's always the risk that your calls could be intercepted. However, they do work well even when cell phone service is unavailable—unless the satellites go down. If you don't have a device that also allows voice communication, you're limited to very short messages, so you'll need to be well-practiced at this. I'd recommend the Garmin Inreach Explorer if you're interested in a satellite phone—this is what I have, and it's served me well on campsites where there's been no cell phone signal.

Communication Strategies

Once you've settled on your equipment, you'll need to think about how you will convey any message you need to send more subtly.

Morse code is one option and would be extremely useful if you needed to communicate with someone in an adjacent room (you could do this by tapping the code on the wall) or across a long distance (which could be done using a flashlight). It requires time to learn, but it would be a fun family project; I can attest to this because we've spent many Sunday afternoons working on it in my family. My boys love it. You could also learn how to send messages using flags, which might be particularly useful if you're planning to use a boat. Again, this will require practice and relies on good visibility. Military hand signals can also be used to quietly convey information, or you can devise your own set of signals for your family. Just be sure that everyone is consistent and knows exactly what each one means. I haven't done this with my family, but I have to say, I do like the idea. No one from outside the group will be able to tell what you're saying, no matter what their training.

★ TAKE ACTION!

Make Your Bug-Out Plan

Every family's bug-out plan will be unique, and there will always be certain elements dictated by the specifics of the emergency. However, to get you started, I've created a template based on my evacuation strategy. Create your own or fill in this one, adapting it to your own needs as you go along. Some sections include an example to give further guidance.

Section 1: Group Members

Name	Phone Number	Special Needs	Skills
Jack	333-333-3333	Nut allergy	Map reading

Section 2: Assembly Points

Assembly Point	Location Name	Specific Location	Exit Point
Primary	*Home*	*Hallway*	*Front door*
Alternative 1			
Alternative 2			
Alternative 3			

Section 3: Bug-Out Locations

Name of Location	Directions	Waypoints	Location of Supply Caches
Primary location	Route 1:		
	Route 2:		
	Route 3:		
Alternative 1	Route 1:		
	Route 2:		
	Route 3:		
Alternative 2	Route 1:		
	Route 2:		
	Route 3:		

Section 4: Emergency Contacts

Incorporate the Family Evacuation Plan you made in Chapter Five here so that you have all of your emergency contacts included in your plan.

Following the advice in every chapter up until this point gives you the backbone of this plan, but you need to make sure you tie it all together and know exactly what you're going to do if the worst happens. This is the final piece of the puzzle, and as you work through your trial runs, you can refine it and make sure it's watertight and ready to see you through any emergency.

PREPARATION FOR ALL

It's never too late to prepare… until it is. As you start putting your bug-out plan together, it's natural that you may start to worry about those who are less well prepared for an emergency. You can help point other people in the right direction simply by leaving a review.

By sharing your honest opinion of this book on Amazon, you'll show new readers where they can find all the information they need to make sure their families are fully prepared for the worst.

WANT TO HELP OTHERS?

Thank you so much for your support. The more people have access to the resources they need to prepare, the more people will stay strong, healthy and safe, no matter what happens.

Scan the QR code to leave your review:

CONCLUSION

You can never be completely prepared for a disaster. Nothing can prepare you for how you may feel the moment an emergency strikes, and there's no way of predicting the way every single detail will pan out. But what you can do is make sure you're prepared to hunker down at home or bug out when necessary, and you now have all the information you need to make a solid bug-out plan. You know what to pack and how to make sure your family is as prepared as possible, and you know how to tell the difference between an emergency that requires you to shelter in place and one that means you must evacuate. Never stop learning; never stop refining, and your plan will begin to emerge piece by piece.

Trial runs will be key to ensuring your bug-out plan is successful, and you may find that your first run leaves you in a state of mild panic. Don't worry—this is exactly what trial runs are for. Keep a determined and focused mindset, and work on those areas of your plan that showed up as lacking.

I've done many trial runs for my bug-out plan, testing each route multiple times, and I can tell you I encountered some steep learning curves in the beginning. But as I honed my plan, I found more and more success with each run, and I'm absolutely confident that my family will know exactly what to do if the worst happens. Every hole you discover in your plan is a learning opportunity. Don't let it dishearten you. Instead, be thankful that you found out well in advance of any emergency and had the opportunity to correct the mistake.

You can reach this same level of confidence. Follow the advice in each chapter of the book, working through methodically and building your plan piece by piece. That dedication and commitment are all you need to make sure you have a solid bug-out plan to see you through any emergency that requires you to evacuate.

If you've come to the end of this book realizing you're underprepared for the possibility of having to shelter in place, view that as a learning opportunity. As long as you realize that there's still work to be done, you've never failed, and every day in front of you is a day you can work on your emergency preparedness. For more details on how to prepare for bugging in, refer back to my previous titles, where you'll find much more detail about preparing your food stocks and other resources. And the bonus is, every extra detail you learn will help you with your bug-out plan too.

Being prepared is a never-ending journey. It's when we sit back and think we've got it all sorted that we're in trouble. There's always more you can do to make your plan better, and when you look at it that way, it's an adventure, and one you absolutely have the skills to embark on.

Always remember: Stay healthy; stay strong; stay prepared.

Ted Riley

A Special Gift to My Readers

Included with your purchase of this book is your free copy of the *Emergency Information Planner*

Follow the link below to receive your copy:
www.tedrileyauthor.com
Or by accessing the QR code:

You can also join our Facebook community **Suburban Prepping with Ted**, or contact me directly via ted@tedrileyauthor.com.

ALSO BY TED RILEY

Would your family survive in lockdown if society were to collapse? Learn how to prepare your home now.

We are used to a world in which our homes are supplied with fresh water, gas, and electricity.

We're used to having our waste removed and our sanitary needs met.

These are all things we've come to expect, but what would happen if they were taken away?

Flooding, hurricanes, and pandemics are affecting areas we once thought were safe from disaster--we shouldn't take anything for granted.

In *When Crisis Hits Suburbia: A Modern-Day Prepping Guide to Effectively Bug In and Protect Your Family Home in a Societal Collapse*, you'll learn exactly what you need to know to prepare your home for an emergency. You'll find:

- The **6 key priorities of survival** and how to make sure you have them covered
- A clear guide for knowing when it's time to stay in, and when it's time to evacuate

- Top prepper **survival secrets** so that you always stay one step ahead of the rest
- A toolbox of information that allows you to choose what works best for your family
- **Practical tips** for preparing your children for worst-case scenarios without frightening them
- How to make sure your water supply is 100% safe at all times
- Comprehensive checklists for everything you need to stock in your home
- **Essential administrative tasks** you should have sorted in advance before a disaster strikes

And much more.

The ideal home is not only the home that keeps you and your family safe in good times, but it's the home that **keeps you safe no matter what**.

Prepare your home for the worst-case scenario and protect your family no matter what.

Do you know how to stay healthy in the face of an emergency? Prepare now to keep your immune system on your side, no matter what happens tomorrow.

The chances of being stuck in our homes for long periods of time are greater than ever, and when disaster strikes, it can be difficult to get hold of crucial supplies.

Preppers have been evangelizing about food preservation and stockpiling for years. It turns out **they were right**, and now it's time to learn their secrets.

In *The Prepper's Pantry: Nutritional Bulk Food Prepping to Maintain a Healthy Diet and a Strong Immune System to Survive Any Crisis,* you'll find a **comprehensive guide** to preparing for good health in the face of an emergency. You'll discover:

- The **#1 way to stay healthy**, no matter what disaster is thrown your way
- Solid nutritional foundations for good health and strong immunity
- The importance of immune health in the event of an emergency
- 4 crucial food preparation **techniques** you'll need to adopt in order to stock your pantry efficiently
- A fool-proof guide to shopping, preparing, and storing your stocks for safe-keeping

- What **cupboard essentials** you should get a hold of now, and how to prolong their shelf-life
- **Lost skills** previous generations had down to a fine art, yet how you can pick these up once again

And much more.

You won't just be preparing to survive: **you'll be preparing to thrive**.

Know exactly how to prepare for good health in the face of a crisis.

REFERENCES

Bobby. (2013, July 29). *Inspirational learning and training quotes | SkyPrep*. Online Training Software | Award-Winning LMS | SkyPrep. https://skyprep.com/2013/07/29/15-inspiration-learning-and-training-quotes/

Brower, H. (2023, January 19). *14 martial arts for survival and prepping*. Survival Sullivan. https://www.survivalsullivan.com/find-right-self-defense-class-preppers/

The bug out bike—Bicycling survival when the SHTF. (2016, September 6). UK Preppers Guide. https://www.ukpreppersguide.co.uk/the-bug-out-bike-bicycling-survival-when-the-shtf/

Bug out cabin tips | How to build the ultimate survival shelter. (2014, October 20). American Gun Association. https://blog.gunassociation.org/how-build-bug-out-cabin/#Tips_for_Building_a_Bug_Out_Cabin

Build a Bugout motorcycle. (2021, June 25). Prepper.com. https://prepper.com/bugout-motorcycle/

C, M. (2021, May 10). *7 Kickass booby traps that keep intruders on their toes*. Tactical Blog | Tactical Gear Reviews. https://www.tactical.com/booby-traps/

C, M. (2022, April 4). *Bugging out on foot: Do you have what it takes?* Tactical Blog | Tactical Gear Reviews. https://www.tactical.com/bugging-out-on-foot/

Canadian Prepper. (2021, May 13). *A Prepper's guide to strength & fitness training for the Apocalypse*. Canadian Preparedness. https://canadianpreparedness.com/blogs/news/a-prepper-s-guide-to-strength-fitness-training-for-the-apocalypse

Chymiy, A. (2018, May 25). *Physical fitness for preppers*. The Prepared. https://theprepared.com/prepping-basics/guides/survival-fitness/

City Prepping. (2020, August 26). *7 tips for bugging in an apartment*. https://www.cityprepping.com/2020/08/26/7-tips-for-bugging-in-an-apartment/

Cobb, J. (2022, January 15). *6 street smart skills you need in an urban disaster*. Urban Survival Site. https://urbansurvivalsite.com/6-street-smart-skills-you-need-in-an-urban-disaster/

Coffman, S. (2016, June 29). *4 foolish mistakes people make when picking a 'bug-out' location (LOTS of people do No. 2)*. Off The Grid News. https://

www.offthegridnews.com/extreme-survival/4-foolish-mistakes-people-make-when-picking-a-bug-out-location-lots-of-people-do-no-2/

Cowbell, M. (2015, June 15). *Waterproof underground PVC cache*. Instructables. https://www.instructables.com/Waterproof-Underground-PVC-Cache/

Data storage for Preppers. (2017, May 1). The Prepper Journal. https://thepreperjournal.com/2017/05/01/data-storage-for-preppers/

Dzr, K. (2020, July 14). *Making cycling a part of your prepping*. The Prepared. https://theprepared.com/forum/thread/making-cycling-a-part-of-your-prepping/

Edwards, T., & Ward, S. (2022, May 18). *Rucking for exercise can boost strength, stamina, and power*. Healthline. https://www.healthline.com/health/fitness/rucking#how-to-get-started

Einsmann, S. (2021, October 15). *The best bug out bags for preparedness*. Outdoor Life. https://www.outdoorlife.com/gear/best-bug-out-bags/

Fishing licenses and regulations. (n.d.). America Go Fishing. https://www.americagofishing.com/fishing/fishing-licenses-and-regulations.html

G, J. R. (2020, February 26). *When to bug out: How to develop a complete bug out plan*. DIY Prepper. https://www.diyprepper.com/when-to-bug-out/

Hendry, K. (2021, July 6). *How to know when to bug out*. Survival Sullivan. https://www.survivalsullivan.com/how-to-know-when-to-bug-out/

Hobel, P. S. (2019, January 4). *Bug-out planning 101*. RECOIL OFFGRID. https://www.offgridweb.com/preparation/bug-out-planning-101/

Holecko, C. (2022, November 29). *The right way to play the classic outdoor game capture the flag*. Verywell Family. https://www.verywellfamily.com/how-to-play-capture-the-flag-1257384

How to build the ultimate survival cache—Mandatory supplies for SHTF. (2021, March 21). ReadyToGoSurvival. https://www.readytogosurvival.com/blogs/prepping-101/survival-cache

Hunter, J. (2022, October 13). *The practical guide to survival cache planning*. Primal Survivor. https://www.primalsurvivor.net/survival-cache/

James, D. (2022, October 6). *Are national parks good bug out locations?* SHTF Blog—Modern Survival. https://www.shtfblog.com/are-national-parks-good-bug-out-locations/

James, D. (2022, July 14). *Bug out communication gear and strategies*. SHTF Blog—Modern Survival. https://www.shtfblog.com/bug-out-communication-gear-and-strategies/

Jarhead Survivor. (2022, June 13). *Selecting a campground as a bug out destination*. SHTF Blog—Modern Survival. https://www.shtfblog.com/selecting-a-campground-as-a-bug-out-destination/

Joe. (2022, July 14). *Using a boat as a bug out location*. SHTF Blog—Modern Survival. https://www.shtfblog.com/using-a-boat-as-a-bug-out-location/

Jones, K. (2019, July 19). *Bug out or bug in—How to know when to go (or stay)*. The Provident Prepper. https://theprovidentprepper.org/bug-out-or-bug-in-how-to-know-when-to-go-or-stay/

Jones, K. (2019, September 13). *Steps to build a successful family emergency plan*. The Provident Prepper. https://theprovidentprepper.org/steps-to-build-a-successful-family-emergency-plan/

Just a moment... (n.d.). Just a moment... https://bugoutbagacademy.com/free-bug-out-bag-list/

Just In Case Jack. (2021, September 16). *23 best prepping quotes from history to motivate & inspire*. Skilled Survival. https://www.skilledsurvival.com/best-prepping-quotes/

Kim, B. (2016, May 16). *Special needs Preppers: The elderly*. The Survival Mom. https://thesurvivalmom.com/special-needs-elderly-preppers/

Kirtley, P. (2014, December 21). *10 bushcraft & survival skills to try this winter*. Paul Kirtley. https://paulkirtley.co.uk/2014/10-bushcraft-survival-skills-to-try-this-winter/

Krebs, J. (2020, April 8). *How to use a compass and map*. The Prepared. https://theprepared.com/survival-skills/guides/learn-compass-map/

Levy, G. (2022, August 1). *A guide to building the perfect bug out bag*. Backdoor Survival. https://www.backdoorsurvival.com/how-to-build-your-own-perfect-bug-out-bag/

Loosli, L. (2020, September 30). *How to really secure your bug out location*. Food Storage Moms. https://www.foodstoragemoms.com/how-to-really-secure-your-bug-out-location/

M, R. (2020, December 12). *The cheapest way to build a sturdy, reliable bug-out retreat*. Off The Grid News. https://www.offthegridnews.com/extreme-survival/the-cheapest-way-to-build-a-sturdy-reliable-bug-out-retreat/

MacWelch, P. T. (2019, September 12). *Survival sanitation: Dealing with the "S" in SHTF*. RECOIL OFFGRID. https://www.offgridweb.com/survival/survival-sanitation-dealing-with-the-s-in-shtf/

Make a plan form. (2022, October 14). Plan Ahead for Disasters | Ready.gov. https://www.ready.gov/plan-form

Marlowe, T. (2022, April 23). *How to build a network of survival caches*. Survival Sullivan. https://www.survivalsullivan.com/survival-caches/

McCarthy, P. (2016, April 28). *Can conventional RVs work in a bug-out scenario?* RECOIL OFFGRID. https://www.offgridweb.com/survival/can-conventional-rvs-work-in-a-bug-out-scenario/

McCarthy, P. (2016, December 10). *Skivvy roll technique for efficient packing.*

RECOIL OFFGRID. https://www.offgridweb.com/preparation/skivvy-roll-technique-for-efficient-packing/

McKoy, S. (2018, February 22). *Preparing for a disaster with a medical condition*. BugOut MAG!. https://www.bugoutmagazine.com/preparing-disaster-medical-condition/

Millerson, M. (2020, November 10). *Bug out bike*. Survive Nature. https://www.survivenature.com/bug-out-bike.php

Millerson, M. (2021, November 1). *All you need to know about a survival cache*. Survive Nature. https://www.survivenature.com/survival-cache.php

Mortensen, K. (2018, December 7). *The ideal diet for 4 year old kids*. Healthy Eating | SF Gate. https://healthyeating.sfgate.com/ideal-diet-4-year-old-kids-2221.html

Murphy, R. (2021, May 20). *Bug out location: 12 qualities of a safe bug out property*. PERSURVIVE. https://persurvive.com/bug-out/bug-out-location/

Perry, C. (2021, August 19). *Survival fishing 101*. The Prepared. https://theprepared.com/survival-skills/guides/fishing/

Planning a bug out route for emergency evacuation. (2016, December 24). Graywolf Survival. https://graywolfsurvival.com/1014/how-to-plan-bugout-route/

Planning your evacuation or bug out route. (2022, May 17). PREPAREDNESS ADVICE. https://preparednessadvice.com/planning-evacuation-bug-route/

R, A. (2019, September 17). *Bushcraft 101: Bushcraft tools and skills you should know*. Tactical Blog | Tactical Gear Reviews. https://www.tactical.com/bushcraft-skills-checklist-shtf/

Ramey, J. (2021, May 10). *Bug in vs. bug out: Why your home is always the default choice*. The Prepared. https://theprepared.com/prepping-basics/guides/bug-in-vs-bug-out/

Reaper. (2022, January 13). *How to test your bug out bag and bug-out range*. Survival Sullivan. https://www.survivalsullivan.com/test-bug-bag/

Renee. (2021, November 17). *Bug out cabins: What they are and how to prep yours*. Survival World. https://www.survivalworld.com/preparedness/bug-out-cabins/

Rogue, M. (2020, August 17). *How secure is your bug out location?* SHTF Blog —Modern Survival. https://www.shtfblog.com/how-secure-is-your-bug-out-location/

Rucker, B. (2022, June 4). *Essential guide on how to learn to hunt (Tips for beginners)*. Survival Cache. https://survivalcache.com/hunting-tips-beginners/

Ruiz, C. (2021, February 22). *How to make a bug out plan*. The Bug Out Bag

Guide. https://www.thebugoutbagguide.com/how-to-make-a-bug-out-plan/

Smyth, B. (2021, July 6). *The essential guide to building your ultimate bug out bag.* Task & Purpose. https://taskandpurpose.com/gear/how-to-build-the-ultimate-bug-out-bag/

SpecificLove. (2015, February 19). *How to make a mousetrap trip wire alarm.* Instructables. https://www.instructables.com/How-to-make-a-Mousetrap-Trip-Wire-Alarm/

Stewart, M. (2018, December 27). *How to bug out if you have children.* The Survivalist Blog. https://www.thesurvivalistblog.net/advice-on-bugging-out-with-children/

Sullivan, D. F. (2022, August 16). *Bug out location: How to find and equip it.* Survival Sullivan. https://www.survivalsullivan.com/bug-out-location-dos-donts-and-the-basics/

Sullivan, D. F. (2022, December 26). *The best 37 survival foods to hoard for any disaster.* Survival Sullivan. https://www.survivalsullivan.com/the-ultimate-37-foods-to-hoard-for-any-disaster/

Survival 101: Foraging for edible plants. (2014, March 17). Be Prepared - Emergency Essentials. https://beprepared.com/blogs/articles/survival-101-foraging-for-edible-plants

Survival Dispatch Staff. (2019, December 10). *Using an abandoned building for shelter.* Survival Dispatch. https://survivaldispatch.com/using-an-abandoned-building-for-shelter/

Tilford, A. (2021, May 13). *Many Americans don't have an emergency go-bag.* Insure.com. https://www.insure.com/home-insurance/emergency-go-bag-survey/

Voh. (2021, September 18). *Increase in natural disasters on a global scale by ten times.* Vision of Humanity. https://www.visionofhumanity.org/global-number-of-natural-disasters-increases-ten-times/

Vuković, D. (2022, October 11). *9 crucial prepping tips for the elderly.* Primal Survivor. https://www.primalsurvivor.net/prepping-tips-elderly/

Vuković, D. (2022, October 13). *Bug out bag first aid kit list: What you need.* Primal Survivor. https://www.primalsurvivor.net/bug-out-bag-first-aid-kit/

Vuković, D. (2023, January 9). *Complete guide to dog bug out bags and bugging out with a dog.* Primal Survivor. https://www.primalsurvivor.net/dog-bug-out-bag/

Vuković, D. (2023, February 2). *The ultimate bug out vehicle checklist.* Primal Survivor. https://www.primalsurvivor.net/bug-vehicle-checklist/

Walter, J. (2018, September 8). *Bug in or bug out: When to run and when to stay*. SuperPrepper.com. https://www.superprepper.com/bug-in-or-bug-out/

Walter, J. (2018, July 11). *How to find the ultimate bug out location (BOL)*. SuperPrepper.com. https://www.superprepper.com/choosing-a-bug-out-location/

Walton, J. (2018, March 22). *If you see these 6 signs it's time to Bugout*. Ask a Prepper. https://www.askaprepper.com/if-you-see-these-6-signs-its-time-to-bugout/

Weston, J. (2018, October 31). *Prepper fitness for self defense: Training for survival*. Backdoor Survival. https://www.backdoorsurvival.com/prepper-fitness-for-self-defense/

What is rucking? Complete guide to amazing benefits & more. (n.d.). GORUCK. https://www.goruck.com/pages/what-is-rucking

Wiley, S. (2012, May 7). *Bugging out with kids*. The Shooter's Log. https://blog.cheaperthandirt.com/bugging-kids/

Williams, C. (2022, October 17). *Ultimate guide to bug out vehicles: How to prepare for when SHTF*. Vinjatek. https://vinjatek.com/bug-out-vehicles/

Yor, C. (2022, November 6). *Bug out routes: Figuring out your evacuation paths*. Survival Sullivan. https://www.survivalsullivan.com/route-planning/

ABOUT THE AUTHOR

Ted Riley is a survivalist, educator, and experienced homesteader, and the bestselling author of *When Crisis Hits Suburbia*, *The Presser's Pantry*, *Prepare Your Home for a Sudden Grid-Down Situation* and *The Bug Out Book*.

With years of studying wilderness and urban survival under his belt, Ted has combined his extensive knowledge with his personal experience of homesteading, resulting in the engaging and informative style that underpins his work. His writing seeks to help the modern family prepare for any potential disaster in a warm and accessible way.

Ted's passion for the outdoors led him to live a largely nomadic life in his younger years, and he has traveled the world, picking up a wealth of skills that feed into his work as a survivalist. His education is a practical one, and it has left him perfectly positioned to teach others in a way that speaks to their unique personal circumstances.

For Ted, no journey is ever truly over, and he continues to push towards greater self-reliance and independence every day. This passion informs his work, and he is highly driven to build on the early foundations he gained as a boy scout through his education work and family life on the homestead.

Ted lives with his wife Kate and their two sons in Oklahoma. With his background as a survivalist and Kate's as a nutritionist, they are confident that their family could thrive in the face of any disaster.

In his free time, you might find Ted kayaking, mountain climbing, or hiking with his family, who he cites as the driving force behind his firm belief in preparing for the unthinkable.

Made in the USA
Monee, IL
24 November 2024

53a8139f-2c56-4783-b713-15843e51e510R01